THE MORRISON STORY 1948–2019

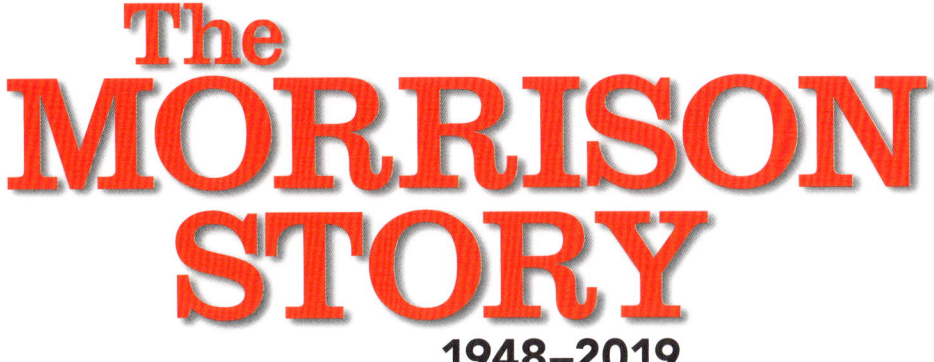

REPUTATION, RISK, AND REWARD

Malcolm Noble

Copyright © University of Hertfordshire

Images © Gordon Morrison unless otherwise stated

Every effort has been made to trace the copyright holders and obtain permission to reproduce this material.

First edition 21st April 2019

Published by
Crucible Books, an imprint of
Carnegie Publishing Ltd
Chatsworth Road,
Lancaster LA1 4SL
www.carnegiepublishing.com

*All rights reserved*
Unauthorised duplication contravenes existing laws

*British Library Cataloguing-in-Publication data*
A catalogue record for this book is available from the British Library

ISBN 978-1-905472-22-2

Designed, typeset and originated by Carnegie Publishing
Printed and bound by Jellyfish Solutions

# Contents

| | | |
|---|---|---|
| Foreword | | vii |
| Acknowledgements | | ix |
| Chapter One | Introduction | 1 |
| Chapter Two | Alex's war | 5 |
| Chapter Three | Starting out: Alexander Morrison Joiners 1948–1962 | 33 |
| Chapter Four | Growing success: Alexander Morrison (Builders) Limited 1963–1974 | 71 |
| Chapter Five | Building capacities: 1974–1984 | 105 |
| Chapter Six | Opportunities beyond the Highlands: a new era 1984–1994 | 139 |
| Chapter Seven | The Morrison Approach: trading on reputation 1995–2000 | 189 |
| Chapter Eight | Afterlives 2000–2019 | 215 |
| Notes | | 249 |
| General Index | | 279 |
| Projects and Places Index | | 287 |
| People Index | | 291 |

# Foreword

*Gordon Morrison*

When my father laid down the foundations of Morrison in 1948, I am sure he had no vision of what the business would achieve 70 years on. He just had a passion to do well for his family and to improve and develop the business year on year. We will never know how his parents influenced him and what impact spending five years in a Prisoner of War camp had on him, but we can say he commenced his business life with strong leadership and entrepreneurial skills along with a determination to succeed.

One of my greatest regrets was that I did not sit down with my parents to hear and note down their life stories. Their experiences and challenges would have filled many books, I am sure. I did try, but not hard enough. They both were not comfortable talking about their past as they did not think they had done anything particularly interesting and were never ones for boasting of their achievements.

Sadly, we did find out that my father wanted to record his war years when he tried to make some notes near the end of his life but, unfortunately, his notes never described action in France.

This book is based on a lot of research and hopefully will make up for what I failed to do in the past.

One theme that extends through all the story that follows is one of determination, pushing aside the barriers that hold so many people and companies back. This not only applied to my father but also to my brother Fraser and me, along with the many thousands of people who worked and still work for the company. I would like to think that the culture developed by my father in 1948 has filtered down through the company even to this day.

From humble beginnings, Morrison, through my father's and then Fraser's leadership, and those who followed, achieved so much taking its skills and quality of work into most parts of the UK and many countries overseas.

From 1974 the Morrison business has had many owners and shareholders, but all have been extremely supportive respecting the quality of the management, helping to take the business forward, developing careers and introducing new skills.

What I admire is the strength and influence of the Morrison management during many times of change. The various parts of the Morrison business came through difficult periods more determined than ever and showed their investors/owners what was possible through innovation and a constant focus on quality.

Construction is a people business and it is the employees of the company who succeed or fail. Failure was not something that Morrison as a business has ever been accustomed to. Yes, we had difficult projects but with determination these were all successfully overcome and laid the foundations for further growth.

Fraser and I left the Morrison business in 2001 and ever since have watched with pride as the company has grown and prospered, its reputation reaching ever greater heights.

Over the last 18 years many projects have been successfully completed but walking over the new Queensferry Crossing ahead of its opening by Her Majesty the Queen in 2017 was a very proud moment for me. Morrison may have had a minor equity stake in the project, but it had a very significant part to play in the management of it. That is a monument that will stand in the heart of Scotland for many decades to come, and the completed structure is one of the great twenty first century bridges with global significance.

The other achievement which I feel particularly proud of is the growth of the Morrison Utility Services business, now part of M Group Services. As you will read in this book this started from virtually nothing in 1988 but what I did have were highly capable people ready to restart a failing business and play their part in the success of the wider company.

To become the largest and most respected player in their industry in just over 25 years is an incredible achievement. Some who shared the dark days in Arlesey in 1988 are still playing a major role in that business.

I passionately respect all the people who worked for Morrison over the last 70 years. Only with their skills and determination would the writing of this history book be possible.

So, could I thank them all and also the current owners of the business, Galliford Try, PAI Partners and the Senior Management, on behalf of Fraser, myself and of course my father?

April 2019

# Acknowledgements

If the Scottish Highlands is famous for one thing, I would contend it is the hospitality offered to visitors; in my experience it seems to have infected anyone with the slightest connection to Morrison, even if they have never set foot north of the Tweed. I must start by recording my deep gratitude to all of the interviewees not only for their time and kind assistance, but the warm welcome received when I visited homes and offices. I thoroughly enjoyed every single one. The people interviewed were: Andrew Aldred, Lawrence Allan, Jim Arnold, Sally Bond, Julie Brinkley, Roger Croson, Ian Cusden, Hugh England, Zoe Gentle, Ken Gillespie, Adam Gosnold, Peter Heathershaw, David Henderson, Stuart Higgins, David Jeffs, Dan MacDonald, Lisa MacInnes, Ian MacKay, Pam MacKay, Donald MacLennan, Stewart MacLeod, Michael Martin, Ron McGraw, Charles Morrison, Sir Fraser Morrison, Gordon Morrison, John Morrison, Allan Russell, Ian Smith, Ken Tallant, and Liz Urquhart.

Many offered additional help with more information or images, and in particular, Roger Croson provided a detailed set of notes. In arranging these interviews a number of people helped, most exceptionally Sally Bond, without whom this book would have taken at least another year. I would also thank those Morrison people not interviewed who helped, including Jayne Broddle, Megan Taylor, Stephen Hewings and Paul Kerridge. At the University of Hertfordshire, Jenny Dart provided help with various aspects of obtaining some material as well as horrible jobs such as photocopying awkward items. I am grateful too to Jane Housham for the help she provided in the early stages around publication, and to Anna Goddard and her colleagues at Carnegie, especially Lucy Frontani and her kind and almost unlimited patience was vital in the final stages of production.

It is a particular delight to have brand new paintings used to illustrate this book, which Gordon has commissioned from a talented young artist,

George Ellis, and we have had the luxury of reproducing in full pages. The customary thanks to various librarians and archivists must be included too, including at the, NA, Highland Life, and LSE archives, as well as the British Library Business and IP reading room. In particular Mhairi Jarvie, Sandy Wood, Debbie Potter and others helped with remarkable kindness: Fred Wellings provided some figures on housebuilding to a complete stranger. With translation of some German material, Dr Julie Attard and my sister Catriona Noble were most patient. Prof. Richard Rodger and Dr Bernard Attard provided valuable advice, and many others encouragement.

In completing a book under great time pressure, my demands of many of these people have been consistently unreasonably and not infrequently outrageous. With great speed David Watt provided a meticulous proofread at short order, and saved me from many embarrassments. My dad Keith Noble also provided a fresh pair of eyes on a complete draft. Such mistakes which remain, of course are entirely on me.

There are two particularly important thanks I would like to extend. Firstly, to Prof. Anne Murphy who has supervised the project, for sharing much wisdom with kindness and good humour. Finally for giving me the chance to tell this remarkable story, and providing so much assistance with almost every aspect, I owe a debt of gratitude to Gordon Morrison.

After all this help, I can only hope it is found to be a 'Quality' job.

January 2019

# THE MORRISON STORY

Looking up towards the Old Tower and Tain High Street, 1940s. (© Tain & District Museum and Clan Ross Centre)

CHAPTER ONE

# Introduction

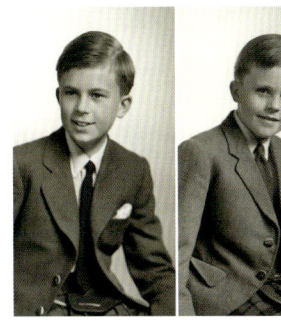

In 1948, ALEX MORRISON set up a joinery business in a remote part of the Highlands of Scotland using some saved army pay and a bag of borrowed tools. A mere seventy years later, one part of the resulting company had a turnover in excess of £1 billion at the last tally, and the people Alex employed have worked around the globe. This book reveals the history of that remarkable company. There are three interlinking stories within the text. The first and most important one is the overarching story of Alex's company, which includes the establishment of the company, its growth, sale, buyback, flotation, takeover, and afterlives. This will perhaps be of interest to the majority of readers.

The second reveals Morrison's history through different projects and people and their many achievements, which are in themselves worthy of great respect. Many will turn to see if their favourite bridge or building is included. It is inevitable, but regretful nonetheless, that not everything gathered in the preparation of this book could be included in it. Only a small fraction of material could be used, and the selection has been designed to ensure the big story can be told, rather than on the grounds of how good any project was or was not.

The third, and perhaps most surprising story, is the way in which the history of Morrison reflects the postwar British state: how it responded to immediate crises in housing, schools and health in 1945, how modern infrastructure was funded and built, how anxieties about the economic future of the Highlands of Scotland were addressed; the policy decisions around the oil boom which began in the 1970s; around the different approaches to these from the 1980s, the waves of privatisation, deregulation, and New Public Management. This story is not the main subject in hand, so at times it may seem oblique, sitting in the background rather than the foreground, but as a construction company, Morrison was frequently fulfilling these different policies about how public services should be provided. I had not

Fraser, left, age 11 and Gordon, right, age 8.

fully anticipated at the outset how much this would be the case, but it became apparent early on, however, that I could not tell the Morrison story without reflecting at least some of this, and I hope some readers will be interested to follow these threads.

It is worth saying too what this book is not. It is not an archival history, although I draw on a number of collections; it is not for an academic audience and I have made every effort to avoid technical terms likely to be unfamiliar to a general reader, but it is not meant to be unscholarly and endnotes are provided. It is by no means a biography, but it is a book primarily about one man's company. The approach taken is to draw on oral history interviews. In January 2018 when I began the research, Gordon Morrison, whose father set up the business, suggested the aims were to celebrate the achievements of the builders, engineers, accountants, marketers, and all the other Morrison people who build the business, and to make their voices heard. I hope that has been achieved.

In the 31 interviews I conducted, I was consistently struck by the candour and generosity with which everyone shared their time and stories. Some readers might be anxious as to how reliable memory can be – some interviewees certainly expressed such concerns that dates and information might not be accurate. But these interviews were done in search of recollections and experiences, not hard facts and figures. With the lightest possible touch, these have been edited so that the eloquence on tape translates to clarity on page; they are quotations, not transcriptions. To prevent the reader from being overwhelmed with detail, I have generally rounded amounts of money and figures. The Morrison group of companies is simply referred to as Morrison for simplicity. Discussion of legal entities and the technicalities of ownership is kept to a minimum. Companies House holds the documentation on this enormous and convoluted aspect.

The book is arranged in broadly chronological fashion, but to make a coherent whole some things are occasionally discussed in thematic groups in adjacent chapters. The story begins in chapter two with Alex's time in the army during the Second World War. He was captured in France and spent years in a prisoner of war camp. His impulse to set up the business came explicitly from spending his formative years in such conditions, so it was vital to spend some time exploring this culture and his experience. Alex started his business soon after the War, and chapter three follows the small jobs and joinery work undertaken as the company built up a reputation and order book, leading to its breakthrough contract at the Invergordon Distillery. Chapter four begins with formal incorporation in 1963, and follows through the company's growing success and expansion, in particular the quarry division, and the

# INTRODUCTION

subsequent acquisition of Morrison by Consolidated African Selection Trust in 1973. This first sale might have signalled the end of the story, but Morrison remained a family firm in many ways which are discussed throughout the book. The story continues in chapter five, with the arrival of the oil and gas industry, which heralded the next major phase for the Highland economy, which, alongside civil engineering and property development, saw Morrison become a much broader-based company by the mid-1980s. Chapter six sees the company move beyond the Highlands to international reach, pursuing in particular an agenda focused around Quality. This in turn was developed into the Morrison Approach to collaborative working, which is the subject of chapter seven, alongside the period of exceptional growth from 1995 when Morrison was floated on the stock exchange and enjoyed remarkable success until takeover by Anglian Water in 2000. The afterlives of the company in chapter eight, look at how the Morrison name, brand and culture are continued, as well as taking stock on the corporate culture. It is a remarkable post-war story, so it must begin with the War; in the very darkest days of the War after the Allies were driven ignominiously from occupied France.

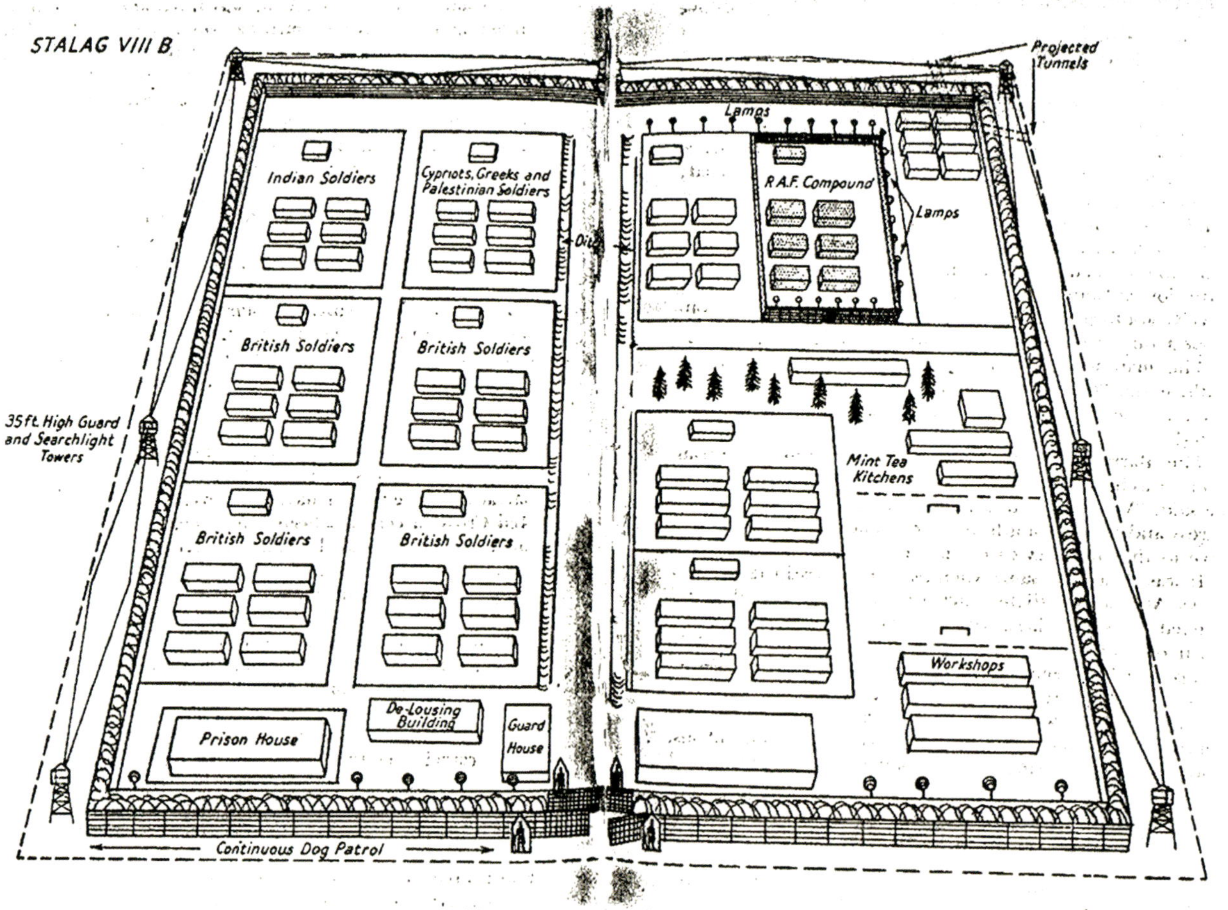

Camp life at Lamsdorf and above, the McSorley plan of the camp. (www.lamsdorf.com)

CHAPTER TWO

# Alex's war

**N**OT A GREAT DEAL is known about Alex Morrison's personal wartime experiences; in keeping with many of his generation, he was not to be drawn much on his time during the Second World War. He gave up his apprenticeship as a joiner to enlist. It might be reckoned that a few days supporting the British Expeditionary Force constitutes heroism enough; and surviving years in a Nazi prisoner of war camp in Upper Silesia would have been more than many could bear. Nobody interviewed for this book could shed any light on what happened. Alex's prisoner of war record provides some limited information about his time. There is, however, a general story to be told and a range of accounts of the War can help us do this, painting a picture of life in the camp in which he spent much of the War, both in the realities of everyday life behind barbed wire and the ways in which prisoners made use of their time.

### The end of the Battle of France and the capture of the 51st Highland Division

On 21 November 1938, Alex joined the 4th Battalion of the Seaforth Highlanders, in the 51st Highland Division.[1] The regiment was the natural choice for a Highlander: the formal Highland dress and its traditions, many friends and it was based close to home. The regiment may have a long, proud tradition, but in the Second World War, the story is brief. The story of the war is familiar. After the so-called 'phoney war', when relatively little happened, things took progressive turns for the worse as the Nazis invaded and successfully occupied much of Western Europe. Despite the efforts of the British Expeditionary Force to help defend France, the Battle of France was soon over and the mass evacuation of British troops from Dunkirk saw Britain facing Germany alone. When Churchill addressed the country on

Alex Morrison, front left, with friends and colleagues prior to leaving Tain as they headed to Aldershot for training. Alex's tartan and the man on the right with the kilt is believed to be Seaforth Highlanders tartan.

# THE MORRISON STORY

Alex with comrades, middle row, second from left.

the wireless in June 1940 in probably his best-known speech, the future looked bleak and the British state faced its most acute existential threat since Napoleon.² The summer of 1940 was a dark time for the Allies. This is a story well known: the doomed heroism has resonated down the years in popular accounts of the war. The story of the men 'left behind' was not generally featured as prominently, as unfortunately sitting in prisoner of war camps does not have the cinematic thrill of the extraordinary evacuation in a plucky flotilla of small ships and vessels. Some of the men left behind were the Seaforth Highlanders, including the 4th Battalion. Amongst them was Alex. Fighting their way to Le Havre hoping for rescue, many unaware of what was happening in Dunkirk, the 51st landed up cornered in the town of St-Valery-en-Caux. The men were obliged to capitulate: the 2nd Division ran out of ammunition; the 4th, in which Alex had enlisted, was ordered to surrender. With France occupied by Nazis and the rest of the British Expeditionary Force evacuated, there was no alternative. After this, as Longden puts it, 'the survivors of an entire infantry division marched off to face almost five years in captivity'.³ With so many Highlanders missing in action, the Lieutenant Colonel wrote to the *Ross-shire Journal* because 'the hearts of so many are desperate with anxiety'. He also addressed any possible shame in a whole division being captured: 'these officers and men knew their duty and carried it out to the fullest limit'.[4] In many Highland towns, the War was making itself known beyond the absence of a substantial proportion of the adult male population.[5]

Surrender was no guarantee of safety. This may seem counter intuitive, but there was always a risk of being shot through vengeance, through misunderstanding or simply through confusion. This was especially the case for small groups of soldiers.[6] At St-Valery, the numbers were so great that this was not a problem. The wounded would not necessarily receive the attention they required. However, for the Seaforths, this appeared to work out well, as one prisoner Captain Derek Lang, remembered that 'a lot of trouble was taken at this stage with the wounded' at St-Valery.[7] Alex and his comrades would have certainly felt exhausted, accompanied no doubt by a range of emotions ranging from shame to relief.[8] After surrender had been accepted, prisoners were searched. This might be done with decency or it might essentially be robbery at gunpoint. Usually, captives were interrogated, often at special camps. In the case of the 51st, no such interrogation took place. Compared to how things might have gone for captured soldiers, the Seaforths had as successful a surrender as might be hoped. Some may have found this quite humiliating – to be considered unworthy of the effort of questioning – but ultimately it saved tired men further ordeals.[9] Large numbers of prisoners threatened to overwhelm the Nazi resources for dealing with the men. The reality of a stretched wartime state meant transfers between permanent camps

Alex with comrades, top row, third from left.

## THE MORRISON STORY

Alex's Army Record of Service. 21 November 1939 to 6 June 1946.

Picture of Alex published in local paper after he was captured at St Valery and at that time missing.

tended to take place on foot, often by minor roads, so as not to impede military logistics. Together, this made for a period of considerable hardship. Underfed, fatigued, marching anything between 13 and 30 miles per day, with feet frequently in bad condition, this certainly was a test of endurance. Around 15 July 1940, Alex and the Highlanders arrived at what was to be their home for the rest of the War: Lamsdorf in Upper Silesia, in modern Poland. After a journey of over 900 km, he would have been in a state of extreme exhaustion.[10]

Stalag VIIIB (Lamsdorf) was part of a network of camps. Prisoners of war were held in different camps depending on their rank, with officers in Oflags and navy and merchant seamen in Marlags. Stalag camps held the majority, however, with ordinary ranks and non-commissioned officers. Within the camps, different nationalities were generally separated. Lamsdorf was the largest camp. Located in Upper Silesia, it was near extensive coal seams and other natural resources the Nazis wished to exploit. It had functioned as a prisoner of war camp in the First World War and was expanded considerably during the Second World War. It functioned primarily as a staging post, sending men to work in thousands of *arbeitskommandos*. Men were not obliged to work, but most chose to do so. The Nazis had a deliberate policy of moving men far from their comrades on the front line, so that escape was more or less impossible: there was nothing like the famous film *The Great Escape* about the experience of being a prisoner for the overwhelming majority.[11] The reality for most was a long period in a camp like Lamsdorf, with hard physical labour.

## Life at Lamsdorf

Life as a prisoner of war for Alex, as for millions of others, was characterised by privations, tedium, frustration and perhaps more than anything, uncertainty and anxiety. On arrival, the camp made quite an impression on prisoners, especially later in the War when it had become a sprawling complex. As one solider, C. G. King recollected:

> Viewed from the air, this Lager [camp] could never have been mistaken for anything else but a prison. With its low rectangular buildings, sandy compounds and hard stone connecting roads it gave every appearance of grim comfortlessness. Except from the outer perimeters of triple stockades of barbed wire there was not a blade of grass, bush or tree to be seen. The interiors of the barracks gave no further encouragement, with their long lines of wooden beds stacked three high, perhaps one wooden table and two o[f] the usual stone built fires, which only gave out a comfortable heat when they were well stoked. This was on rare occasions, for the ration of coal was very meagre indeed…[12]

The layout of the camp meant that there was little prospect of easy communication between the huts within it, as the compound was rigidly subdivided:

> Basically, visualise a noughts and crosses grid, with the two uprights a double line. These were access roads, and every line was a high barbed wire fence. Surrounding everything was an even taller fence, two fences in fact, separated by about three yards of "no man's land".

THE MORRISON STORY

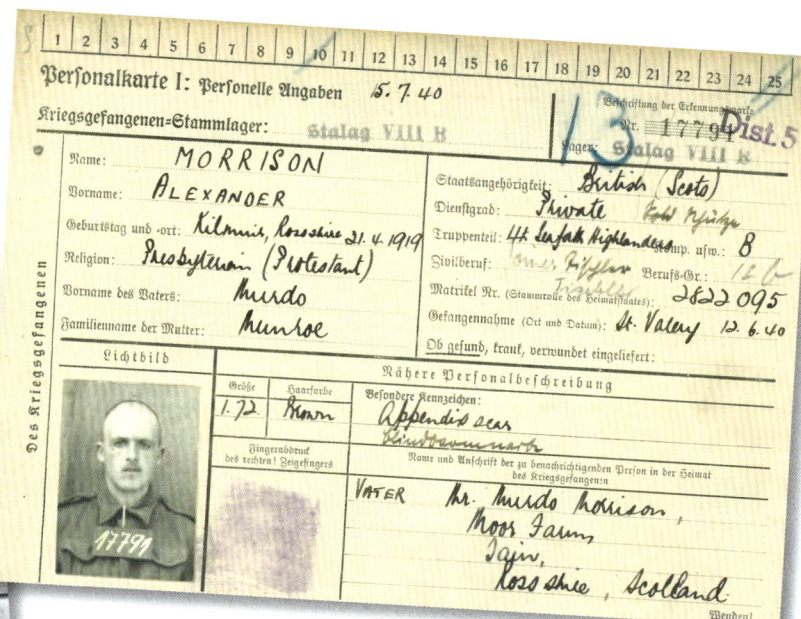

Alex's Prisoner of War Record created on his arrival at Lamsdorf. The National Archives, ref. WO416/263.

Alex setting off for war.

Alex, back row third from left, in a another team at Lamsdorf.

Above, Alex, back row fourth from left, in a rugby team at Lamsdorf. Pictures such as these were Nazi propaganda and gave the impression the men were having a much nicer time than they were in reality.

ALEX'S WAR

Alex on his way to fight. It was likely taken at Aldershot where Alex received his army training before travelling to France.

The *Clarion* was the magazine produced in Stalag VIIIB by the prisoners. June–July 1943. (www.lamsdorf.com)

Images such as these were of great value to prisoners, and were carried back on their return. This is a picture of Alex's mother sent to him at Lamsdorf in which she is feeding a lamb from a bottle on the family farm.
On the rear, she has addressed it to Alick.
On the left, a picture of Alex's parents.

At intervals of about 200 yards, and at each corner, there was a guard tower continually manned by two guards, equipped with binoculars and machine guns.[13]

The camp itself was built around an existing stable block. In another context, the alpine charm of the place would be striking, and in some letters home, and in memoirs, there is evidence that the picturesque qualities were not lost on all prisoners. In one letter home, David Lidstone wrote to his parents: 'The little village here is surrounded closely by hills and is very pretty under a heavy coating of snow'.[14] 'On the east was a dense pine forest… To the west was open moorland as far as the eye could see, and on a fine day we could see the Carpathian and Tatra mountains. The Moorland extended to the north…'[15] Looking back, Denholm Elliott, who went on postwar to become a famous actor, noted 'fir trees silhouetted on the little hills all around the camp' on his arrival at Lamsdorf.[16] The climate oscillated between scorching hot summers and ferociously cold winters.[17]

## Camp conditions

Once inside the camp, prisoners were faced with conditions which can reasonably be described as Spartan. It was in the sleeping quarters that most time was spent. Elliott described the beds stacked in 'three tiers with the top bunk 2½' from the ceiling and the bottom tier virtually on the floor', and that '[t]he mattresses were sort of sacking filled with straw and we had to take them out once a week and hang them in the sun to get the fleas out of them'.[18] Lidstone also noted that bed bugs were rife in the camp.[19] Unhygienic conditions in the camp were exacerbated by its continual extension. When Lidstone arrived the camp, he was housed in one of the old stable buildings which 'had previously been used as stabling for German Cavalry', but could soon see new buildings – 'row upon row of long wooden huts… in time the real Stalag VIIIB'.[20] Lamsdorf grew rapidly holding 'well over 10,000 prisoners in six compounds'. The camp's conditions were always poor with a reputation for being the worst.[21] Lidstone complained in October 1942, in a letter to his mother, that '[t]hey are talking of having some more [prisoners] here soon, but I have no idea where they will sleep; we only have a small room here.'[22] Long days began with morning roll call, some coffee, strolling around the barracks, soup at lunch, a meal at five o'clock, and '[t]hen to bed in an attempt to get through the long night'.[23]

Conditions deteriorated over time, largely due to overcrowding. By October 1943, there were 30,000 prisoners in Lamsdorf, which caused problems in providing space for eating and sleeping, not to mention inadequate water supply and latrines.²⁴ King noted that in that month it 'was a very dismal place with its ill lit barracks, lack of fuel and sheer boredom'.²⁵ Major expansions meant that by the end of the year, a new camp was built, as a supplement to the old one.²⁶ Given that it was the largest camp it is unsurprising that a propaganda film encouraging the British public to donate to Red Cross parcels came in response to a fictive letter from the camp, exhorting people at home to contribute to the cost of 'parcels bringing food, medical comforts and books to make their lives bearable'. The film does not show the actual camp: there was no footage available, but allusion is made to it; doubtless Lamsdorf was selected because it would encourage the largest number of people to donate.²⁷ These parcels would prove a vital lifeline for Alex and his comrades in captivity.

As the War entered a crisis phase for the Nazi regime, different ranks and nationalities were mixed together and new guards were installed at Lamsdorf: men suitable for fighting were too scarce a commodity to be left merely to guard prisoners, especially those severely weakened by many years in captivity. A toxic mixture of German men too old to fight, those unable to fight due to injury and those too young to fight – the Hitler Youth, for example, were sent and were generally much harsher and less respectful than the 'real' soldiers.²⁸ In short, the conditions in Lamsdorf deteriorated as the camp expanded, and as the War continued.

## After Dieppe

The most significant example of misery being inflicted came over the Dieppe Raid in August 1942, after which, it was rumoured, that prisoners of war captured by the British were handcuffed, in breach of the Geneva Convention. It is not entirely clear whether or not the alleged handcuffing actually occurred, but certainly Churchill handled the situation badly. The upshot of this was that by November many British and Canadian prisoners had their hands bound in retaliation, first with the string from Red Cross parcels, and then with metal handcuffs.²⁹ Failure in diplomacy meant that prisoners like Mead, '[f]or twelve long months, we were handcuffed every morning at 8 o'clock, and released at about 6 [o'clock]'³⁰ By one estimate, 2,300 British and Canadian prisoners at Lamsdorf were manacled in this way.³¹ Handcuffing made life very difficult for prisoners, and if 'found by their guards with the string loosened, smoking in their barracks… [they] were kept for several hours with wrists bound harshly together and drawn up

In retaliation for alleged handcuffing of Germans taken prisoner by the British after the Dieppe Raid in August 1942, many British prisoners of war had their hands bound, such as Sergeant Albert Willis here. (www.lamsdorf.com)

tightly behind their back, nose and toes touching a wall'.[32] If the guards ever showed any discretion or kindness, it was not over this; other than inflicting misery, it achieved nothing: it was, as Mead put it, nothing more than a 'little Wehrmacht vengeance'.[33]

## Maintaining order

Few jobs can rank as more thankless than that of Senior British Officer. At Lamsdorf, Regimental Sergeant Major Sidney Sheriff filled the role for five years, indicating that he did a decent job walking the tightrope between the needs of his men and the willingness of the camp authorities to listen.[34] This role required making constant representations to and demands of the Nazi administration, when negotiating from a position of fundamental weakness, as well as persuading British prisoners to do what was asked of them. The Nazis did not care about the King's Regulations, and the experiences were highly variable. 'John the Bastard', an unteroffizier responsible for prisoners working in a coalmine in Silesia was infamous for the reasons his nick-name suggests; on the other hand another was sufficiently popular to be extended an invitation to a prisoner reunion after the War in London, which he accepted.[35] In the context, it probably took relatively little humanity or decency to earn respect or even gratitude.

Maintaining order within the camp would have bothered the Nazis less than keeping prisoners in it. In the winter of 1943, a police force had to be established at Lamsdorf to deal with violent gangs extorting food to feed their members at razor-point.[36] This was not, however, the common experience. A strong *esprit de corps* and a sense of solidarity amongst prisoners meant that such events were relatively rare.

## Starvation rations and Red Cross salvation

All of this was exacerbated by food which was at best barely adequate and thoroughly unappetising and at worst far below meeting the nutritional needs of the prisoners. Lidstone described the food provided as 'feeble and ineffective in keeping our minds and bodies in any state of fitness'.[37] This precluded any escapes, as prisoners simply did not have the energy to fight their way very far, and no rations could be saved. It also made for very poor health. Modern estimates reckon that the diet on offer to prisoners gave them 1,666 calories per day, woefully short of the 2,150 required by adult males with adequate sleep but taking little exercise.[38] The nutritional need of those doing hard labour was much higher. In late 1940, when material conditions had become seriously dangerous, some prisoners were losing hair and teeth due to malnutrition.[39]

The food served by the Nazis was very different to the Highland fare to which the Seaforths had been used. Breakfast was ersatz coffee made from acorns, and at lunch only a very thin 'primitive soup of swedes floating in water' with a few boiled potatoes was served.[40] It was possible to keep a scrap of bread from supper for breakfast, but 'your saving could be stolen while you slept or paid a trip to the night-tub'.[41] Potatoes certainly offered familiar food. Bread had become a more important part of the Scottish staple diet since the Victorian period, but oats remained an important food of the Scottish poor, alongside wheat.[42] The kind of German dark rye breads provided by the Nazis, perhaps similar to those now sold at high prices in supermarkets, were entirely unknown. In the afternoon, there was 'a small portion of dark brown bread together with a minute slice of wurst or some cream cheese and marg'.[43] This was miserable fare and wholly inadequate for a cold climate and hard labour.

There was little point wishing for anything else by way of food, but some remarkable innovations were made by prisoners with what was on hand. Elliott noted some rudimentary cuisine:

> Your one meal in the evening was the one you looked forward to because that was the one you need if you were to sleep... We used to get a bit of ersatz cheese made from old fish and some red jam made from turnips and that sort of thing occasionally. In the centre of the hut was this green tiled German/Polish stove which heated the place with a great chimney going up and in this stove there were little gates in which you could put your billy-can with this bit of stuff and people, including myself, used to mince up the bread and put a bit of jam on it and try to do something with ersatz cheese. And then the evening came and you would take it out and eat it very slowly, with relish.[44]

In the Camp magazine, the *Clarion*, 'Cheffie' offered 'Stalag Recipes', suggesting that a cooked potato could be scooped out, mixed with 'margarine, meat loaf, sausage or fish paste' and baked in the stoves in the fashion described by Elliott. Not only did such efforts improve the taste of the food, but perhaps more importantly they enabled prisoners to take control of some small aspect of their material circumstances, when they were otherwise denied any influence. Another article, 'Cookery Nook', stressed the value of

Distribution of Red Cross parcels. (www.lamsdorf.com)

gardens and growing a few vegetables, something those on some work parties might manage to do.[45]

The most important result of the poor catering was that the prisoners were absolutely obsessed with food; nearly every account of life in the camp mentions this. As David Lidstone put it: '[w]hatever conversation we carried on with companions, the subject was very soon discarded and we were talking about FOOD!'[46] As Elliott half-joked: 'Everybody talked about food, non-stop. Whenever we did have a full stomach we talked about sex but food was always the first thing we thought of.'[47] To supplement diets, cigarettes could be 'bartered for rations of bread'.[48] For many the situation was compounded by nicotine cravings.

In the context of this persistent under-nourishment, the importance of Red Cross parcels, which offered vital calories and cheer, cannot be overstated. Internationally, the Red Cross struggled with the necessary scaling up of its operations during a time of scarcity and logistical difficulties.[49] Given that most of the 51st Division was captured at once, it is easy to see how this would have presented severe challenges. In the summer of 1940, the supply routes which had ensured the parcels arrived during the first stages of the War were disrupted, leaving prisoners 'to subsist on what the enemy was able and chose to supply' until they were reinstated.[50] The Nazis were not inclined to overfeed prisoners of any creed, even if the British fared better than others.[51] The state was stretched anyway, so it is questionable how much better food could have been supplied. The food in these parcels was much more nutritious and included, in basic formulations: 'cheese, milk, biscuits, margarine, some vegetables, syrup, jam, sausages, bacon, oatmeal, tinned meat or stew, beef cubes, rice pudding, marmite, custard, chocolate, sugar, and – of course – tea!'.[52]

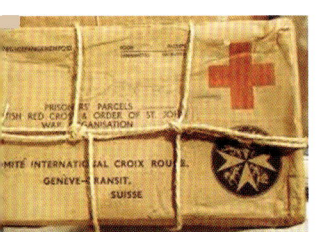

A Red Cross parcel, which were literal lifesavers to many prisoners. (www.lamsdorf.com)

The quality and contents of Red Cross parcels varied according to their point of origin. Elliott reckoned 'the Canadian ones were probably the best' and there were even special festive ones with Christmas puddings in them.[53] Parcels might be for shared or personal consumption. They were spectacularly valuable and proved too tempting for some. One hungry infantry sergeant major stole a parcel and was 'thrown into a latrine' as punishment.[54] Modern readers will understand why someone stole such food out of desperate hunger, and also why there was such anger in response; because, as King put it 'I am quite sure that the rare issue of these parcels saved our lives'.[55] The Red cross also delivered invalid parcels, containing the basic medical supplies lacking from camps, as well as parcels containing clothes and books.[56] With cold winters, poor general health, and extreme tedium, these consignments were literally vital.

Contents of a typical Red Cross parcel sent from England

| | |
|---|---|
| 1 tin meat roll | 1 packet tea |
| 1 tin stew | 1 tin cocoa |
| 1 steamed pudding | 1 tin cheese |
| 1 tin condensed milk | 1 tin biscuits |
| 1 tin bacon | 1 tin margarine |
| 1 tin salmon | 1 tin soup |
| 1 tin jam or marmalade | 1 slab sugar |

Source: IWM Documents.3802/A, C. G. King, 'A Wartime Log', contemporary notes in small journal received from YMCA 24 June 1944, p.106.

The material conditions for prisoners in the camp were fundamentally poor. As Mead put it: 'Our miserable confinement sometimes bordered on despair'.[57] It might be considered miraculous that any of the men survived. Yet a number of things made the situation bearable for them, and the following section will explore how prisoners like Alex structured their time as prisoners, through work, through reading and study, music and entertainment and special occasions. It has already been shown that tedium could be kept marginally at bay through some little efforts at cookery, and that the meagre rations provided could be enhanced. This relates to questions of agency: prisoners were not merely passive recipients of their situation but tried to assert control in a remarkable number of ways.

## Health at Lamsdorf

Clearly, the material conditions in camp were not conducive to good health. Red Cross parcels delivered not only some basic nutrition required to survive, but healthcare parcels provided some basic medical supplies. There was no guarantee of a doctor or qualified medic on hand to help care for sick prisoners. With no guarantee of medical salvation in the event of illness, it boiled down to luck.[58] Alex spent some time in Lazarett Scharley, the hospital attached to Lamsdorf, where he went from an *arbeitskommando*. He spent three weeks there in 1942, which indicates a considerable illness. Unfortunately, the nature of the condition which led to his admission is illegible on his record.[59]

The mental strain of indefinite incarceration was significant. Release came in many forms. Work – hard physical labour – might be better for mental health than sitting idle.[60] Major G. B. Matthews made a wartime enquiry into the mental health situation for prisoners, whom he reckoned would need rehabilitation on their return to Britain. Matthews identified four causes of melancholy: lack of privacy, frustration, monotonous and depressing surroundings.[61] The prisoners were not altogether without control over some of these circumstances: they could choose to work, and they could engage in a broad range of activities in the camp. For individuals such as Alex, imprisoned for long years, their experience of the War and their ability to transition successfully back to civilian life, hinged partly on what they chose to make of it.

## Work and play: making a life in the camp

Modern readers might be surprised that prisoners of war volunteered to work for the enemy. Many did, however, primarily to relieve the tedium and to get out of freezing cold huts.[62] King signed up because of 'a rising dislike of the continuous monotony of the camp life'.[63] This was part of the function of the system. The Nazi regime relied heavily on foreign and often unwilling labour. In December 1940, there were 1,178,668 prisoners of war deployed as labourers. The majority, 54 per cent, worked in agriculture, to feed a hungry country during total war. Around a quarter worked in construction, nearly 20 per cent did other work and an unfortunate two per cent worked in mining.[64] Whilst farming was the best job for prisoners, mines were the worst, given the negligible regard for safety.[65] A dangerous occupation in any context, but with no concern for the wellbeing of an entirely expendable workforce which was underfed and in poor health, the conditions faced by those sent down these mines were dire. Any hopes of extra food provided in these assignments were likely to be dashed: the situation was much less secure in that regard than inside camps, and any dietary supplement was unlikely to make up for the higher calories expended.[66]

The resilience which survival in this context required must have been remarkable. The merciless treatment of the workforce by the Nazis showed Alex the damage done through that lack of compassion. As will be discussed below, Alex's concern for friends and the willingness to go to any length to help them sits in sharp contradistinction to his experience of digging coal in the Nazi mines. Salt, copper and lignite were also extracted from Silesian mines.[67] Kochavi suggests eight hours per day of work in the mines, plus considerable travel on foot to and from the site, was typical.[68] It was no secret that labouring in these mines was hard. Lidstone's mother identified the working party in which her son had been placed, and having met J. S. Couper, a veteran, subsequently wrote and asked what might be entailed. He explained: 'E719, I take is a coal mine well your son has my deepest sympathy and I have spent three years down one and so I know what it is like.'[69] In May 1945, now that an end to the fighting was in sight, it was perhaps safe enough to talk about the dangers a little, without offering any detail.

The euphemistic description of the scenes in the Nazi mines as 'quite frightening' is hardly surprising.[70] The workforce was made up of large numbers of men, wholly unsuited to the task, without experience doing it – an apprentice joiner from the Highlands like Alex would surely be singularly unsuited to working in confined spaces, with negligible health and safety precautions.[71] Lidstone recollected his time at the Castelengau mine, a pit near Gleiwitz, where he was transferred in February 1941. This might even be the same mine in which Alex worked from 12 September 1942, but there were many mines in Gleiwitz.[72] At Castelengau, better food was served, the huts were warmer and Red Cross parcels arrived weekly for Lidstone. Each day, the prisoners were woken at 4:30 am and left their camp at 5:15 am. They changed into clothes for mining after a considerable walk. No helmets were provided, and conditions in the mine were dangerous: '[a]long the dark tunnels the floor was uneven, wet and lined with pit props. Water sometimes dripped through the roof making black mud under foot.'[73] Accounts like this, of long days, dangerous, toxic conditions and unimaginable exhaustion, are as close as we can get to Alex's experience of mining.

If mining was some of the most hazardous work prisoners at Lamsdorf undertook, it was not the worst. In August 1943, Major Woolley was assigned to a British arbeitskommando sent to build a fence to incorporate Birkenau and Auschwitz concentration and extermination camps into one. It being quite apparent that mass killings were taking place, he sent a coded letter back to Britain. Woolley also helped some Jewish people in their attempts at escape by providing a plaster sheet so they could scale the barbed wire fence; when they were caught, Woolley faced some kind of trial in Berlin, but the Swiss interceded and he was sent back to work.[74] If such atrocities were known, it is all the harder to comprehend why some men joined the British Free Corps. The brain child of John Amery, son of Leo Amery, Secretary of State for India during World War Two, the BFC recruited a small number British, including Commonwealth, prisoners of war to fight *for* the Nazis against the Russians.[75] In May 1944, recruitment leaflets were seen by one prisoner at Lamsdorf, George Beck, as a sign of desperation: 'Germany must be in a state now, printing stuff like this for prisoners.'[76] Few took up these offers, and Courts Martial quietly and with leniency dealt with these individuals after the War.[77]

The scale of these operations had implications for the labour market, with ten per cent of the foreign workforce in Germany comprised of

THE MORRISON STORY

French prisoners.[78] Camps such as Lamsdorf were designed to work as staging posts for a large workforce distributed across many placements. In May 1942, there were 5,678 in Lamsdorf itself, but 13,319 prisoners across 272 arbeitskommandos. The scale of the operation was remarkable.[79] Most arbeitskommandos had a code number and a place-name recorded for it on a prisoner of war's record, but there is no index to these. Beyond this, information is very scarce. It is known that Alex worked in coal mines and, given that the work assignments noted on his card were near coal deposits, it is a reasonable conclusion that what was taking place in these was mining.

Alex's locations during his time at Lamsforf, based on his Prisoner of war record

| Date | Where |
| --- | --- |
| 3 August 1940 – until 26 November 1940 | Bunzlau district, Eichberg |
| 6 December 1940 – [unknown] | Labour Camp Winzenberg E82 |
| 13 June 1941 – 11 September 1942 | Mechtal Preussengruber E46 |
| *Except 30 June 1942 – 21 July 1942* | *Lazarett Scharley (hospital)* |
| 12 September 1942 | Gleiwitz district, Knurow. E75 |

Source: NA WO 416/263/1 Prisoner of war record for Alexander Morrison.
Information in this box is rearranged from original source to aid comprehension.

A little something is known from War Office and Red Cross reports about two of these work parties, both of which were mines. Work party E46 was where Alex started working in June 1941. When visited in August 1942, concerns were raised about the amount of work prisoners were expected to do on Sundays. The most alarming thing was the suggestion that men were forced to carry out 'some dangerous work… in certain parts of the mine called "Feile"', which was 'definitely dangerous for non-professionals, which is the case of most of the prisoners working now in these mines'.[80] This is presumably the same place as the 'Pfeiler' noted in an earlier report which noted this was 'where the seams of coal are at an almost vertical angle', meaning that the coal was extracted 'from below up to the ceiling… up to 20 metres high and [the men] are exposed constantly to being hit by pieces of coal falling from the ceiling'.[81] Another report from May 1942 noted that the men had to work 9¾ hours per day in the summer and twelve per weekday in January, with '18 hours over week-end when the shifts were changing'.⁸²

Alex spent most of his time in work party E75, which was a coal mine. The mine worked round the clock, in '3 shifts of 8½ hours', with other men also doing surface work.⁸³ Against such gruelling labour, the provision of entertainments was clearly important and much space in these reports is spent discussing this. In March 1943 there were hopes that a recreation room would soon be provided and that a civilian canteen might be used for 'concerts or theatrical performances', with 'two bands in the camp, one large one with about 30 instrumentalists and a smaller one with about fifteen', as well as hopes for 'some lectures on different subjects'.⁸⁴ The control or agency asserted by the men over their conditions in this regard is striking.

A report in February 1944 by Gabriel Naville for the International Committee of the Red Cross stated that the rooms were cramped but broadly acceptable: 'adequate accommodation for a short period but inadequate as permanent sleeping and living rooms', and a recreation room had 'been put at the permanent disposal of the prisoners'. However there was a want of sports and music equipment, including 'music manuscript paper'. Of the essentials, the food had 'improved', with 'a good stock of Red Cross food parcels'. Working conditions were poor, not least because the 'working clothes and boots… are… not of very good quality and require frequent repairs', and a second cobbler was needed'. Naville also noted that '[n]o rubber boots have been issued, but fortunately this mine is rather dry'.⁸⁵ Ultimately luck was a clear factor in determining individual experiences.

## Arts and Ents: the intellectual life of the camp

The intellectual life in the camp reflected the richness of working-class culture in Britain at the outbreak of the war. In brief this was centred around curiosity, self-improvement, radical education, studying and appreciating art and many of other topics, listening to and performing a broad range of music. This might seem extremely remote in the current age, but before c.1960 there was great enthusiasm for education either for self-improvement or for personal betterment, as well as broad cultural engagement with forms of art now seen – problematically – as high culture or elite. As Rose puts it: 'the withering away of the auto-didact tradition has been a great loss'.⁸⁶ This is a crucial context because what happened in the camps cannot be understood without appreciating the richness of working-class intellectual traditions; these were particularly strong in Scotland with a longer history of mass literacy since the days of John Knox. Whilst things had moved on from the kailyard myth of the 'lad o' pairts' able to work through village school to university, widespread optimism of the prospects opened up by education continued.[87]

Years later, Alex's obituary in the *Herald* newspaper noted his 'emphasis on the value of further educational opportunities organised by the prisoners themselves'.[88] If Alex had the idea whilst in the camp to set up his own business, then it hardly seems a surprise that this became a company which placed a strong value on individual training and continued development. With this in mind, it is worth considering the opportunities available. Indefinite stays, where inmates were often underemployed, left scope for education. In a grim echo of the lucubrations of Parisian workers in the nineteenth century spending evenings reading and dreaming of socialist utopias, prisoners at Lamsdorf had much more time on their hands, and imagined the better world and lives they would build when they were released.[89] In his idle hours, Alex imagined that he would work for himself, and provide good employment for some of his comrades.

At the centre of the intellectual life in the camps were books. At first, these were not readily available – they were like 'gold dust' at first, but soon 'quite extensive camp libraries' were amassed, with the YMCA dispatching over 250,000 volumes to different camps.[90] Whilst newspapers and magazines could not be sent, books could be dispatched directly from book sellers via the Red Cross, or included in parcels from home, subject to changing rules. For example, during 1942 there was a new requirement that books to be packed individually. All the same, subject to delays and some restrictions, a note home requesting something to read would lead to a very slow 'mail order' service. The modern reader anticipating next-day delivery might find this intolerable, but for the men in Lamsdorf, any deliveries were very welcome. When the postal systems worked, letters took about six weeks to arrive; at other times, they could take much longer.[91] Almost every letter sent home by Lidstone requested more material or discussed things he had already read. As well as enjoying a *Life of Wellington* 'the best book I have read here by far', he also mentions Priestly, Woodhouse and Hugo, amongst many others.[92] After a while, there was clear change in Lidstone's thinking, towards what would be useful for the future, not simply diverting from the present. In February 1942, he wrote home:

> It is a difficult question about books, as I don't know exactly what my position will be when I get home. Perhaps a shorthand Manual & Dictionary would be O. K. What do you think?[93]

Here a young man of 21 was planning for a new world. The imagining of the future constituted an act of resistance and was vital to morale. A high volume of books soon flowed: Lidstone noted having received eleven books in three parcels on one day in October 1942.[94] We know that Alex claimed to have started thinking about setting up a business whilst in the camp.

Access to books was not contingent on the ability of individuals or families to pay for them and arrange despatch. Some of the books sent to Lidstone were paid from the South Wales Argus Fund, in which his aunt had some role.[95] Charitable endeavours operated at a more general level, but also very informally. Lidstone noted in a letter home that '[a]ll the books you sent me have been a great success here', strongly implying he was sharing his material.[96] Readership figures for individual copies of books seem likely to have been high. Evidence for this is provided by the printing of the camp paper the *Clarion* at one copy per ten men; this suggests that material was read by many.[97] Reading was clearly a popular and widespread pursuit. The *Clarion* contained a joke in 1944 about suitcases being full after the most essential books were packed as men prepared to leave the camp, a particular kind of bibliomania appeared to have taken root.[98]

The production of the *Clarion* was possible due to YMCA's donation of paper, and the Camp Welfare Fund met the cost of printing.[99] It contained news, articles and topical information. Nothing of great substance, but it does offer a window on camp life. Articles included one on work by Lutyens to plan postwar London as early as January 1943, as well as lectures on linguistics.[100] All speak to a general, broad appetite. The *Clarion* ought not to be confused with the propaganda paper *Camp* produced by the Nazis.[101]

The music and theatre in the camps might be filed under the continuation of ordinary working-class culture, of which classical music and theatre were important parts. It could also be considered as a response to the particular conditions. There was a vague requirement for such things to be encouraged 'so far as possible' under the Geneva Convention and this offered opportunities to alleviate boredom, or in some camps to provide a backdrop for escapes.[102] At Lamsdorf, where there was little prospect of escape, there was a rich variety of entertainments. As soon as instruments could be obtained, a symphonic orchestra was established at the camp: several in fact. When one prisoner complained that 'there were *only* ten sets of bagpipes', his concerns were tempered by the news that 'the Provost of Inverness had started a fund to buy drums to complete the Stalag's pipe band'.[103] More common sources of instruments were the Red Cross and some loans from the Nazis.[104] Sufficient musicians and instruments were gathered to enable three orchestras, a dance band, a military band and a string orchestra to be established.[105] Music performed in Lamsdorf catered for all tastes, and must have constituted a blessed relief.

Thanks to the bagpipes arranged by the efforts of the Provost of Inverness, in 1944 Burns Night was celebrated in Lamsdorf with a concert, albeit one without any alcohol. Even if Alex and his comrades missed a drop of Glenmorangie, there was still a taste of home in the celebration. The *Clarion* reported that it 'was enjoyed by a large and appreciative audience (consisting mainly of Scotsmen of course)', and that it had been 'so successful that the Scots are now looking for an excuse for another'.[106] This was a clear assertion of identity.

Other kinds of music could articulate resistance. Beethoven's Fifth Symphony, with its memorable, thundering opening passage, came to be known as the 'Victory Symphony' during the War; as one American musical commentator noted in 1944, it 'has symbolised the unceasing fight against the ruthlessness of the dictators'.[107] The famous opening bars in which Beethoven evoked thunder 'da da da duh' are the Morse code for the letter 'V'. Some 14,000 prisoners at Lamsdorf wished to hear it when the camp orchestra played it.[108]

The mustering of resources to create a makeshift theatre in the camp in which many plays and at least one operetta were staged is striking for its ingenuity. Seats were made from tea chests, for example.[109] But what fine entertainment the *Mikado* must have provided to men bored and frustrated by hardship and tedium! A production of *Twelfth Night* was so well-received it toured a number of camps and some nearby oil refineries, with costumes borrowed from the Breslau Opera for the actors.[110] There were rich seams of talent on which to draw; given that the men in the camp came from all occupations and walks of life, this is hardly surprising. One name amongst the thespians amongst Lamsdorf stands out: Denholm Elliott. Elliott went on to have a glittering career and his film credits included *Raiders of the Lost Ark* (1981) and *Indiana Jones and the Last Crusade* (1989), in which Nazi attempts to obtain the holy grail are thwarted by scholars. Credits at Lamsdorf included *Pygmalion*, which he produced and in which he played Eliza Doolittle, 'the Hackney flowergirl'.[111] He had a 'keen following among the guards' too; in the context it was not unusual for some of these entertainers to obtain a substantial number of fans in the camp.[112] In May 1944, in addition to Gilbert and Sullivan's satire *Mikado*, there was a production of *Hayfever*, Nöel Coward's country house comedy.[113] A common theme is that these entertainments were just that – providing much-needed light relief.

*High days and holidays*

Emeljanow identifies 'initiative and humour' as 'the basis of viable survival strategies' for prisoners in the camps.[114] Language barriers enabled 'humour at the expense of their captors to become a standard device'.[115] Conditions may have been miserable, but there were occasions when mass efforts were made to forget trouble. The *Clarion* carried reports of two carnivals in 1944. The Whit Monday Carnival featured tableaux by various of groups of prisoners. With so many Highlanders in the camp, it was not surprising that:

> Freaks of nature abounded. The Loch Ness Monster had been persuaded to parade, accompanied by a bodyguard of four braw Scotties. Judging by their appearance they only persuaded it after a titanic struggle.[116]

A second carnival followed in August, which included 22 tableaux. According to the *Clarion*:

> Like a Goldwyn extravaganza our second Carnival unrolled itself before the eyes of an appreciative audience on Sunday, August 6th.[117]

These occasions were vital not just for escapism, but because they constituted 'attempts to create a sense of community'.[118] But these performances went further, as they also helped constitute a functioning community in a real and practical sense, not just in their conception, planning, execution and for spectators, but in the purpose they served. The Whitsun festival raised 61,000 cigarettes for the welfare fund.[119] Cigarettes were the de facto currency in the camp, and with them almost anything might be obtained.[120]

Lotteries run in the camp enabled the winner to obtain astronomical numbers of cigarettes.[121] Little is known about how the Welfare Fund and Camp Comforts Committee functioned. It is not unreasonable to assume they were linked. The Fund was the economic centre of the camp as it enabled a range of things which made life bearable. It offered grants to wounded men, as well as loans, and payment for postage; it was funded by a mixture of subscriptions and donations. In January 1943, it had about 11,500 Reichsmarks on hand, or £48,730 in 2017 money.[122] The Committee also collected practical goods to help new prisoners or those otherwise in need: between November 1943 and January 1944, it collected 6017 articles of clothing, 3110 articles of 'small kit', 2526 items of toiletries, and 13,578 cigarettes, all of which were accounted for and reported in the *Clarion*.[123] The sense of community was created not only through such formal occasions, but also through sports. Given that Alex and both of his sons shared an enthusiasm for sports, it seems very likely he would have been involved in a wide range which were played in the camp.[124]

## The War back home

For those at home, the trauma must have been in not knowing. In most cases, next of kin would receive a note from the army informing them that their son, husband, father or brother was missing in action, perhaps stating that they had been taken prisoner, but more likely their fate was less certain. They might have been informed of a camp 'in Germany', but with Hitler's conquest of much of Eastern Europe as part of the Lebensraum policy, the term was hardly specific. Reference would be made to a specific camp: Stalag VIIIB, Germany. That was it. The *Soldiers and Airforce Families Association Newsletter* produced a special issue on Lamsdorf, with the inevitable upbeat tone which 'played down the difficulties and suffering of [prisoners] who were employed in the mines.'[125]

Letters would take weeks and often several months to arrive, with strict censorship of each and every letter. Inmates were restricted to a postcard or a single side of letter paper, which was usually filled with family tittle-tattle, non-committal reassurances of good health and fair conditions. Complaints, however justified, were unlikely to help anyone. Bad news was a dangerous commodity in such an environment. The infamous 'Dear John Letters' sent from home ending relationships could cause acute distress. Information about the War was scant: even if BBC broadcasts could be picked up on ingeniously constructed radio sets, which were forbidden in the camps, the information this relayed was neither impartial nor unrestricted.[126] For families at home writing to their sons, husbands, brothers, fiancés or friends, the composition of an appropriate message was a challenge. So much so that the Red Cross prepared a guide entitled *What to Tell Him* including advice on suitable subject matters for discussion including 'money you've saved' and subjects better avoided, or '[w]hat not tell him', including 'dinner you ate', 'cold you caught' or the 'vase you broke'.[127] The enclosed letter from Andrew Fraser, who would later become Alex's brother-in-law, is indicative of the wistful chit chat which often filled letters home from prisoners of war.

Providing families with information and facilitating regular contact between home and prisoners was a major task and the reality is that the

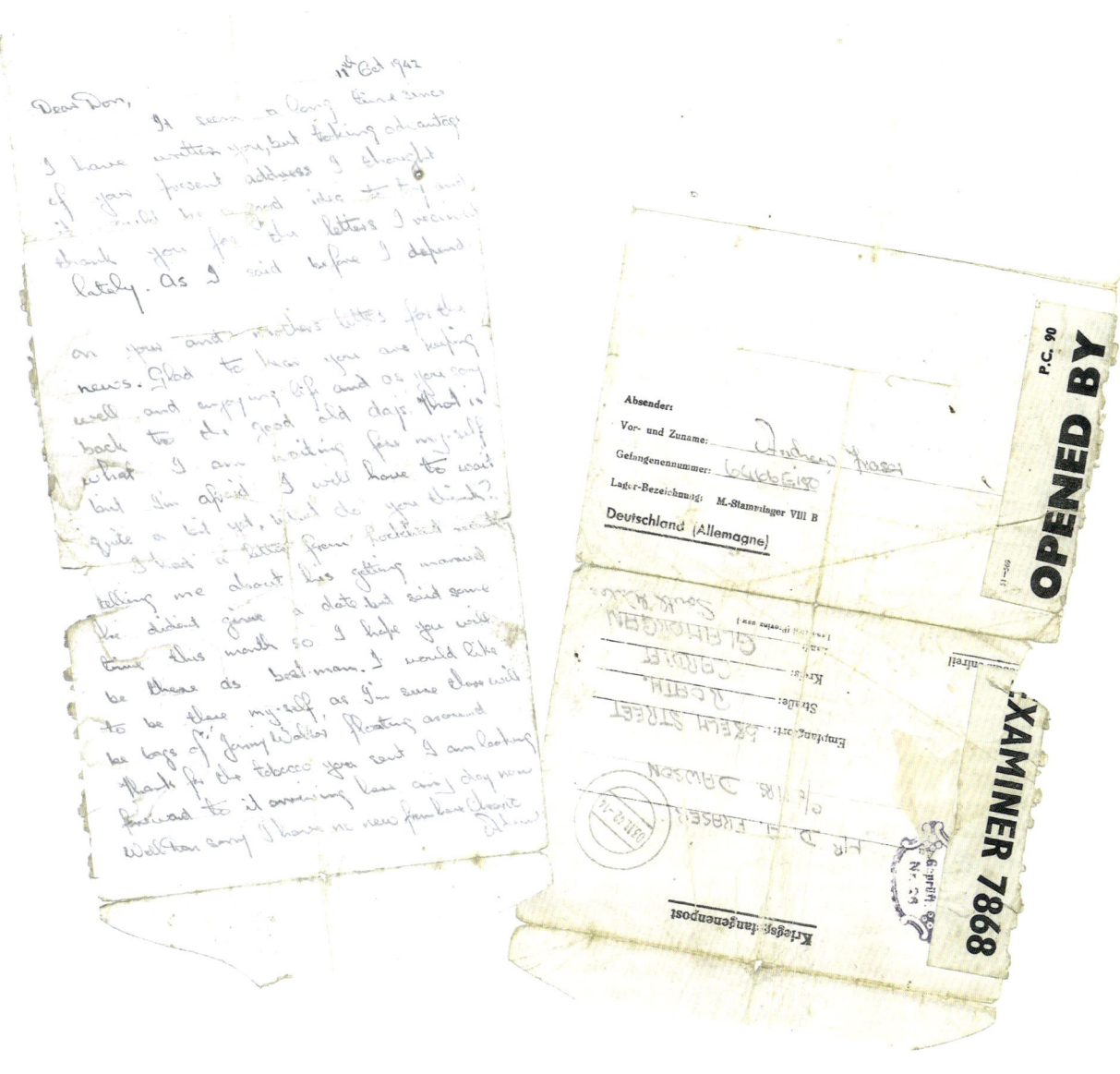

Andrew Fraser's letter home to Don Fraser from 11 October 1942. Don was also in Stalag VIIIB.

British state was fundamentally underprepared for the scale of it, relying heavily on improvisation.[128] More generally, the numbers are striking: of 80 million men in the conflict world-wide over the course of the War, some 35 million spent some time in captivity. In February 1943, 100,000 prisoners were taken in one day at Stalingrad.[129] When Alex was captured, he was amongst a large influx, meaning information home about him was delayed, hence the need for the division to post some information in the local press.[130]

## The end of the War

It became apparent in the first months of 1945 that the Nazis were going to be defeated on the Eastern Front and as a result, plans started to be made about the considerable number of prisoners of war held in occupied Poland and other territories likely to be liberated. This was a time of great misinformation in the camps. For men like Alex the thought of freedom would have been a source of joy – they would be back home in the Highlands in time for long summer nights. Yet there were apprehensions about what exactly emancipation would look like. For the Nazis, this meant that they started moving men westwards. Mark Mead was given one hour's notice on 18 January 1945 that he and other prisoners would leave on foot, and a 1000 km 'death march' followed. The term is surely justified, given that around 1,000 of his RAF comrades left; there were only 200 of them remaining by the end of March: 'dysentery, frostbite and malnutrition were rife', and '[a]lmost no food was provided' – perhaps only one solitary Red Cross parcel. These marches were bloody and futile and there were many such evacuations. Some small numbers simply refused to go.[131] Leaving Lamsdorf, Elliott reckoned that with 'heavy snow on the ground and endless road ahead, [it was] rather like Napoleon's retreat from Moscow'.[132] International negotiations meant that in April 1945 the Nazis agreed to leave prisoners in the camps; by the 1 May 1945 such movements had ceased.[133]

Death March.
(www.lamsdorf.com)

The question of remaining in situ was a complex one. At Lamsdorf, plans were afoot for the men to be 'secretly organised into fighting units which would be the hard core of any resistance to the Germans, if that proved necessary'.[134] There were real concerns: the Nazis had proven they were capable of anything – might they execute all prisoners of war? The death marches had killed enough to demonstrate lethal policies, to say nothing of the genocide against Jews and others deemed ideologically undesirable.[135] The collapse of Nazi regime and the liberation of Europe is written so firmly into the postwar story that it is hard to imagine alternatives. These narratives tend to miss out the behaviour of emancipated troops, too. After years of captivity, a long and bloody war, and rumours of atrocities hitherto unimaginable, what kind of response might be expected from men released from camps? Moving hundreds of thousands of men in poor physical and mental condition presented serious challenges in any case. The plan was that men would go to RAMP (Recovered Allied Military Personnel) transit centres, then by air to south east England, then to ex-prisoner of war centres where they would be issued with identity cards and other necessities, before final journeys home.

The Highlands remained remote from Upper Silesia in 1945, even after the War had finished[136]

Orderly repatriation may have been the plan of the British military, but it was not always what happened. This was partly because the American military had much less concern in this regard. Woolley wrote of his concern that the Americans would simply let prisoners go. His fears were proved correct:

> The inevitable happened and within a couple of hours there was hardly a woman who hadn't been raped or a house that hadn't been set on fire. I didn't understand the Americans and still don't.[137]

These were exceptional times. For example, the Mayor of Memmingen surrendered to Woolley as senior officer; but he had little idea what to do in response.[138] Normal rules of life – or even war – seemed not to apply. Vehicles, food and drink were simply commandeered by hungry, frustrated men. Some British prisoners jointed with American GIs in the summary executions of Nazis. It should be stressed that most prisoners were horrified at the barbarity and violence from liberating troops towards the Nazis and in some cases even shielded their former captors. The reality was that many struggled to move or think for themselves after years of confinement.[139]

There is no real certainty about Alex's journey home. It is known that he escaped during one of the death marches and hid in a barn to evade detection.[140] It seems he took the first opportunity to escape, as doing this from the camp during the War was more or less impossible.[141] Questionnaires were issued to all former prisoners of war. Alex's contains little detail other than a short account:

> ESCAPED ON APRIL 1945, MARCHING IN GERMANY. STAYED IN SHED TILL U.S. F[ORCES?] CAME & RELEASED. 28 APRIL.[142]

Fraser is adamant that 'he wouldn't make it up or add colour'; this fits with the assessment of his character offered by every interviewee, but in reality, very little is known.[143]

There is then a gap in the record until Alex was found with some Marines in Leipzig where he had helped with guarding German prisoners. The PM office, on whose behalf the note was written, was responsible for prisoners of war and those missing in action.[144] It is impossible to know exactly what happened. From this episode, certain things can be inferred: Alex had

# THE MORRISON STORY

charmed a marine into writing a note for them; he was likely leading things, as the note was found among his papers, despite there being four others involved.[145] It also raises a series of questions about what helping meant, how he came to be there, and many others, which simply cannot be answered and about which Alex was modestly reticent after the War.

To Whom it may Concern:

These five (5) soldiers assisted the P. M. Office of Logistics[?] in guarding and handling of German prisoners. I'll appreciate any help given them back to thier [sic] own troops.

Thank you

Wesley G. Flood

1st Lt PM Office

Source: family papers.

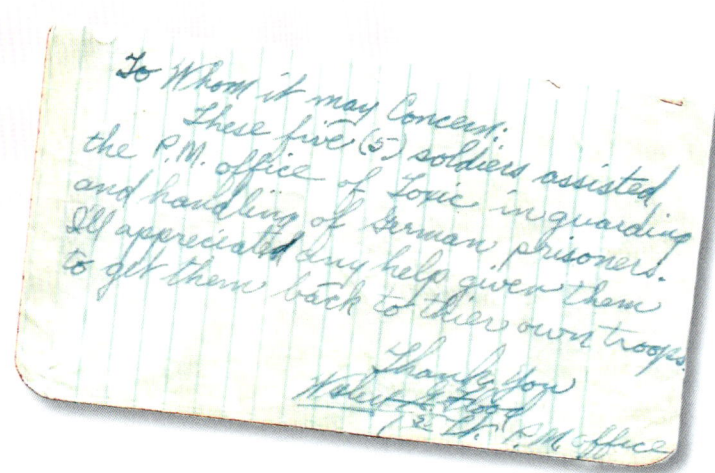

## 'Should do very well indeed': home at last

Alex arrived back in the UK safe and sound 'shortly after the end of the war'.[146] He remained in military service until 7 February 1946. His Release Certificate praised his conduct as 'exemplary', and an officer noted

> A man of above average intelligence. Very tidy at his job (especially joinery) & good at it. Cheerful & hardworking with pleasant manners. Should do very well indeed.

The officer writing this, Anthony Slocombe could hardly have anticipated just *how* well this young carpenter would do.[147] Equipped with little more than a flattering two-line reference and some saved army pay, Alex was released and finally free to go and build a new life. As we shall see, he wasted time neither in setting up a family nor a business. Aspects of his experience at Lamsdorf foreshadow the character of the business he would build. Harsh working conditions and appalling safety conditions sit in stark contrast to what would be the culture at his company. The entrepreneurial impulse, which he claimed consistently was a resolution during his imprisonment that he would not work for anyone else ever again, clearly comes from this time. A direct line can be drawn, too, between Alex seeing so many of his comrades spending time learning and planning futures as they took the initiative with education and the Morrison approach to training. The emphasis on treating friends and family very well and with real loyalty, and providing practical help whenever it was needed, comes straight from the esprit de corps shared in the army. Perhaps, these are all coincidences, but the contrasts are stark, nonetheless. Alex got home, finished his apprenticeship and got to work in showing that officer just how well he would do.

Alex in 1947.

Alex pictured shortly after the war, before he set up his business, 7 June 1946.

CHAPTER THREE

# Starting out: Alexander Morrison Joiners 1948–1962

TWO YEARS AFTER RETURNING to Tain, Alex established his firm of joiners in 1948. Within a few years, he had found his feet, won work, hired men, set up a workshop, and acquired a corporate fleet of vehicles, including vans, buses and trucks. A diverse portfolio established the company's quality reputation, through a large number of minor jobs and some larger contracts. The work undertaken by the company in this period included different types of construction including, both dwelling houses and commercial buildings, as well as various contracts for local and central government. This occurred in the context of the postwar recovery, which provided an economic boom in many sectors, especially building, as the national housing stock required urgent repair, replacement and renewal. Scarce resources were used on priority projects: housing, schools and building industrial capacity for a postwar economy.[1] From the earliest stages, Alex's company responded ambitiously and flexibly to these opportunities. Alex achieved all this whilst building a happy home life with his wife and two young sons. By 1959, the company had annual sales of nearly £61,000, or £5m in 2017 money.[2]

After the War, it was a positive time for Scotland in many ways. Despite being a country exhausted by war, traumatised by the revelations of the Nazi regime, and with national finances struggling to cope due to the scale of government borrowing, some found sources of optimism. After heroic efforts, the Axis powers had been defeated, and many were dreaming of a better world which might come to be put in its place. The prospect of meaningful international co-operation in defence, through NATO, in economic development, through the European Steel and Coal Community – what would become the European Union – and towards global governance through the United Nations, all pointed to a peaceful world. Strong economic growth with the task of rebuilding and the shift to high mass consumption, suggested a future

Alex just before he set up in business.

of plenty and comfort. Some were even thinking about the things which make life richer: in 1947 the first Edinburgh International Festival celebrated art and humanity, and brought lovers of music, theatre and art together. The optimism of the period following total war ought not to be underestimated. There have been few better times to start a small joinery and construction business.

## Alex Morrison's early life (1919–1938)

Alex had been born in New Tarbat, Kilmuir Easter, just a few miles from Tain, prior to moving a short distance to Moor Farm where his father Murdo Morrison had found a new farming job. Sitting on the Dornoch Firth, an hour or so north of Inverness, Tain was, and is, a quiet Highland town – in 1951

Alex on right aged around 6 with his older brother Donald-John.

STARTING OUT

Tain High Street in the late 1930s.

of over 2,300 people.³ Those who have not visited can easily imagine almost endless summer nights, the glittering North Sea and hills of bracken, heather and peat. In 1952, local minister Rev. Begg described Tain as 'of pleasant aspect, firth and field and wood blending beautifully from season to season'.⁴ It is a source of considerable pride to residents to claim that Tain is the oldest Royal Burgh in Scotland, having been granted its charter by Malcolm III in 1066.⁵ With Royal Burgh status, came the right not only to hold a market, but to trade internationally. Over the centuries, some successful exports have served to put the town on the map rather more than might be expected for its size. Few are unfamiliar with Glenmorangie whisky or crowdie soft cheese. A pivotal moment for the export trade from Tain, as with many towns, especially in the north of Scotland, was the arrival of the railway in 1864. For any produce which was time-sensitive, quick access to markets in the south opened up new possibilities. In particular, Tain's productive mussel beds became highly valuable.⁶ Substantial volumes of mussels were required by the fishing industry for use as bait, which supported the development of fishing in the town as well as sales of bait. In essence, it was a small trading community dominated by agriculture and fishing, supplemented by some exports. Alex's wife, Connie, remembers it as being the sort of 'place where "everybody knew each other"'.⁷

The agricultural community into which Alex had been born predominately grew staple crops: 'hay, wheat, oats, barley, potatoes'.[8] Begg noted in his account of his parish that 'modern machines indicate a progressive farming community who are concerned to make the fullest use of the opportunities presented to them by the ample natural resources of their parish'.[9] Even after the urgent increases in output during World War Two, between 1950 and 1990 substantial growth in the output and yield of Scottish farming were needed to feed a growing population.[10] Scottish farming was still dominated by oats until the 1980s. The major change in farming postwar was the supplanting of human labour by machinery, and of larger but less diverse farms.[11] The other local product worth noting – sandstone – came from the local the quarry which in the Victorian era had 'produced some of the finest local sandstone'.[12] This is important, as different quarries would form part of the Morrison story later on with the development of the aggregates business, which in the context of the oil industry became a valuable resource.

A quiet place, then, which has attracted little attention from historians.[13] A measure of the town is this: soon after Alex's business was underway, there were complaints about building activity on the Sabbath which was then more strictly observed in the Highlands than in metropolitan areas, and more in Scotland than in England.[14] There was plenty to occupy the outdoors type: curling, cricket, football, tennis, and golf. Indoors, at the community centre, known as the Town Hall, whist, bridge, and a Speaker's Club met in 1952.[15] All of these recreations were in line with what might be expected, but their scale suggests a vibrant community.

For most living in the town, occupations were of the sort which had existed for centuries: fishing, farming and some light manufacturing jobs making whisky and cheese. So important was the export of this cheese, that when Caboc started selling to Harrods in London in the early 1960s, David Henderson remembers having the day off from school in order to watch a consignment being dispatched to the famous department store.[16] That such an occasion warranted this attention speaks not only of the significance of this trade to the town, but also that teachers in the local schools were keen to promote commerce in the minds of students. Ultimately, this was an economics lesson.

The War had been a very busy time for Tain. Morrich Mhór was used by the Air Force, with hundreds based there in simple brick huts.[17] Many public buildings were commandeered and, of course, a good number of the town's young men – including Alex – were in the 51st Highland Division. The capture of 'no fewer than 40 Tain lads' at St Valery had seen considerable volumes of Red Cross parcels dispatched. In the previous chapter, it was made very clear how valuable these were.[18] The hardships certainly were lesser in Tain than they had been in Lamsdorf, but the war had certainly made itself known in this small community, through missing sons – of whom fortunately most returned – a great deal of worry, rationing and a substantial military presence.

With the longed-for peace came new priorities and some urgent tasks for the British state. Firstly, there was a need to invest substantially in housing stock. This entailed building new houses when resources remained scarce – rationing of building material continued until November 1954.[19] This meant producing large numbers of houses quickly. Experiments in a range of pre-fabricated types continued after the War in an attempt to alleviate pressure, but these were only ever designed as a short-term solution. The second strategic priority which followed this was renewing infrastructure, primarily electricity and road systems. In other words, there was unprecedented demand for building work, followed by major engineering projects. As will be considered in future chapters, from a north Scottish perspective the boom caused by oil meant that even the smallest places felt the consequences of global market forces with engineering requirements and housing demand responding to global oil prices. This was a period of reconstruction and therefore great and prolonged opportunities too.

## Family life

Family life for Alex was clearly very important. Many of those interviewed for this book met Alex during their working lives but had little knowledge of his personal character. Despite rising quickly to prominence in this small community, Alex's family life remained fairly private. The details of it have no bearing on the business history, other than it is clear that he had a loving, stable home, and that he cared deeply for his wife and sons. Alex built a family quickly. He was married to Connie on 3 April 1947. After a short spell at Connie's parents' home at 21 Academy Street, Tain, they moved in together at their first home, 10 St Andrew's Road, Tain. On 20 March 1948, their first son, Fraser, was born followed exactly three years later by their second son Gordon. Aged only six months, Gordon contracted tuberculosis, and spent six months in hospital.[20] This must have been a period of considerable worry for two young parents, and it is perhaps unsurprising that the family remained close-knit. Connie remembers:

> There was a lot to do with two boys at home. I liked to cook and bake, and also to knit and sew. Alex helped at home and helped with the shopping. I recall decorating the house together. Alex had started the business because he wanted to provide for Fraser and take care of the family, which would later include Gordon.[21]

Despite this privacy, there is no doubt that work dominated family life. In holidays, the sons went to visit building sites, encountering first-hand the hard work of labouring. Later, after both studied civil engineering at the University of Edinburgh, they joined the business at board level, and had hands-on experience. At home, much table talk would have been business, but the family all had keen interest in competitive sports as well. This included cricket, football and shooting as well as skiing. Given that this required a car to participate, it suggests that his business was doing well. Amongst all this Connie was very much present. Lawrence Allan remembers Connie taking 'a great interest in the business' and offering much support and discussion to Alex about such matters. She 'guided him in many ways… she had quite an input'.[22]

## Small beginnings

When Alex returned to Tain, he was 26 years old. Having sacrificed long years in a prisoner of war camp, he set out with vigour to achieve his goals. Before the War, Alex had begun an apprenticeship, but this had been left unfinished when he had gone to war. After completing it on his return, it is less clear what he did next. For a while, certainly, he was clerk of works on a council housing scheme at Glebe estate and he may have worked on the Campbell estates.[23] David Henderson reckons that 'as I understand it through Gordon, his father always had a vision when he was a prisoner of war, at the end of it all, that he would start up his own building company'.[24] For a newly-wed, with his first child on the way, branching out on his own and setting up a business was a bold move. His son Fraser explains this quite simply: 'in his nature he was entrepreneurial. I suppose, when you've been a prisoner of war… taking a bit of a risk in a business context' would be much less daunting.[25] And as David puts it, this means 'clearly Alex had a tremendous vision and competence… a certain determination to succeed'.[26] Alex Semple said when he asked Alex Morrison during his final years if he had always aimed 'to be a tycoon?', Alex replied:

> No, but all those years I was a prisoner of war I spent a lot of my time reading and thinking. I decided I'd rather have people working for me.[27]

Setting up in business was not especially difficult. Alex did not register a limited company and neither the joiner nor the contractor's trade is a capital-intensive one – that is to say that it does not require substantial investment in equipment or anything else. Thanks to around £200 of saved army pay – worth less than £7,000 in modern money, Alex had a new motor car, a Morris Eight, and a handful of tools. A school friend of Gordon's, Alistar Stenhouse, says Alex 'borrowed a hammer and saw from his father to help undertake some work… family gossip is that he never got the saw back'.[28] It can be safely concluded that the Morrison business did not start with a large amount of expensive equipment.

Starting out, Alex did not immediately take the formal route of incorporation, and the business was not officially registered with Companies House until May 1963.[29] In this context, personal contacts were important. Alex had, rather importantly, cultivated a good relationship with the bank manager. This was his response to the fundamental challenge of

> develop[ing] his own credibility to secure funding, to deal with banks, to be able to expand – the rate of progress was pretty phenomenal. He may not have had the formal education that subsequent generations enjoyed but was financially very astute.[30]

In a way which may seem quite strange now, the local bank manager was a figure of respect and, indeed, some prominence in any local community, especially a small town like Tain. They exercised a much greater deal of

Connie sitting in Alex's Morris 8.

THE MORRISON STORY

An early Morrison truck, the progenitor of many hundreds of Morrison vehicles which would follow in the decades ahead.

A glass model of the lorry with registration 'DJS 4' presented by the employees to Alex on the occasion of his company's 50th anniversary.

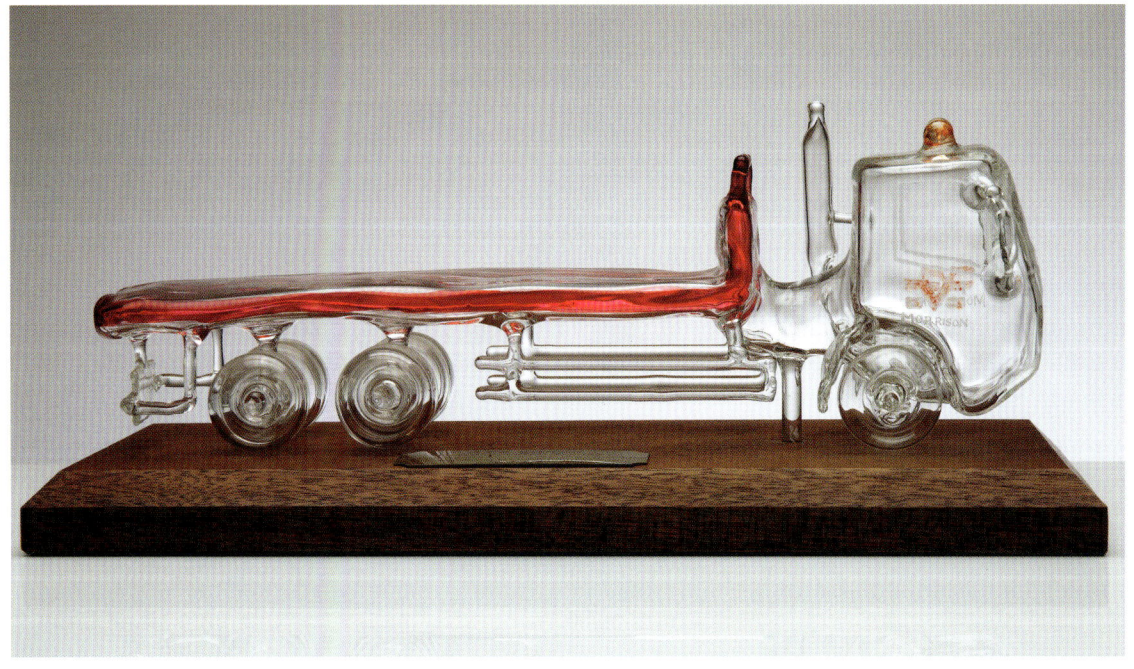

STARTING OUT

Everything stops for lunch and a cuppa: Alex enjoys a break with Connie, 1964.

discretion at a local level, making decisions based on the personal credit and character of individuals, rather than calculated credit ratings from agencies. It is important to understand this context, as this relationship was vital to the social role provided by the banking sector and how small companies like Alex's functioned. Lawrence Allan remembers one occasion when Alex was away and, therefore, could not sign the cheques to pay the men's wages. Mr Gibson, the bank manager, was prevailed upon to release funds on the authorisation of Connie, Alex's wife – this would have been a very large sum. Albeit exceptionally, the bank manager used his discretion to ensure the business survived and that the employees were taken care of by the business. This is a theme which will recur in subsequent chapters. When Alex needed a lorry – perhaps the one in the photograph below – Mr Gibson extended the overdraft facility to pay for this. Gibson might have questioned the wisdom of his approach to risk here when the lorry, with registration DJS 4, suffered a minor collision on its first day in use.[31] The relationship between businessperson and bank manager was pivotal not only to the business thriving and expanding, but to its basic functioning.

What was it like to work for Alex in the early days? Construction and engineering were male-dominated industries, and to a large extent still are. There were some female workers in the office – for example Christine McGillivray and then Margaret McEwan who were responsible for processing wages.[32] In writing this history, a concerted effort has been made to include as many female voices as possible, however female employees of the firm took

Alex's yard at Chapel Street, Tain, sketched by George Ellis, 2018.

STARTING OUT

administrative or office-based roles. The final chapter will see the beginning of the changes in this regard. As it is, much of this story is about men.

The gender of division in the kind of work done also extended to the conditions in which it took place. In the office, Alex provided nice lavatories for the ladies and somewhere to make tea; in contrast the male facilities were somewhat more Spartan. This certainly reflects a parsimonious tendency on Alex's part, but also the attitudes of his workers. The war generation found ways to make do and mend. Close at hand, Billy Louden's grandmother supplied the men with hot water to make tea to accompany their mid-day break when they took a teapot to her house to be filled. She was presented with a tea set by the men in gratitude for this when she was finally supplanted by a gas ring. Tea breaks were short – even shorter when Alex was present. Lunch was a thirty-minute unpaid break at half past twelve.[33] The heat given off by the stove to make tea and melt glue required for joinery work did little to stop the workshop hut being very cold; Tain may enjoy milder winters than elsewhere in Scotland, but they are cold enough. The first workshop the company had was on Chapel Road in Tain, near Connie's parents' house.[34]

The term 'industrial welfare' describes the provision of better facilities in workplaces in the mid-twentieth century. These included improvements such as holiday pay, better lavatories on sites rather than buckets, or steps taken to make working outdoors less unpleasant. The response to this was mixed, especially in the building trades, where there was a general preference for more cash payments.[35] This is important to the Morrison story, because even if conditions working for Alex were rustic, the men may not have perceived this as any great hardship. All the same, as Fraser notes, Alex was 'quite tough – a hard taskmaster' and 'you would not get away with this today'.[36] A consistent theme which emerges in the later chapters of the company's history is an early, vigorous and sincere commitment to health and safety through the quality agenda.

43

## Seizing opportunities

Alex's company thrived. Quickly. Within five years of Alex starting out, the family were already enjoying the material benefits of the booming business. In 1953, the Morrisons were one of few families in Tain to have a brand-new television on which to watch the coronation. The company had grown, and in 1951, its tenth employee joined the business.[37] In these early years, Alex seems to have acted confidently if perhaps a little impulsively. A small Tain builder, Hugh Mackay, found himself in financial difficulties in the spring of 1950. Alex bought his business and took over his order book, so expanding Morrison.[38] This is an example of Alex taking advantage of opportunities. Undoubtedly this reflects his judgement which was clearly generally good, but also raises the issue that chance plays some role in much of the story of many businesses.

Getting the right staff was something over which much care was taken and was mentioned by many interviewees. In the early days, Alex made some rather more spontaneous decisions. In May 1953, for example, Billy Louden was summarily appointed by Alex after he left the forces. It might be noted that Alex made a decided habit of appointing ex-military men. Jackie Grant, Alexander Urquhart, and Billy Paterson were all veterans employed by Alex. George Morrison, Alex's brother, joined the company after he left the navy.[39] Johnny Morrison, one of several employees bearing that name but no relation to the founder, worked for Hugh Mackay the troubled Tain builder whose business Alex had taken over in 1950.[40]

## 'The first priority of all is housing'

House building was a major strategic task for the country and the building sector in the period immediately after the end of World War Two. In his book published in 1948, the same year Alex set up his business, David Hall assessed the task of what building work was needed to reconstruct Britain after the War, and reckoned 'the amount is colossal', and identified '[t]he first priority of all is housing'.[41] There were plenty of jobs to be had as Hall noted this raised the prospect of full employment for the sector. With a mixture of an underlying housing shortage in 1939, the loss of 200–250,000 houses in the blitz, deferred maintenance and what was, in effect, the opportunity cost of 1.5 to 2 million homes not built due to the War meant the scale of the task was considerable.[42] In terms of Scotland, between 1933 and 1939 an average of 24,000 houses were completed each year, suggesting that between 1940 and 1947 148,000 houses were not built.[43] In Tain, a major programme of renewal had been underway since before the War. Between 1918 and 1952, the Council had built 158 homes, of which 20 were pre-fabricated; a further 64 were under construction, for a population of 2,176.[44] The net effect of this was that: '[w]hen all these are completed, it will be true to say that one third of the population of the burgh is housed in new houses'.[45] For an ambitious young building firm, this meant a range of opportunities. It should be remembered that Morrison had a larger hinterland than simply Tain: even from quite early days the firm operated in a wider regional context. Firstly, new homes could be built for a range of clients. Even if Tain Town Council never gave Alex work, the District Council did award him contracts. Maintenance had been deferred during the war on housing stock which had not been in a particularly good condition in the first place. The problem was pressing in rural areas as well as in towns.[46] The aerial bombardment of many cities and towns – although not Tain – had increased the urgent demand for more and better houses. Radical solutions explored were the relatively expensive pre-fabricated houses, which offered speed or used less precious resources, but at a higher price than traditional options. Designed only as a temporary solution, but with lasting appeal to many, a substantial number of these were built. Morrison entered the building industry at a time when local authorities – including town and district councils – built most houses completed in Scotland. As is shown in table 3.1, the public sector dominated new-build housing. It can also be seen that it took a number of years for the industry to regain capacity, partly as a result of the very real scarcity of raw materials, partly as a result of policy problems.

For Gordon, 'there was always housing… [as] part of the package, [but]… it was not a primary part of the business'. Alex did not win contracts to build for Tain Council. Gordon suggests that, like many councils and other aspects of Scottish public life, Freemasons held considerable influence over Tain Council. Alex 'always suspected the reason he never got work from Tain Town Council was because he was not a Freemason'.[47] It is impossible to know, but perhaps this does indeed explain why his firm did not win such work. Alex did, however, receive contracts from district councils. Perhaps the lack of work in Tain forced him to look further and develop a more diverse order book, ultimately strengthening the business.

Table 3.1: Scottish Housing Completions (1945–62)

| | Local Authority (%) | Other Public Sector (%) | Total Public Sector (%) | Private Sector (%) | Total number of completions |
|---|---|---|---|---|---|
| 1945 | 86 | 5 | 91 | 9 | 1,569 |
| 1946 | 77 | 11 | 88 | 12 | 4,310 |
| 1947 | 73 | 15 | 89 | 11 | 12,149 |
| 1948 | 78 | 14 | 93 | 7 | 21,211 |
| 1949 | 77 | 18 | 96 | 4 | 25,847 |
| 1950 | 81 | 16 | 97 | 3 | 25,811 |
| 1951 | 78 | 17 | 95 | 5 | 22,928 |
| 1952 | 72 | 20 | 93 | 7 | 30,947 |
| 1953 | 75 | 19 | 94 | 6 | 39,548 |
| 1954 | 77 | 17 | 93 | 7 | 38,853 |
| 1955 | 71 | 19 | 90 | 10 | 34,069 |
| 1956 | 69 | 16 | 86 | 14 | 31,901 |
| 1957 | 75 | 14 | 89 | 11 | 32,437 |
| 1958 | 70 | 17 | 87 | 13 | 32,170 |
| 1959 | 68 | 16 | 84 | 16 | 27,293 |
| 1960 | 63 | 15 | 77 | 23 | 28,592 |
| 1961 | 62 | 12 | 74 | 26 | 27,230 |
| 1962 | 61 | 10 | 71 | 29 | 26,761 |
| Mean | 73 | 15 | 88 | 12 | 25,757 |

Notes: For simplicity, Other Public Sector means all non-Local Authority housing: New Towns, Scottish Special Housing Associations, Other Housing Association, and Government Departments.
Calculated from figures in 'Appendix A: Completed Houses – Scotland, 1919–1987', in R. Rodger (ed.), *Scottish Housing in the Twentieth Century* (Leicester: Leicester University Press, 1989), pp.236–7.

THE MORRISON STORY

After the Second World War, successive Conservative governments pursued agendas of a shift towards working-class home ownership. Peter Malpass has characterised the provision of housing as the 'wobbly pillar' of the welfare state, largely as a result of the capital intensity – that is large amounts of public resources being required to provide them, but also because of an ideological shift which sought to reduce state responsibility and place the onus on individuals, either through ownership outright or through the private rented sector.[48] The idea of a property-owning democracy emerged during the interwar period, although it was some time until the major transfers of public housing took place as part of central government policy.[49] Table 3.1 shows the increasing number of private homes being built in this period.

As a small-scale operation at this time, Alex's company was well-positioned to undertake a range of housing contracts, including small Local Authority schemes, as well as some individual properties for private clients. Morrison was not a speculative builder at this time, even if the property development wing of the company would do this later on in the company's history. At several points in this story, Alex and each of his sons were a few steps ahead of the curve. Treating house building as 'a personal activity' and allowing private clients to choose internal design

Early houses on Morangie Road, Tain, from 1950s by George Ellis, 2018.

and paint colours, is symptomatic of how interviewees saw Alex's approach to business: that it was both personal in nature, and personable in the way he approached it. The approach was cautious, too, in that this was not speculative building. He started with three bungalows on Morangie Road, Tain, built to order.

The personal touch was evident even at this early stage, as whilst the basic designs were the same, 'the buyer could select one of three types of bathroom, with the costs varying according to how luxurious the fittings were'.[50] Alex's wife Connie is still in touch with the family of the purchasers of these first Morrison houses. A similar approach of selling one house at a time was employed in small developments such as at Knockbreck Avenue and on Scotsburn Road in Tain. On Scotsburn Road, Alex built six more for local professionals including two teachers.[51] Morrison built houses for Gordon and Fraser's maths and French teachers. The invoice for Mr Melvin, the French teacher's house in Scotsburn Road is shown. Alex described himself as 'Carpenter and Joiner, Building Contractor' – it might be added that he did so with exquisite typography, offering a little polish to the company's emerging image. Ten years in and Alex was already offering extras by encouraging clients to feel they were getting a good deal with

# THE MORRISON STORY

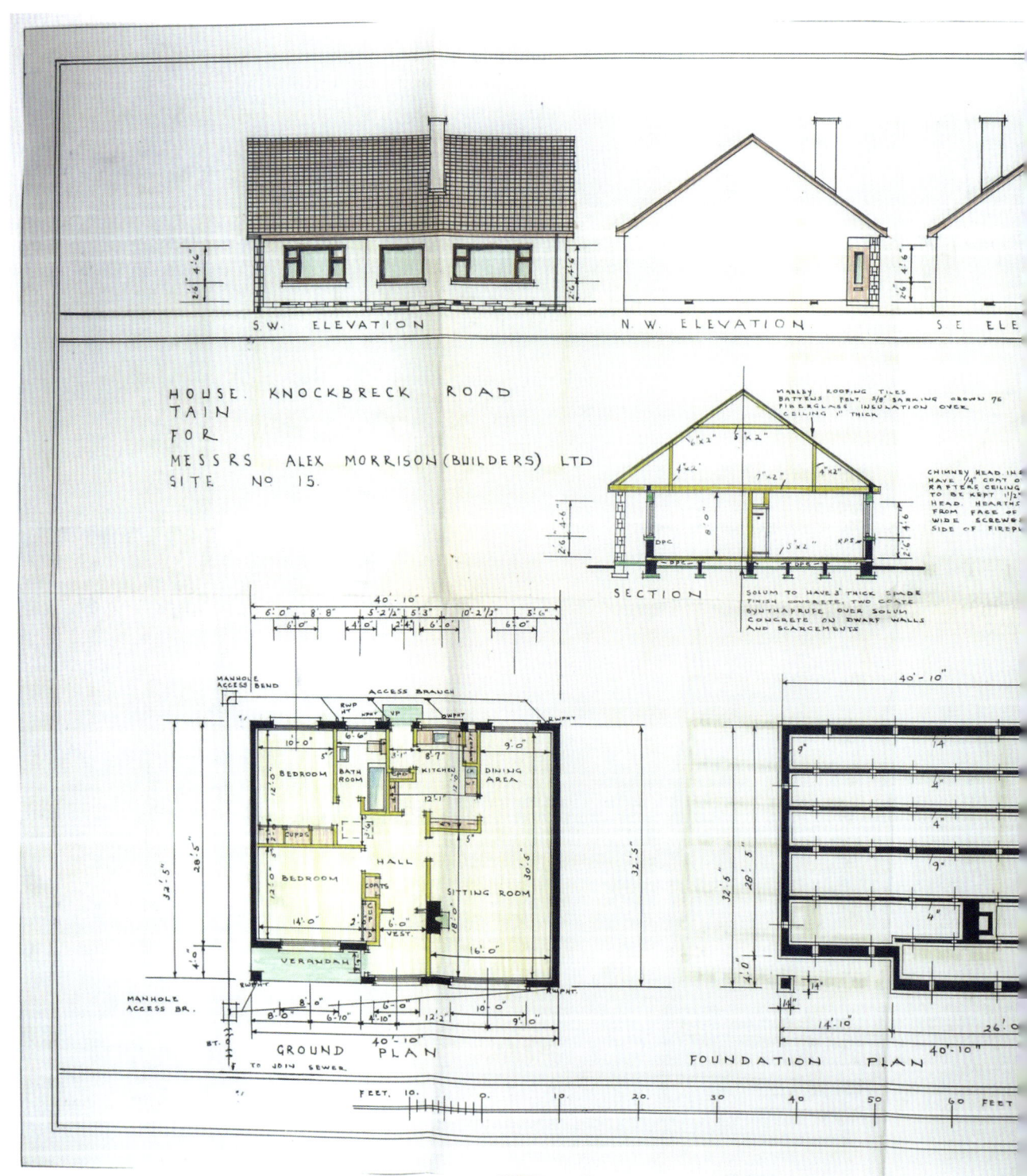

STARTING OUT

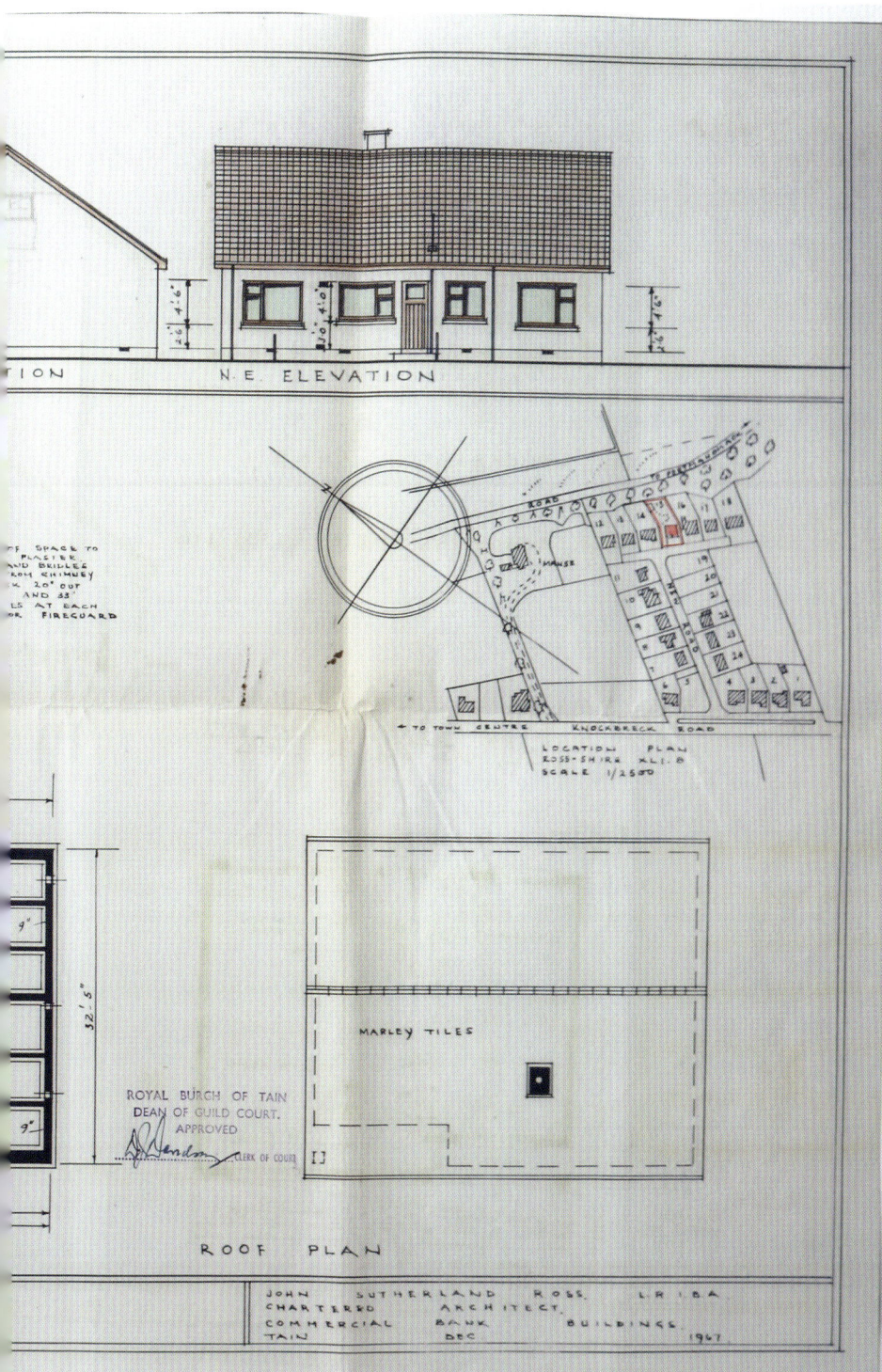

Plans for a bungalow on Morangie Road, Tain, which was never built, 1954. Drawn by John Ross, relative of Connie. (BTN/3/1/28, Highland Archive Centre)

THE MORRISON STORY

Invoice for Mr Melvin's house, 1958.

```
                        TELEPHONE 202
        TO...
        ALEX. MORRISON
        Carpenter and Joiner, Building Contractor
            STATION ROAD ... TAIN

Mr. G. Melvin,                          September, 1958.
   Scotsburn Road,
   Tain.

        To building bungalow as per offer.     £  3282  -  -
        Extra for trellis as per offer £40 done for   25  -  -
        Extra for outer wall as per offer.            20  -  -
        Extra for fireplace £9 15s.   No. charge.
                                         £  3327  -  -
                    Less amount paid        2500  -  -
                                         £   827  -  -
                    Less Discount               27  -  -
                                         £   800  -  -

22nd October 1958.   £  s.  d.
Rec'd from              800: -: -
Mr G. Melvin
Scotsburn C. Tain.        By
p.p. Alex Morrison      Cheque.
Sig. S. [illegible]
```

such things as discounted trellis work and a free fireplace, as well as a bill rounded down from £827 to £800 on the final instalment. Mr Melvin not only became neighbours with Alex and Connie, but also a lifelong friend. Building the houses one by one provided a granular development which was cautious but supplied a 'trickle' of work to help keep Alex's men in work between the larger contracts. Alex's efforts to keep his in men in work earned their devoted loyalty. At the same time, it maintained the flexibility to scale up operations quickly when larger contracts were awarded, preventing the company from over-reaching.

One of the most important houses that Alex built was his own on Scotsburn Road, completed in 1958. Certainly, it made for a handsome family home, but more than anything it served as a statement: less than ten years in business and he had been able to build for his family. His wife remembers 'I recall laying the foundation stone of the house we built together, and I liked the house very much.'⁵²

The Mansfield Estate, Tain, was a larger project which saw 80 houses built by Morrison in five years and a further 40 followed.⁵³ This was the largest scale project in these years and was undertaken for Ross & Cromarty District Council. A three-bedroom council house cost £26 per year to rent in 1952 in Tain – £1800 in 2017 money.⁵⁴ It also shows the problems of the postwar reconstruction era, in that building works were hampered by the inadequacy of the brick supply.⁵⁵ The Edderton Council Housing scheme which began in 1954 was an important project for Alex's company in its early years, with contracts worth £4,520 adding sheds to the ten houses in the first development. Another council housing contract was at Evanton where the firm built 20 houses, with contracts for site preparation, brick work, carpenter work, plumbing and plastering totalling £11,600 between 1961 and 1963.⁵⁶ Finally, the Alness scheme saw Morrison build 181 houses.⁵⁷ For a young business in a small rural place, this is evidence that, even if snubbed by Tain Town Council, the firm quickly established a reputation in the broader local area.

Alex laying the foundation stone of his house.

Wartime and postwar construction had seen experimentation with new approaches and non-traditional building methods.⁵⁸ Given that building houses by laying bricks or stones was essentially timeless, it is perhaps unsurprising that there was an expectation in the 1940s in particular that new technologies and ways of building should be found. Various kit and pre-fabricated homes were developed. One historian has called these houses 'participatory forms of architecture'.⁵⁹ This might mean those which saved on resources: energy, bricks, time assembling on site. Very rarely were they cheaper than traditional methods. The Scandinavian type, for example, was:

> Built of short waste lengths of tongue-and-groove boarding, they were quickly erected in rural areas and had excellent insulation standards; although redesigned by British government architects, the plank construction was distinctively Scandinavian. Local authorities provided sites and services, from 1945 using prisoner-of-war labour, but although 10,000 houses were promised, only 2,444 were erected because of restrictions on dollar imports imposed in 1947 that limited softwood supplies until November 1953.⁶⁰

The construction of these houses occurred within the context of postwar economy: practical realities were to the fore, such as securing enough raw materials and the problems of managing foreign exchange when the state

Alex and Connie Morrison's new house in Tain, in 1958 by George Ellis, 2018. To the right, part of Mr Melvin's house can be seen.

had stretched the economy almost to the limit, in order to meet the needs of total war. The term 'total war' means conflicts where the entire resources of the nation-state are mobilised for defensive purposes, leaving very little capacity for other economic activities. These houses were erected as part of a programme launched in 1945 to install 2,500. By February 1949, there were complaints in the House of Commons that the government had insisted on using no more than four large companies, largely because of concerns about finding the expertise 'accustomed to building in remote areas'.[61] Morrison was not yet of a stature to bid for the initial work, only the upgrades; but the story tells something of the climate in which Alex's company was operating.

These houses – not erected by Morrison – were found wanting, soon requiring upgrades and improvements. Problems included woodworm, non-compliance with fire-regulations, 'chimney stacks in roof space[s]… [which] had not been cement rendered' were identified. Even when new windows were added, they were 'letting in even more water than the old type' with 'dangerous water penetration into power points below the living room and bedroom windows'.[62] Morrison won a contract from Caithness Council to add porches to the Swedish system houses they had installed, leading to a profitable six-month job.[63] These were the type of houses imported 'flat-packed' from Sweden described by Harwood above. The need for the porches speaks of the challenges of Highland weather when designing and building structures. Over the years, Morrison would come to win contracts in many inhospitable places – not only in the north of Scotland, but even as unforgiving as the Falkland Islands and Antarctica on the basis of this expertise. The aesthetic and cultural value of these houses has become celebrated, and some have been listed.[64] In the late 1950s Morrison won a contract to put up Slingsby kit houses.[65]

## Other building work

Around 1953, Alex's firm began a strategy of diversification, taking on a broader range of tasks. This made growth possible and creates a more resilient business. This included both public and private clients. Some of this work was a range of jobs for the Highland Council, particularly from the mid-1950s onwards. Some representative examples of these are: a small contract erecting a fence in front of Culrain School in September 1953 for £30; '[r]epairs to windows and internal decoration on change of headteacher' at Inver Schoolhouse, for £137 in June 1954; carpenter work at Kilmuir Easter School and Schoolhouse in 1958 worth £121 in 1958. As the company expanded its

Taylor's Garage, Invergordon, c.1960. Back row: Alex, Hughie Macintosh, Dan Mackenzie, Max the Pole, Alec Semple, Johnny Morrison, David Vass, Donny McLaren, Robert John Mackay, Jock MacRae, Donnie Mackenzie, Billy Louden; Front row: Dickson Ross, Alec MacLennan, Bobbie Hart, Ian More, Alistair Munro (or Wilson), Hamish Ross, unknown, Ian John Ross, Jock 'Peg' Ross or Vass.

scope, this came to include more than just joinery, so that in December 1959 Alex's company carried out site works, brick work and joinery work worth a total of £8233.[66] A decade after starting out Morrison was moving towards being the one-stop-shop for all construction needs it would later become. One project was Taylor's Garage in Invergordon, where the company built a new showroom and offices for the Ford dealer. In the Highlands private motor cars were very popular given the difficulties of getting around without them.

This was an important job for the firm as it saw Alex fulfilling his ambition of having men work for him. This can be seen in the photograph: there are 22 labourers and tradesmen, but Alex is in a suit on the right; by 1953, he was already managing rather than labouring himself. Moreover, for this project he employed men from another business in order to complete a larger job. On the left of the photograph, a shed bears the sign 'Alex Morrison, Tain, Building Contractor'. Any job might therefore be undertaken, because

## THE MORRISON STORY

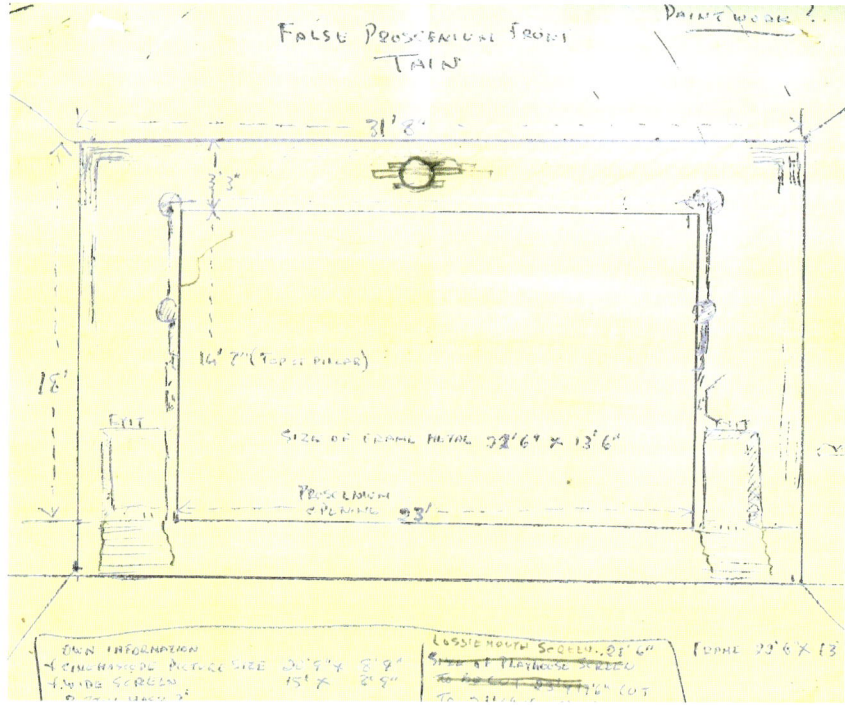

An informal 'back of an envelope' construction drawing, 1954, for Tain cinema's new screen.

as many skills or workers could be brought in as needed. Morrison was no longer a small building company but could take on larger contracts requiring greater human resources and a wider range of technical skills.

The famous Glemorangie whisky distillery had suffered due to Prohibition in the US before World War Two, and the consequences of the economic collapse during the Great Depression. During the War, agricultural products were too scarce to be used for making whisky and the plant was shut down in 1941. After the War, however, the distillery enjoyed a period of steady growth, and expanded its capacity considerably. The distillery's archives hold no information about the nature of the work Morrison was completing there, however, anecdotes have survived about it.[67] Working there in 1953 offered some happy perquisites to Alex's men: they were offered a dram before work, at noon, and at five o'clock. For those whose thirst remained unslaked by this generous serving during working hours, the combination of appropriate tools and substantial warehousing of whisky has left some inevitable stories of the distillery's products being purloined by workmen. Some tales involved tool boxes with false bottoms, others suggest filling lengths of copper pipe with whisky. It is very hard to know how much truth there was to any of this, but it would be unfortunate for company folklore for there to be no such stories.

# STARTING OUT

Even if the stories were fabricated, they speak of the camaraderie shared by Alex's early workforce.

In 1954, the company built a cinema screen in Tain. This was not a major undertaking, but it shows several things: firstly, that the company was getting work locally; secondly, the diversification of the company's order book. Finally, something of the influence of modernity was coming to Tain, as the older screen installed in the 1920s in the converted town hall was upgraded.[68]

## Invergordon Distillery

One of the most important contracts in the Morrison came at Invergordon Distillery. The distillery itself was the brain child of Frank Thomson, as part of the efforts to stimulate the economy which followed the closure of Invergordon as a major naval base. Morrison won a contract to build a substantial number of additional warehouses. Lawrence Allan considers it to be

Founded in whisky country, it is not surprising that Morrison should undertake various distillery warehousing contracts for whisky producers. Above is Balblair Distillery and left is Glenmorangie.

the big jump… from being a small-time building contractor to a much larger concern… because that gave him the confidence to take on the larger jobs. Also, with the sort of security of having that big contract, he was able to invest in more plant.[69]

In a real sense, this contract represented a major turning point. Alex had taken on this work with encouragement from Thomson. Thomson was an entrepreneur and Chairman of Ross County Football Club, and was responsible for getting Morrison invited to tender. Once again, personal connections proved so important to the company's growth.[70] Gordon suggested in his book *Men of Tain* that it led to a payroll of over 200.[71]

With more men working on site, Alex had his first taste of dealing with industrial relations during the Invergordon project. The demands were for overtime and travel time, things which were increasingly common in the sector. Alex agreed promptly, and a strike was averted. This is a telling incident, as it marks the shift from Alex simply employing family and former comrades to becoming a serious operation. People may have enjoyed their work and what they did, but they wanted to be paid properly for it and have decent conditions in which to do it.

## Workplace culture

Working at Morrison in the early days would have been very different to later years with the company. Alex himself was, by most accounts, economical. He would not allow materials to be wasted or for his men to sit idle. Yet if they were worked hard, and pay was relatively mean, men did not leave the company. This was another enduring feature of the firm. In these early years, there are many reasons why men might have stayed with the firm, but money was not one of them. A lack of alternative sources of employment partly explains this. Whilst the postwar period saw high levels of employment nationally, options within small places like Tain were limited. His parsimony earned him the epithet "Mr Shilling-a-Foot" for his exhortations to treat materials as the valuable resources they were, particularly in the postwar era. Overtime pay was resisted for a long time. There was an implicit deal: in return for working hard when times were busy, Alex kept on his men when times were lean. It is perhaps unsurprising then that he inspired great loyalty.[72] Alex also had great faith in the men whom he employed and people with modest experience or few formal qualifications but plenty of potential would be nurtured.

Another reason men may have stayed with the company for long periods of time were acts of kindness. Some of these were small: buying rounds of drinks or sending each of his men a turkey at Christmas.[73] Whilst the men will surely have appreciated Alex's own version of workplace welfare, they possibly would have preferred overtime pay. However, from quite early days, Morrison was a company with which it was worth remaining. There was scope for promotion – from the early days and, as will be shown, this is still the case. Billy Louden joined the company in 1960, was promoted to foreman in 1965 and became a site agent in 1970; Johnny Morrison enjoyed a similar career trajectory.

When John Fisher Ross, an ex-army man, suffered with poor eye sight and arthritis, Alex simply found him a job in the workshop.[74] In the picture below Alex is with John Fisher Ross by the sundial he gave to Tain as a civic gift to the benefit of the town, in 1966. This was part of the celebrations of 900 years of Tain's status as a Royal Burgh, when a new rose garden was created. Providing the sundial – offered some positive publicity for the company and quietly supported Alex's local community.[75]

As the company became bigger, the transport needs of the workforce expanded. Alex started with a Morris, then a Land Rover by June 1953,

INCOME TAX YEAR 1965-66
CERTIFICATE OF PAY AND TAX DEDUCTED

John George Morrison
(Name of employee and Works No., if any)

Code No. at 5 April, 1966 (Enter "E" if an Emergency Card is in use at 5 April, 1966) 633

District Ref. (if any)

1. Pay and tax in respect of previous employment(s) in 1965–66 taken into account in arriving at the tax deductions made by me/us ... ... ... ...

2. PAY AND TAX IN MY/OUR EMPLOYMENT ...

| Gross pay £ | s. | d. | Tax £ | s. | d. |
|---|---|---|---|---|---|
| | | | | | |
| 1036 | 16 | [illegible] | 63 | 2 | . |

I/We certify that the particulars given above include the total amount of pay (including overtime, bonus, commission, etc.) paid to you by me/us in the year ended 5 April, 1966, and the total tax deducted by me/us (less any refunds) in that year.

6th April, 1966 ....Date ....Employer

TO THE EMPLOYEE. Keep this certificate. It will help you to check any Notice of Assessment which the tax office may send you in due course.

P60 (1965)

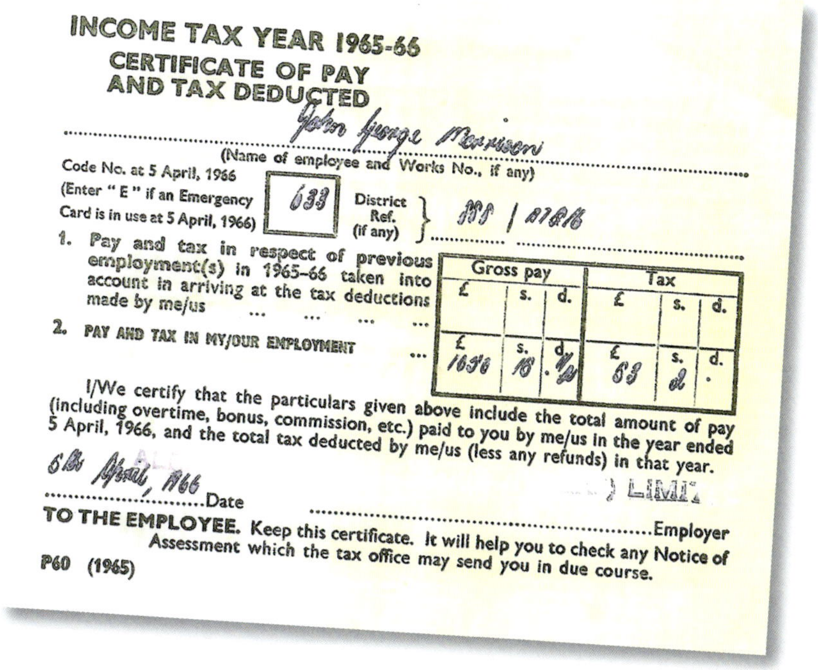

Johnny Morrison's first annual salary of over £1,000, April 1966.

# THE MORRISON STORY

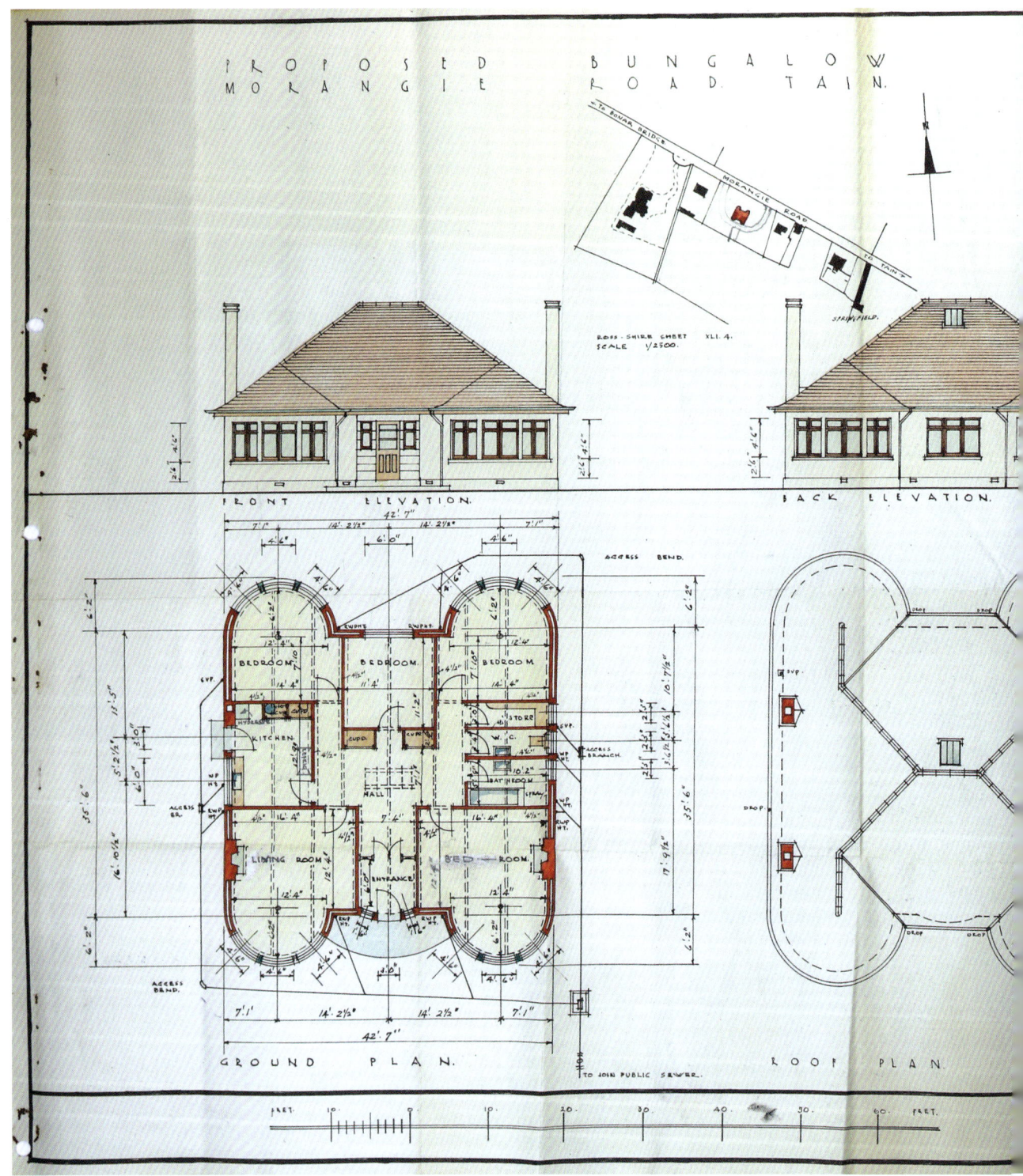

# STARTING OUT

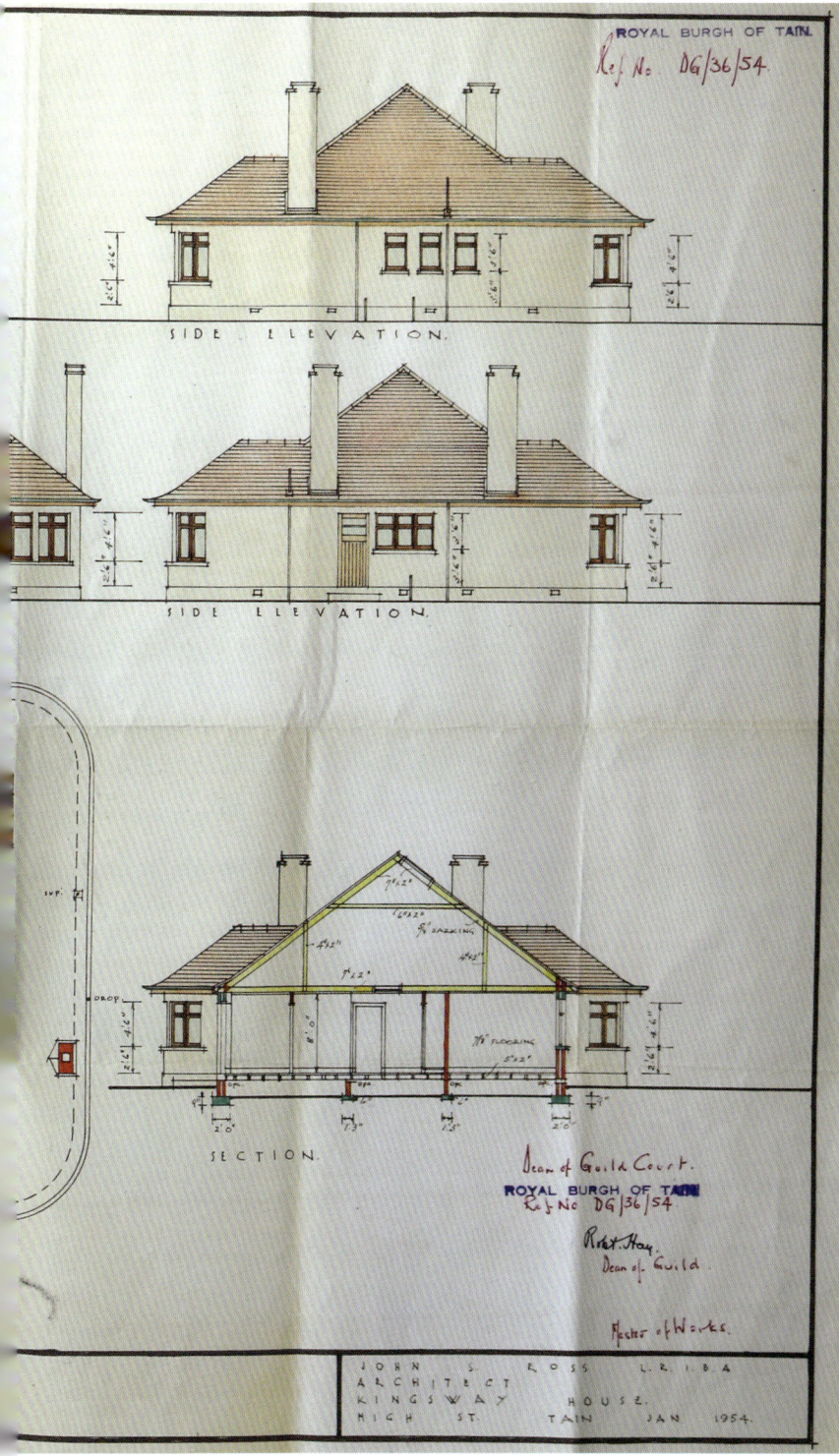

Plans for a bungalow on Morangie Road, Tain, which was never built, 1954. Drawn by John Ross, relative of Connie. (BTN/3/1/61, Highland Archive Centre)

THE MORRISON STORY

Inver Housing, near Tain.

then a Hillman Minx. In 1958, the crew bus "Trojan" had been acquired. Lorries were also needed to move around construction materials.

The company was growing rapidly and perhaps even Alex was taken a little by surprise by how big his company had become when the lorries were lined up one holiday at Knockbreck Avenue in 1964.[76] Clearly the fleet was important to Alex and on the fiftieth anniversary of the company he was presented with a glass replica of a lorry.[77] A growing fleet of vehicles was a visible sign of modernity and success for the company (see picture on page 66).

John Fisher Ross and Alex with the sundial which Morrison presented to Tain civic garden in 1966.

STARTING OUT

Alex and Connie are presented to HM the Queen Mother during celebrations to mark the 900th anniversary of Tain's Royal Charter, 1966.

Fraser and Gordon with their grandfather, Dan Fraser (Connie's father), on Coronation Day, 2 June 1953.

A Morrison Bedford lorry being put to good use as a float in the annual Tain Gala, July 1954.

THE MORRISON STORY

Crew Bus 19 July 1958. The Trojan pictured on Coronation Park.

A proud and impressive line-up: parked up for summer break, 1964. Seven Thames Traders and one Commer.

## Financial growth

Only very limited information is available about the company's finances in this early period. Nonetheless, the trading summaries in table 3.2 reveal a good deal. Between 1951 and 1959, cash figures, which are nominal and, therefore, not adjusted for inflation, reveal quite a lot. Firstly, business done, materials, wages and costs had increased tenfold; net profit had fallen from 13.4 per cent to 3.5 per cent of sales. This most likely reflects the decline after the immediate postwar boom, as a 13 per cent return would not have been sustainable.

Table 3.2: Trading summaries for Morrison (1951–59) (£ Nominal)

| YEAR ENDING 31/5 | Sales and Work Done | Materials | Wages | Costs | Gross Profit | Net Profit | (as % of sales) |
|---|---|---|---|---|---|---|---|
| 1951 | 6,208 | 2,575 | 1,880 | 5,040 | 1,168 | 831 | 13.4 |
| 1952 | 8,351 | 3,602 | 2,898 | 7,052 | 1,299 | 820 | 9.8 |
| 1953 | 11,589 | 6,119 | 3,444 | 10,017 | 1,572 | 975 | 8.4 |
| 1954 | 17,573 | 10,596 | 4,563 | 15,899 | 1,674 | 1,017 | 5.8 |
| 1955 | 25,321 | 16,650 | 4,762 | 22,307 | 3,014 | 1,947 | 7.7 |
| 1956 | 38,288 | 24,623 | 8,796 | 35,281 | 3,007 | 1,994 | 5.2 |
| 1957 | 54,046 | 26,248 | 15,761 | 50,392 | 3,654 | 2,055 | 3.8 |
| 1958 | 61,122 | 25,039 | 20,409 | 56,640 | 4,482 | 2,589 | 4.2 |
| 1959 | 60,822 | 28,363 | 21,223 | 56,063 | 4,759 | 2,154 | 3.5 |

Notes: based on typescript sheet in family papers. Provenance unknown.
Costs include both costs of sales and work done; prices are in nominal £.
Per cent calculated to one decimal place.

There are different ways in which this information can be considered. Adjusted for inflation, the growth in sales was healthy. These figures show a more realistic representation of the value of work done.

These figures only provide very rough estimates, but they show that the company was getting bigger in every way: more men, more work and growing profits, even if the margin fell. Several strategies sat behind this. As has been shown, Alex was happy to pick up work from other, failing companies. With cashflows reliant on bank overdrafts, it only took a small number of contracts to go wrong for a company to find itself in financial difficulties. During the building boom, Alex's company got work from local farmers and their friends. A large number of small jobs added up to provide quite a diverse order book, alongside larger ones.[78] Around 1960, the company won a contract to work on the pier at Kinlochbervie. Whilst the job involved wood and joinery, it was a proper civil engineering job, and meant working with the tide.[79] This gave a taste of what was to come: within two decades the company would be undertaking some very technically challenging engineering projects in roads, bridges and other complex structures. The pier saw the company take a first step in that direction.

Table 3.3: Estimated Number of Employees (1951–59)

| YEAR ENDING 31/5 | Wages (£) | Estimated number of employees | Average Annual Nominal Earnings (£) |
| --- | --- | --- | --- |
| 1951 | 1,880 | 5.5 | 344 |
| 1952 | 2,898 | 7.7 | 375 |
| 1953 | 3,444 | 8.6 | 400 |
| 1954 | 4,563 | 11.0 | 414 |
| 1955 | 4,762 | 11.0 | 434 |
| 1956 | 8,796 | 18.4 | 478 |
| 1957 | 15,761 | 32.3 | 489 |
| 1958 | 20,409 | 39.7 | 514 |
| 1959 | 21,223 | 39.6 | 535 |

Notes: the wages here are given as nominal prices – so they have not been adjusted for inflation. The total amount spent on wages has been divided by the average annual earnings to indicate the approximate number of employees.

## Conclusion

In the twelve-year period, from 1948 to 1962, Alex's business was established and enjoyed remarkable growth, becoming a profitable company, with a diverse order book of housing, commercial building and other jobs on any scale. That first foray into engineering offered a taste of what was to come. The company had become a contractor, able to scale to any size of job. The first pivotal project was the Invergordon Distillery warehousing contract, which offered security of work on which to build corporate capacity, buying plant to save on the cost of hiring. It also formalised workforce relations as Alex came up against the reality that to be a major player he would have to compete on the same terms as other contractors with his workers; camaraderie, loyalty and a Christmas turkey would only take things so far. Alex's business was becoming a much more impressive outfit; even if these staff-related issues may have felt like troubles at the time, they were in fact growing pains. The world of work was beginning to become more modern and the company moved with the times. One of the defining characteristics of both the sons in their later leadership of the company was to be several steps ahead of the competition. The flexible, bold approach Alex had demonstrated in grasping opportunities and taking risks foreshadowed this.

The company was a product of the postwar period, reflecting the building boom and type of work which was on offer. It was a product, too, of Alex's time as a prisoner of war. If, whilst languishing at Lamsdorf, he had dreamed of having others work for him, then he saw this materialise; it seems likely he dreamed of a comfortable home and a loving family, and he certainly got these, too. Alex had leveraged a car, some tools – perhaps borrowed, and personal connections, to a business making a healthy profit of £178,000 per year in 2017 money.[80] He had a happy family which lived in material comfort. Through a mixture of good judgement, luck and circumstances, Morrison was in an ideal position to seize opportunities. As the company continued to grow, it would take on some important jobs. Moreover, as it scaled up its capacities, it became well-placed to take advantage of the major oil boom heading to the North, but with diversity to hedge against downturns and price fluctuations.

CHAPTER FOUR

# Growing success: Alexander Morrison (Builders) Limited 1963–1974

**O**N 31 MAY 1963, Alexander Morrison (Builders) Limited was incorporated, with a nominal capital of £20,000. This represented an important moment in the development of the company, not least because Alex was no longer personally liable for any debts incurred by the business. Control was kept firmly in the family: ownership was split between Alex and Connie in equal proportions and the qualification for directorship was a 50 per cent shareholding. The Memorandum of Association defined the objects of the business as to take over 'and to carry on business':

> as builders, contractors, manufacturers and erectors of concrete, stone, wooden, steel, plaster or other dwelling houses, outhouses, works, buildings, fences, roofs… [and as] painters, decorators, plumbers, masons, bricklayers, plasterers, joiners, wood workers, wood merchants, engineers (structural, mechanical, electrical and gas and water)… [and as builders of] houses, buildings, works, fences, roads, drains, ways, workshops, warehouses, shops, stores and buildings of all kinds…[1]

These show how broad Alex's operation had become, albeit still a family one with strong local roots. The extent to which the company was actually engaged in all these activities is a separate question, but they do reflect flexibility and ambition. Having already become a contractor – meaning that scale was not an obstacle – scope was being expanded, too. Over time the addition of other capacities – or disciplines as they are sometimes called such as civil engineering and property services, saw the company was able to undertake any project that came its way.

If the company had gained a formal legal personality with limited liability and was making some first steps towards corporate oversight and governance, the sense of the smaller family operation clearly remained. The objects also permitted the company:

> [t]o support and subscribe to any charitable or public object and any institution, society or club which may be for the benefit of the Company or its employees, or may be connected with any town or place where the Company carries on business; to give pensions, gratuities or charitable aid to any person or persons who have served the Company, or to the wives, children or other relatives of such persons, and to form and contribute to provident and benefit funds for the benefit of any persons employed by the Company.[2]

At some point in the process, Alex ensured that he would have sufficient constitutional powers to make a wide range of discretionary payments.

The registration of the business as a formal company was not the only thing changing in 1963. Lawrence Allen arrived in April 1963 to be the company's first full-time accountant after Alex 'had been told by his auditor it was about time he got somebody in to look after the paperwork of his business, rather than trying to do that himself.'[3]

Lawrence's appointment was important because he was a professional, the first qualified person appointed to such a role within the company, with only one examination left to sit before becoming a certified accountant. Alex showed confidence in him and appointed him. Not only was Lawrence responsible for keeping the accounts, but he also had to manage the office. The scale of expansion meant that more elements of management were needed to keep control over the business.

Even as things were being put on a more formal footing in terms of business management, Alex's style of business remained warm and personal. Lawrence remembers arriving in Tain to stay with a friend's relation.

> I was taken to the bed and breakfast… an hour or so after I arrived there, there was a knock at the door. This was Alex Morrison. He'd been told where I was staying… [and] this was him to welcome me. He picked me up and we went touring around the town, and then I was up [to his home] for a meal before I started… on the Monday morning.[4]

GROWING SUCCESS

Such was Highland hospitality. From the start, Lawrence formed a good impression of Alex, as his new boss arrived to pick him up in a smart motor car. Lawrence contends that the various luxury motors Alex had over the years were to 'put out that air of authority', and they certainly feature in many of the stories involving Alex. At one point Alex even had a Bentley, 'but he only kept it for a short period of time… it was a bit much'. The warm welcome clearly worked: whilst Lawrence did not want to move to Inverness when the firm did, he remained firm friends with Alex and Connie and until she moved to London to be nearer her sons more recently, paid her regular visits.[5]

The next day, Lawrence went to his office at the new Station Road workshop, where the firm had its first proper offices. This had more modern facilities, including a first aid cabinet, proper lavatories, and 'state-of-the-art machines' for wood working, including saws and planers.[6] A portion was divided out for his office, but the furniture had not yet arrived.[7] The separation of space to provide a specific place for administration and book-keeping was the start of a process of increasing bureaucracy necessary for project management, compliance and corporate control. In the workshop proper, a range of goods could be manufactured: doors, windows, and staircases.

An outing in his Mercedes-Benz: Alex and family members at Logie Quarry, 1965.

# THE MORRISON STORY

GROWING SUCCESS

Morrison's second office and workshop, 1960s, by George Ellis, 2018.

A move to a larger workshop in the early 70s allowed the pre-fabrication of timber framed houses and chalets. These reflect experimentation in types and ways of constructing buildings, particularly around the idea of concentrating work in factories. Even if pre-fabricated housing did not lead the building industry towards a fundamentally different mode of production, increasing use was made of fabricating parts of houses off-site in factories. Later in this story, Morrison used pre-manufactured bathroom units in the new Edinburgh Royal Infirmary. In the 1960s, the innovations were simpler and related to the joinery business that sat at the core of operations. The eight men or more who Lawrence remembers from the new workshop were, in effect, consolidating the supply chain within the company: a small-scale version of vertical integration.[8] This sits in sharp contrast to the disaggregated supply chains that characterise modern commerce.

The 1960s were also a formative period for workplace safety culture. At the start of this period, the provisions were wholly inadequate. One historian has described the safety regulations in place as 'highly fragmented', so that 'a third of the entire working population received no statutory protection from accidents and illnesses resulting from work'.[9] In 1961, the first construction health and safety regulations for factories were issued, as part of an uneven system. Given that it was not until 1989 that hard hats became compulsory,

Alex hard at work at his desk at Shandwick House offices.

it requires little stretch of the imagination to realise how dangerous building sites were. In 1965, the accident rate in the United Kingdom was 84 per cent higher than the United States. The harsh reality such statistics reveal is that there was a higher chance that the UK workplace would be a site of injury or even fatality than in America, or than in the modern workplace with its safety measures. Over the period with which this chapter is concerned, the situation was improving, with the number of workplace deaths nationally falling: 250 occurred in 1963–64; in 1989–90 this figure dropped to 140; in 2009–10, 45 people were killed at work in the UK. This improvement was achieved through a number of initiatives. During the consultations which preceded the Health and Safety at Work etc Act 1974, the Robens principle that voluntary self-regulation where possible should be pursued held much sway.[10] In the early 1960s, there was a very long way to go in ensuring everyone returned home safely at night; within a few decades, the company would become a leader in health and safety, and it would become a major distinguishing factor for Morrison in a crowded market.

Not dissimilarly to the workplace welfare discussed in the previous chapter, the growing need for health and safety regimes was met with hostility or concern by some. The figure of the suited inspector, perhaps brandishing a clipboard, became something of a spectre haunting sites. Lawrence Allan bore witness to this in an oblique way. The Invergordon Distillery warehouses contract, which was so important to Morrison's development, started around 1963. He remembers one occasion having reason to visit the site and the men being somewhat alarmed. 'I had to go out from the office… to [make] a proper inventory of our plant and equipment.' As he arrived on site, 'the foreman… saw from a distance these two men… he recognised one right away… the other was a chap in a suit… he thought I was some sort of official' and was very much relieved when it transpired he had not arrived to make some formal inspection perhaps of the arrangements for the storage of bonded whisky, on which duty had not been paid.[11]

Building sites became subject to greater scrutiny and inspection and, even if it was frustrating, over time this was part of what made them safer places to work. This happened in the workshop one day when 'a stranger in a suit walked in and introduced himself. "I'm from the Health and Safety Executive," before asking to see the lavatories and first aid cupboard'. If this is remembered correctly, then it must have been after 1974 when the Health and Safety Executive (HSE) was established.[12] With the encouragement of officialdom, these necessities were provided with promptitude – within a week some basic provisions had been made.[13] Gordon remembers his father co-operating with such a visit from the HSE. There was a great gap from how things were in the earliest days to how they ought to be in workplaces which did not have hard hats or other basic precautions. At Invergordon distillery in the mid-1960s, when Gordon was around 15, he used to go and drive his father's car to visit all the bonded warehouses. On another occasion, Gordon was driving a vibrating roller, earning a reprimand from the Health and Safety inspector for a teenager operating such a potentially dangerous machine.[14]

Perhaps over time as workers and employers alike saw the benefits of safer workplaces, at least at Morrison, wariness gave way to wholehearted embrace. As will be shown, over the following decades a proactive and frequently industry-leading safety culture developed within the company. Initial changes centred on removing unsafe practices and acquiring basic safety equipment, as well as establishing a cultural change. No statutory instrument could mandate the internalisation of responsibilities – this would take considerable time to develop. Through these earliest steps, a modern workplace culture was emerging. Safe business is good business, as it tends to be more profitable.

## Tain Royal Academy

If housing was the first postwar construction priority, the provision of schools was probably the second. The growing importance of this task is highlighted by one statistic: In 1948, 8 per cent of Local Authority buildings constructed were schools; ten years later they represented over one quarter of this output.[15] Not only was the population growing, but the raising of the school leaving age meant that more schooling and, therefore, school accommodation were required. The leaving age was increased to 15 in 1947 and 16 in 1973, with strong pressure for pupils to continue beyond this age. New comprehensive schools also meant new and modified buildings.[16] Nationally, 'severe strains' were caused in supporting the programme of building and expanding schools. Financially and logistically, the scale of capital investment need, raising both local-administrative and national-policy issues.[17] For Alex's business, however, there was the chance to provide a range of services at any scale.

Schools presented a particular challenge in the Highlands, as there were a great number of them, many of which catered for tiny numbers and almost all of which needed urgent improvements. When visited in 1963: '[o]f the 112 day schools in the County 100 of these were at present sub-standard', and the problem was sufficient significant for the Scottish Education Department to be involved.[18] Some of these only required relatively small works such as Scotsburn Schoolhouse where Alex went to school in 1924 walking several miles each day from Moor Farm and where Morrison did '[s]everal works' for £941 in 1963.[19]

Particularly in small and remote places, providing accommodation for teachers was important. The diversity of services offered by Morrison came into play and various County Council contracts followed: Gledfield School, Ardgay, had a new floor covering for £283, Tain Primary School had a new lavatory extension for £4470, and at Inver School House, re-decoration provided £130 of business to Morrison.[20] The size of these contracts won varied, and being willing to take on even small contracts enabled the company to pick up much business leading to a steady flow of work. This attitude continued even as the business expanded considerably to become a major force in the construction sector.

Some schools required more serious investment than simple maintenance, and a lengthy procurement process..[21] By the late 1960s this was becoming pressing and, as an interim measure, Morrison set up some temporary classrooms at Conon Bridge School in 1969, for £6182, and at Dingwall Academy completed several contracts totalling £10,739 for the '[e]rection of temporary classrooms'.[22] The major work remained: there was no substitute for building the new schools which were needed. In 1963, Morrison was on the shortlist invited to tender for Fortrose Academy and Invergordon School. Alexander Hall of Aberdeen won the Fortrose contract, but Morrison won the one at Invergordon.[23] There must have been a certain amount of rivalry between the two. Hall had won the County offices tender too, for £148,000 against £160,000 from Morrison, with a key factor being the cost of quarrying and transporting stone.[24]

The Invergordon School contract was clearly a difficult and demanding one. The architects, George Watt and Stewart, designed it in 'the Festival of Britain manner'.[25] In November 1966, there was a meeting to see if it was possible to expedite the building works. The County Council, architects, quantity surveyor, heating and electrical contractors were all there, as well as Alex:

> Mr Morrison stated that certain of his trades were at a standstill because of the lack of heating and the hold up in connection with electrical installations.[26]

With more complex jobs, and more contractors, burdens arose in management and not everything was in Alex's control. Something of his acuity comes through in the outcome of this meeting:

THE MORRISON STORY

Construction work gets underway on the new Invergordon Academy, 1970. Excavator is a 'Drott' from International Harvester and driven by 'Tosh', a machine operator for many many years.

Invergordon Academy.

> At the request of Mr Morrison both these firms [James Scott and R. Finlayson] agreed to provide in writing the assurances… on receipt of which it was agreed the private architects would draw up a programme with the main contractor.[27]

Clearly, it was not Morrison holding up business. Indeed, subsequently Alex had the retention monies held by the Council to mitigate the risk with the project reduced from £25,000 to £16,000, a considerable boost to Morrison cash flow. Nearly a year later, he asked again for it to be reduced to £8,000, which was accepted as this 'would be sufficient at this stage of building operations'.[28] Eventually, Morrison claimed £1937 above the contract price to reach a commercial settlement.[29] Clearly, the company was building up good working relationships, networks and reputation if such an agreement could be reached.

Building on this reputation, the company successfully tendered for the Tain Royal Academy contract. Building a modern secondary school was a project of some importance to the small town but crucially underscored the

Tain Academy during construction in severe winter conditions, 1967.

firm's local reputation. Fraser remembers his father's delight at having won the contract noting, 'he was particularly keen to win… and it was a very competitive tender', and 'it would not have been in his nature to live terribly well with Alexander Hall building the Academy across from his front door'.[30] Indeed, the school entrance was literally across the road from the family home on Scotsburn Road. In 1939, a new school had been approved, but nothing happened, as the War diverted capacity away from such projects.[31] As early as 1949, a site had been identified and planning consultants brought in to assess its suitability.[32] A 1962 report recommended 'that a new secondary school for Tain be included in the Capital Works Programme with a high priority', to accommodate an estimated 16 teachers and 330 students.[33] The

View from the Tain Academy construction site with the Morrison family home in the centre background.

GROWING SUCCESS

Tain Royal Academy Opening. (© Tain & District Museum and Clan Ross Centre)

first cost estimate was £250,000.³⁴ Initially, Morrison appears to have bid too low – there was certainly some problem, but they won it all the same in 1966 for £378,000.³⁵ Alex attempted to trade on the company's reputation to have the Council waive the guarantee bond, on grounds it was 'totally unnecessary for a firm of their standard and repute', but this was declined.³⁶ The job was an important one for the company – it was a large contract, it was very prominent in the firm's home town, and it led to more business. Given that it was 'one of the pivotal… contracts', it was convenient that Alex could keep a very close eye on the site. There was little need for concern as

Tain Royal Academy.

THE MORRISON STORY

GROWING SUCCESS

Construction of Tain Academy, painted by George Ellis, 2018.

Dingwall Swimming Pool. Another Sandy Duff Project.

Sandy Duff was in charge of the school site whom Fraser remembers as being 'a hugely successful and powerful and charismatic individual'.[37] The school was successfully completed and opened by a former Lieutenant Governor of British Colombia, Frank Ross, on 2 October 1969.[38] Gordon was amongst the pupils present at the opening of their new school.[39]

Around this time, clearly having impressed the County Council, Morrison won further work building houses. In 1968, three contracts were worth a considerable sum of money: 10 houses at Balintore worth £37,000, and 24 houses at Milton, worth £87,500, and eight houses at Lochcarron worth £41,500.[40] A willingness to take smaller contracts meant that Morrison was useful to have on the informal list of suppliers used by the Council. At Edderton, Morrison was paid £588 in 1968 for the 'taking down and rebuilding of the chimney stacks of the four houses at Station Road'.[41] Even smaller was a 1964 contract to clear the site ahead of the third development at Edderton, for £35.[42] These may not have been as prominent as the new Academy contract, but they were important work to keep men employed and business ticking over.

## Family home and family life

Alex continued to have a happy and comfortable home life at Scotsburn Road. Labour-saving luxuries such as an automatic washing machine and a car each for both Alex and Connie made for a high material standard of living.[43] Gordon went to school at Tain Royal Academy where he met his future wife, Mary, whom he married at 23. Support for learning was inculcated in both Gordon and Fraser by their parents. In turn, this translated into a corporate culture which invested in training when they led the business. Both Alex and Connie supported education generally, but there was neither pressure nor assumption for their sons to enter the family business. The boys thrived at school, but both had more interest and aptitude in maths and science, rather than the arts. This set them up for any number of possible careers. Fraser wanted at first to be a doctor, then wanted to read chemical engineering. Only when he got to the University of Edinburgh did he decide to study civil engineering. Gordon also studied civil engineering at Edinburgh before going on to work for Tarmac. However, by 1973, both sons had joined the family business.

As shown, even from the earliest days, Alex took care of his extended family. This included close friendships, too. In 1956, David Henderson, the son of a close family friend, broke his leg in the school playground. Alex

GROWING SUCCESS

Fraser and Gordon with friends David and Eric Henderson, 1956.

drove him 46 miles in the back of his car to the nearest hospital. On another occasion, David had managed to embed an axe in his knee. The Morrisons being one of relatively few families to have a private telephone, Connie ran to call the doctor. The point is not to give the impression that David was accident-prone, but rather, as he put it, that Alex was 'always there for our family'. After the Hendersons moved away to Forres, both Alex and Connie always kept in touch. In June 1974, David's father was 'involved in a horrific car accident from which he never recovered. The very first person who was in touch with us was Alex Morrison', making a serious offer of any help which might be needed.[44] A consistent feature in the story of both the family and the company is the creation of enduring relationships. Perhaps this gives the strongest sense of Alex: how he behaved towards those who he knew were not necessarily in a position to help him.

Much of both family life and friendships revolved around cricket. David and Eric Henderson's father was an accountant at the Clydesdale Bank. He was a great enthusiast for the game and the two Morrison sons got 'their first interest in the game through my father'. With so few cars around, the four boys could safely play cricket in the street. Alex himself liked many sports, including target shooting, but unlike many in the north of Scotland, he was not a golfer. Alex had a good sense of fun, but was fiercely competitive too, as David recalls:

> He was competitive. We were on a treasure hunt one night, and I was in Alex's big Rover. We were travelling many miles in and around Tain to pick up clues… We discovered at the end of the evening it was a dead heat, and a question was put to the driver of each car: what was the distance to travel to London not driving on any motorways.

When asked by Alex, David guessed 600, only a few miles out, meaning they won the competition, much to Alex's delight.[45]

Kindnesses extended beyond friendship networks to the community as a whole. Both Alex and Connie were regular church-goers, but never held offices. David Henderson remembers Alex's style was to give discreetly to charitable collections. If the bank manager, solicitor and teacher were the pillars of the community, Alex stood alongside those as a figure of prominence and respect. This is important for the corporate story because as the company became a major national and even international enterprise, both the family and the business retained strong local links. This all gives a sense of Alex as a well-rounded individual – happy at home, successful at work and respected in his community.

## A Highland business

By the early 1970s, the relatively easy prosperity of the immediate postwar years was giving way to more mixed economic circumstances. Not least, inflation, which in the later part of that decade would be so great as to present real challenges to the construction sector, was creeping higher.[46] This was a particular risk with Local Authority contracts at a fixed price.[47] The economic situation was a deteriorating one. The heavy manufacturing sector suffered sustained job losses. Over time this would only worsen, resulting in what historian Bill Knox described as the 'general attrition of manufacturing'.[48] At the same time as this decline, substantial investment was required in almost every area of collective life to meet the promises of public services and public goods from the postwar settlement. Whilst upgrades to schools and housing have already been discussed, other major capital-intensive infrastructure programmes were still needed; for example, upgrading existing roads and constructing a motorway network presented major civil engineering opportunities.

The low population density of the Highlands required more intensive investment in public facilities if service levels were to be maintained. This challenge had been tackled by policy-makers. It was not by coincidence that what is often called the precursor of the National Health Service, the Highlands and Islands Medical Service (HIMS), was set up in sparsely populated areas with low disposable incomes where it was difficult to attract doctors and for them to make a living. The romanticised world of Dr Finlay was some way from the reality. In 1915 the HIMS had been established 'to meet the problems of access to medical services in the islands and northern half of Scotland'.[49] The Highlands would continue to be an important area for policy experimentation, but the hard fact was that if modern medicine was to be provided by the new National Health Service, substantial investment in hospitals required major building projects to high specifications with careful budgetary control.[50] Some of these programmes were disproportionately capital-intense in the sparsely populated Highlands: there were many difficult miles of roads to build, and many very small schools for a handful of pupils. South of Inverness, however, road-building offered benefits to a large number of people. A 1967 report on the Moray Firth Development Area suggested that 'the private car, when available, will be the first choice of travel mode, and one of the attractions of the area will be that people will be able to use their motor cars freely', without the congestion found on urban roads.[51]

If these astonishing programmes of urgent public works presented a headache for the Treasury looking to finance them, for an ambitious building firm like Morrison, they offered real opportunities. Had Alex set up a company which was focused solely on building houses, it seems unlikely that he would have succeeded in creating a thriving business in the medium term, due to the consolidation within the sector which followed the initial postwar boom.[52] Morrison pursued big contracts, like the Invergordon Distillery warehouses job, but remained flexible enough to take on small ones, too. As Donald MacLennan put it: 'we did almost anything. I remember somebody saying, "if there is a roof on it, we will build it"... we built anything and everything: houses, schools, industrial buildings.'[53] Morrison was willing to pick up contracts of any size; for example, in 1964 Morrison built a nurse's house and garage in Tain for the Ross and Cromarty County Council at a cost of £4200.[54]

The Highlands caused particular economic anxieties for Whitehall: questions about productivity, levels of economic activity, sustainable populations and agricultural efficiency dogged policy-makers for decades. The policy answers to these in the 1960s had implications for Morrison because they provided business: firstly, the creation of the Highland and

THE MORRISON STORY

Islands Development Board (HIDB) which sought to develop the economy of the region; and, secondly, the various Board of Agriculture funding schemes for farmers to increase productivity. For example, the Farm Improvement Scheme provided a steady flow of work for Morrison by supporting various modest building works, including 'provision and installation of new fixed plant and machinery; [and] the construction and improvement of silos'.[55] Official anxieties about the Scottish economy were nothing new. During the late eighteenth and nineteenth centuries, major programmes of clearances had seen traditional communities of crofters removed as landlords sought higher incomes by turning over their lands to sheep farming. Existing tenants, perhaps failing to make even a subsistence living from their land, were often far behind on rents. As centuries of relationships were swept away, populations were sometimes moved to marginal spaces and sought to eke out a living on coastal shores. Many others emigrated, with financial assistance from some landlords and private charities, to the settler colonial dominions, leading to a long relationship between Scotland and the white settlers of Canada.[56] Demographic problems became a constant worry after this, as a sustainable population was seen as vital to a productive economy.

At the same time, mass enthusiasm for the Highlands led to a highly romanticised image of the region. Walter Scott's pageants for George IV's visit to Edinburgh in 1822 spread a widespread view of Scotland as being Highland. Queen Victoria had a great enthusiasm for the Highlands at the same time as the railways started to make them increasingly accessible to tourists. Yet this was a highly emotional view, and there were serious

Alness Police Station, mid 1970s.

A wonderful background for the Kyle houses, here under construction, 1968.

questions for public policy. In the 1880s, a distinct 'Highland Policy area' had been created. In the interwar period, there had been further attempts to deal with the particular problems of the area. For example, in the 1930s there had been attempts to create a Commission for the Highlands.[57] During the Second World War, the expediencies of the wartime economy to produce food and wood from farms and forest had taken priority.[58] There was a very real concern 'that the Highlands could not sustain a modern economy, based on a growing population'.[59]

By the early 1960s, therefore, Highland economic development had become a pressing issue. In 1964, the Labour manifesto had promised the establishment of a powerful agency.[60] The result was the creation in 1965 of the Highland and Islands Development Board, which sought to look beyond the mystique of the region and create a more robust economy.[61] The agency had considerable discretion, including the flexibility to support small but risky projects, to offer higher levels of support than the government would generally allow. This was in recognition of the competitive disadvantages and barriers to entry in the region due to its remoteness, high transport costs, and lack of local expertise. As a result, the HIDB was not obliged to apply standard Treasury tests with normal vigour. The HIDB could offer applicants grants-in-aid of up to £25,000, and loans of £50,000. Above these levels, applications would have to be made to the Board of Trade as usual.[62] The intention was clearly to provide relatively modest funding where there was chance of it achieving some success, but perhaps with levels of risk which would not ordinarily have been considered acceptable for public money.

Morrison remained agile, opportunistic and continued to network very effectively within the Highlands. Agility meant building what was needed: this would lead the company to civil engineering before long. Projects were diverse. In 1968, the company built 33 houses at Kyle of Lochalsh, excavating peat and blowing up rock in order to do so. The Highland geology produced a range of challenges. Large lumps of granite were in the way and explosives were applied to make the remains portable. When the process was repeated to forcibly excavate a cattle grid, rather too much explosive was applied, so that the detonation had sufficient force to shatter some windows in neighbouring houses. Of course, a firm of builders was well placed to put this right. At Fearn, a project of fifteen houses began in 1972. The men struggled due to very heavy rainfall causing a flood on site and a supply of timber had to be elevated to higher ground. This is an example of the difficulties the Highland weather could cause. In 1974–75, Alness Police Station saw the company build a particular type of building: a modern police station able to withstand heavy use.[63] The company was building up a portfolio of completed projects that supported its tenders for even more ambitious ones, demonstrating thorough competence within the building discipline.

## Agriculture

Another persistent anxiety was around agricultural productivity in the region. As discussed in the previous chapter, Tain was an agricultural community. A crucial change which took place during the twentieth century in Scottish farming was what one historian, Campbell, identifies as an agricultural revolution in Scotland, with 'the emergence of owner-occupation of the land where most agriculture is practiced', with a change from very high rates of renting to owner occupation.[64] In 1901, Sutherland, Caithness and many other counties were over 90 per cent rented; by 1960, only Bute was in this category. The rugged Highland landscapes – sublime to behold – had meant that farms tended to be very small, making it hard for them to be sufficiently profitable to warrant capital investment in upgrades to enhance productivity.[65] Even after the concerted efforts of total war, considerable investment was needed. Under the Agriculture Act 1957, there had been attempts to support the growing numbers of small owner-occupier farmers. The 1966 Agriculture Bill promised support to small farmers from the Agricultural Board. The Farm Improvement Scheme offered a larger range of funds and a higher proportion of support than had been previously available.[66] When this particular sun shone, Morrison made hay. Alec Semple remembered hundreds of small farm extensions and improvement works, such as building somewhere to store machinery. As farming became more mechanised, it was imperative to offset some of the comparative disadvantages faced by small, remote farms. Morrison came to the rescue as old barns were adapted and new ones raised to provide garaging for combine harvesters and other equipment. The scheme was renewed in the 1970s.[67] This is another example of how the Morrison willingness to do any and all contracts, regardless of size, helped generate business. And it demonstrates the usefulness and versatility of the new Tain workshop in which Alex had invested. Much of the broad range of services promised in the company's Memorandum of Association were now being offered.

## Quarries

In 1966, Alex took on leases for a quarry at Tarbat near Tain which produced concrete, sand, gravel, and slabs.[68] Firstly, this was a typical Alex act impulsive – or at least apparently so – but also very profitable. Secondly, it enabled the supply chain for the company to be controlled and consolidated. Lawrence Allan notes the importance of the concrete blocks it produced to the building industry.[69] In terms of procurement, it was vital to have a local supply of these heavy, but relatively low value items. This was set in the context of high transport costs as a result of remoteness and relatively poor roads, until upgrades and improvements were made in the later 1970s and 1980s, especially north of Inverness – many by Morrison, leading to quicker, cheaper journeys. Lawrence Allan reckons 'by bringing that [supply] into his control I think that made quite a difference to the financial success to the business'.[70] Alex was proud of his quarries and David Henderson remembers being taken to see them as a child.[71] Finally, the acquisition reflected the importance of local contacts and connections. Alex and Connie socialised with the Factor of Tarbat Estate, Bill Hunter, from whom the quarries were leased.[72]

As part of efforts to rebalance the Highland economy, the HIDB supported a major investment in the £40m Invergordon Aluminium Smelter, on which work started in 1969 and which opened in 1971. It was designed '[b]y the British Aluminium Company's own architects with Penton,

## THE MORRISON STORY

Always smartly turned out, Alex poses at his quarry, 1960s.

Howard, Wood Associates as consultants'.[73] The area was suffering from relatively low incomes, high unemployment, and falling population – the underlying demographic problems for much of the Highland economy.[74] It had been a moment of great hope after decades of speculation about the suitability of the Highlands for such investment, because of cheap and plentiful electricity from hydroelectric generation, and the expectation of further related developments. A 1978 report concluded that it has 'brought a substantial improvement in the economic fortunes of Easter Ross through the provision of over 700 secure and well-paid jobs'.[75] It transpired that these

Loading shovel continues its journey to the New Quarry.

GROWING SUCCESS

Alex at the commissioning of Logie Quarry, 1964.

Alex with Fraser, left, and Gordon, right, at Logie Quarry, 1968. Morrison was firmly a family business.

Having fun: Fraser gives Alex a ride at the blockyard, Logie Quarry, late 1960s. What Alex's tailor thought of these antics is not recorded!

jobs were not secure, as the smelter was very unprofitable and, losing £200 per tonne with a capacity of 100,000 tonnes per year, it is unsurprising that under heavy debts, it was closed in 1981. However, whilst the transportation costs for ingots of produced aluminium were sufficiently low, the cost of moving goods made with it was too high and it never provided the related activity which it was designed to create.[76] The failure of this expensive policy notwithstanding, it had provided a sustained demand for the quarries, as well as some construction work for Morrison.[77]

A singular transformation occurred in the Scottish economy in 1969 when oil was discovered for the first time in the North Sea. This would lead not only to considerable exploration and offshore production but provide a considerable economic boost to the entire region, running up the coast from Aberdeen.[78] As oil began to flow, so did inward investment. Before a drop of oil had been sold, there had been great expectations, leading to a period of sustained growth for the region. The same themes as before became amplified: more housing to accommodate new workers and their families; roads to provide infrastructure; and a wide range of onshore servicing. Especially in Aberdeenshire, the region's economy was pegged to the price of Brent crude: inward investment and jobs would exist as long as extraction costs allowed a profit. The amount of commercially recoverable oil rested on volatile market prices. For any flexible, ambitious construction company there would be many opportunities presented by this situation.

The economy booming in response to the prospect of oil was even better news for anyone owning quarries in the right place. There has been no suggestion that Alex anticipated this exceptional demand when he opened his quarry, but it would prove extremely important. Even before the oil, it had been a good decision, as the business was profitable, and output grew at a healthy rate. Alex's building output in 1973 had grown by 56 per cent when the increase in Scotland had been 27 per cent; estimated that the 1974 output would be at least 25 per cent higher again.[79] The products from the quarry were used to make concrete, build houses and used in civil engineering projects. Prospects were, indeed, healthy: over four years after February 1974, the Scottish Office reckoned 11,000 new houses and business worth £132 million would be needed in the Highlands to meet the needs of the oil industry. In addition, major road upgrades would be vital, including portions of the A9 were to be built or upgraded, and bridges across the local firths; the oil industry required aggregates for onshore work, offshore platforms and even office blocks.[80]

The oil industry will feature prominently in the next chapter, but its discovery immediately vindicated Alex's lease of the quarry. There has never been any suggestion that this was an investment made with a view to supporting the oil industry, merely that Alex struck it lucky, when a move designed to consolidate his existing broadly based business interests turned out to be a very desirable commodity. Estimates were that the market for aggregates in the local area would double by 1978. Combined with additional concrete demands for offices and platforms, a 1974 report prepared assessing Morrison for possible takeover, reckoned Alex's quarry could sell 400,000 tonnes annually by 1978.[81] Alex's investment turned out to be in exceptional demand in exactly the right place, and at the right time

## Sale to CAST (Consolidated African Selection Trust) 1974

In 1973, tax reforms led a mining company, Consolidated African Selection Trust (CAST) and its parent company Selection Trust, to look for investments in the UK. Its Annual Report noted:

> …we are also seeking sources for more immediate revenue, particularly in the United Kingdom, because under the new system of Corporation Tax this is now especially advantageous to the Company. We have therefore recently negotiated interests in three businesses and are continuing to look for similar opportunities.[82]

In February 1974, after discussions H. J. Codrington, CAST's Managing Director, made Alex an offer of £1m for 80 per cent of his business, of which 60 per cent would be in CAST shares, and £400,000 in cash.[83] Morrison was making a taxable profit of around £150,000 annually, and estimates were that this might be doubled.[84] Fraser suggests there were two reasons CAST bought the company: the pursuit of UK income – partly for the reason of taxation reforms – and in the expectation of concrete oil rigs being developed.[85] The purchase of the quarries was a gamble that had more than paid off: without them, there is no obvious reason why CAST would have made an offer for the company.

The Report prepared for the CAST board offered some assessment of Alex's company. Of its history, it suggested it started with 'a small yard and an overdraft of £100'.[86] It also noted '30 bonded warehouses for Invergordon Distillers Ltd and many public works for Ross-shire County Council'.[87] These contracts had been advantageous for Morrison because they had increased corporate capacity, for example with the investment in plant. The business had a healthy order book with various council housing projects worth £3m and £1m of other work in progress. A further £1.2m contract was being negotiated at Invergordon for more housing. Current contracts were outlined as follows:

> '(1) South Lodge Primary School, Invergordon.
> (2) Coulhill Primary School, Alness.
> (3) 200 homes at Tain for the Town Council (phased over four years).
> (4) 181 houses at Alness for County Council (phased over eighteen months).
> (5) Swimming pool at Dingwall.
> (6) Private development of houses at Tain.
> (7) Supermarket complex at Alness.'[88]

The list shows several things. Firstly, that housing was responsible for a considerable proportion of Morrison's order book, with a large number of council houses and a small number of private houses. Secondly, it underscores why the Tain Royal Academy job had been so important to the company's development: it had proved competence and capacity and led to further contracts, with two schools under construction and a swimming pool. Finally, a succession of major contracts provided a boost for the plant owned by Morrison, as the company could buy more of its own so saving on the cost of leasing, and also providing a revenue stream by hiring out when not in use internally.

Major contracts had enabled a period of sustained investment in transport and in-house plant. It is interesting that CAST's engineer assessing the equipment suggested 'the plant and transport seen… is… better maintained than one normally expects for a company of this size', but repairs and maintenance could be streamlined to control costs.[89] That such care was taken squares both with the pride of having a fleet and its symbolic value, and also Alex's thrift. On one hand, this indicates a cautious, careful workplace culture; on the other, within the small business, more advanced techniques for management were not generally in play. The same report highlighted that 'the quality and methods of book-keeping, costing and stores control would not meet with the standards required for a public company', suggesting that this could be remedied by hiring the right accountant and noting that Fraser was trying to do this.[90] Before he worked for Morrison, Hugh England had 'dealt with them as a supplier'. The company was known for its casual accounting: even if 'the whole industry at that time was almost quite informal, unstructured', Morrison was especially so, with rumours of

An excited Gordon takes a closer look at the Morrison fleet of Thames Traders, 1960s. Two of these lorries have a canvas hood on the back that was used to transport the workforce to sites.

'Kellogg's cornflake cartons full of invoices… and it was run from a shed in Tain'.[91] At the time of takeover, these were lessons the company had yet to learn. The arrival of some external pressure accompanied with expertise and constructive suggestions would ultimately prove a positive influence.

One day Alex summoned Johnny Morrison, one of his most loyal workers, for a chat in his car. As many would, he feared he had committed some transgression. In fact, Alex had accepted the offer from CAST for his business. Everyone's jobs were safe, and Alex was now Chairman of the company. CAST had wanted at least 75 per cent, but Alex sold 80 per cent, leaving him with 20 per cent – Fraser posits that this was perhaps ten per cent each for Fraser and Gordon.[92] This left the family with an important financial interest in the business, but not control over decisions. At this time, CAST also purchased another nearby quarry business, Invergordon Sand and Gravel, which was consolidated into Morrison.

## The next generation joins the family business

The purchase by CAST was not the end for Morrison, by any account. Even in this new ownership structure, it remained a family business. The agreement included provision for Alex and Fraser to enter the business immediately and for Gordon to join, probably subject to a time delay after he finished his training at Tarmac. Alex could also nominate three directors to the board of the company under this new ownership: himself and his sons.[93] Under the terms, there were non-compete clauses for Alex, Fraser and Gordon, and both parties had right of first refusal in the event of any future share sale. These conditions guaranteed continued family involvement. In particular, Alex was invited to:

> continue as Managing Director and that your son Fraser will continue in his present capacity since we consider it vital to the company that you both continue to manage its day-to-day affairs.[94]

For Alex, this was quite a compliment: he had no formal management training or experience outside his own business, and a transnational company valued his input sufficiently to wish to preserve it. Indeed, it shows the value he had created as well as the capital produced by his firm's building activities. For Fraser and Gordon, as two young, newly qualified civil engineers, the deal was securing future careers for them. Both had been around the workshops and sites from childhood, so were already well-placed to start working there.[95] If Fraser had initially wanted to be a doctor but changed his mind several times before settling on civil engineering, Gordon was much more fixed, having considered it to be his 'destiny'. Ostensibly, the family were left to get on with things. Gordon joined the company in 1974 but notes that 'not a lot changed – nobody from the acquiring company [was] present at all'.[96] Over the coming decades, the competence of both Gordon and Fraser would be proved time and time again through the company's success and continued growth under their leadership.

Despite the sale of the business Morrison was not integrated into a faceless transnational corporation. Rather this transition triggered the beginning of a clear management structure and culture. At a young age of 54, Alex, if not quite retiring, did take a different kind of role as Chairman rather than de facto Managing Director – a term almost certainly never used to describe him. In the space created, Fraser stepped up and at the same time Gordon entered the family business. Both sons would take the business to places and sectors which Alex could hardly have imagined back in 1948. They would transform the business into a FTSE-listed company within a little over twenty years.

Gordon's first roles in Morrison were to look after joinery and a council housing project at Evanton. One of the lessons Gordon learned at this stage was the importance of 'getting to know your customer'. This sometimes led to some unusual obligations. He remembers one example of spending an evening with Alasdair MacKay drinking port with a customer from whom they had secured a large aggregate supply contract to RAF Leuchars.[97] It was an evening difficult to forget as it must rank as the worst hangovers that Alasdair and Gordon had experienced. The client was, however, very appreciative and the order was extended. The Morrison attitude of keeping customers satisfied would come to be important. Gordon found markets for aggregates and sand. Initially, some were shipped to Sullom Voe. After a local supply was developed there, some were shipped to Germany.

It was at this point that management started to receive higher pay, as Fraser sought 'to elevate these senior foremen to management status, and open up a gap between their earnings and the men's', as well as creating a bonus system and a pension scheme for the first time.[98] Much of what was being paid here was catch-up: more money would be needed to keep talent. All the same, this policy probably marked the sharpest change in leadership styles under the new company, as Fraser was positioning these men to take greater responsibility and initiative. When Alec Semple wanted to leave, Fraser made him Workshop Manager and offered him a pay rise.[99] Fraser – at only 25 – was showing a degree of prescience. This was a context where the supply of skilled labour was already short and would become shorter. Moreover, it would be subject to considerable inflationary demands due to the oil sector, a highly profitable industry requiring technical expertise with immediacy of demand for which it was willing to pay.[100] At the same time, a culture of empowering those with expertise within the business set the scene for the remarkable entrepreneurial culture that was to form the basis of the company's success in the 1980s and 1990s. The company bought by CAST had approximately 425 employees, a 'nucleus of whom are claimed to have exceptional loyalty to Mr Morrison, since he has paid off a minimum number during lean times and because many started with him as apprentices (he trains 60 a year).'[101] Gordon put this more poetically. Against the 'constant stress in the background' of keeping hold of the workforce against the lure of the rich oil industry, 'loyalty then becomes extremely important. And that's something my father's company was awash with, so that certainly eased the journey'.[102]

One of the ways that this loyalty was rewarded was by membership of a very exclusive association: the Twenty-Five Year Club. This had a value beyond money. It could not be bought, only earned. This was Alex and, subsequently, Fraser and Gordon's way of saying thank you to their most loyal staff – strictly for those having served their quarter century. Annual outings were invariably a real treat, especially in the early days, when there were only a handful members. In 1976, as discussed below, Morrison was a subsidiary of Shand which was owned in turn by Selection Trust. The two Twenty-Five

# THE MORRISON STORY

Clubs held joint events. One year, the Morrison members flew to Matlock for dinner, as this was where Shand had its headquarters, in a specially chartered Piper aeroplane.[103]

Soon after Gordon entered the business, he took over the running the quarries division. This was an area where he cut his teeth in management, complementing his technical expertise from studying civil engineering at university. Gordon recruited Alasdair MacKay to help with the quarries and the two soon became firm friends: 'He and I worked hard and played hard'.[104] The overwhelming impression given in the 31 interviews conducted for this book is that people enjoyed going to work. In due course, Gordon and Alasdair made the quarries business an important element within the company and further sites were added in the Borders, as well as at Huntly and Lossiemouth. Accordingly, Morrison became an increasingly important name: Hugh England, who joined Morrison when they took over civil engineering firm Alexander Sutherland of Goslpie, knew the company already as a quarry supplier and as a major 'force in the North'.[105]

Alex was able to enjoy the material success and see his family set up very well in life. Despite his enthusiasm for motor cars and appreciation of a good

Alex hard at work, 1964. His smart shirt and cufflinks suggest he was helping after a day in office.

cigar – many interviewees mentioned both of these – he was 'never flash' as David Henderson put it, but always a 'respected figure of the community'.[106] Where many might have taken the money and stepped back when the company was sold, the family involvement only intensified.

## Springboard for success

To summarise in just over two decades, the business had made remarkable progress. With registration as a limited company, affairs were put on a more formal footing. Alex positioned his business to profit from opportunities which subsequently arose. Shandwick House in Tain expanded capabilities, with office space allowing for administration. A move towards vertical integration and consolidation was made when Alex acquired his own quarry to secure a supply of aggregates, and a workshop capable of manufacturing various parts of buildings. Outside of Alex's control, government policies aiming to help the economy of the Highlands provided valuable work in a regular supply of small contracts to improve farms, and larger ones through the HIDB. Crucially, these were not the counter-cyclical infrastructure demand which dominated economic thinking, but structural attempts to support a poorer region. For the region, the oil industry had arrived, and would be enormously important. Even if this drove up labour costs, good treatment and fierce loyalty secured the services of the men he valued most. For the region, and the company, the public sector and oil would be key driving forces. Oil also led CAST to make a bid to Alex for his company. This gave him a fortune, but also forced the company to improve its management expertise. Despite all this change, the company remained a family one cemented by the arrival of both sons into the business. Takeover did nothing to diminish the brand or the company's ethos. The company was now in an ideal position to expand yet further: with two ambitious young directors, it was ready to expand its capacities and geographical reach beyond anything Alex could have imagined in 1948.

One of the wheelbarrows produced to promote Total Quality Morrison.

CHAPTER FIVE

# Building capacities: 1974–1984

IN THE DECADE PRECEDING the takeover of Morrison by CAST in 1974, the company had established a reputation as an extremely competent and reliable builder and contractor, as evidenced by a succession of public-sector contracts to build schools and houses, as well as industrial facilities. The company had come a long way from a small joinery business run from a shed. In the decade that followed, however, the company would use its position within CAST as a springboard for major success, expanding into new disciplines. As demonstrated later by the case of the spectacular and technically demanding Kylesku Bridge project in Sutherland, the company could operate at the cutting edge of construction capabilities. Underpinning this was an expanded corporate structure that set the stage for these successes as the company went beyond being a northern Highland business to a nationwide Scottish one. This chapter deals with these topics thematically rather than chronologically. It starts with the geographic expansion out of the Highlands, then the disciplines in turn: engineering, civil engineering and property development. It concludes with discussion of the corporate structure and culture underpinning this expansion.

New clients had to be won in different ways and a real change was needed in how the company marketed itself. This chapter draws on the in-house publication *Morrison News*. Whilst this was designed to advertise the company's services, its contents were substantial, and it is more than glossy puff pieces, even if it was not quite the 'journal for the construction industry' it was billed as. The person responsible for this was PR expert Michael Fraser of Michael Fraser Associates in Ardersier, as he was advising the company on how to promote itself.[1] Creative ideas designed to distinguish Morrison from its competitors followed from this period for the next three decades.

Stewart MacLeod remembers:

16 Carden Place as mentioned on page 133.

> Something I got involved in was the production of a brochure, something that we could use as a marketing tool, and Morrison got hold of a very good photographer, and the photographer and myself toured central Scotland taking photographs of contracts that we had built or were building… It was A5 landscape [in format]. That was 1976/77.
>
> Unlike some of my colleagues in Inverness… I was quite in favour of marketing and publicity, which cost money.
>
> It meant we were able to describe to clients in central Scotland who the Morrison group was, because at that time… the group was not at all well known, whereas its parent company, Lehane, Mackenzie and Shand was… Morrison did not have a major track record of civil engineering contracts, whereas Shand did have, so it was a good way of getting in the door of consultants and other potential clients.[2]

## Out of the Highlands

There was a limit to how much building work Morrison could reasonably take on whilst it remained a Highland contractor. Of course, the Highlands were a tough but effective training ground in terms of logistics and environment: if you could build there, you could build in the most remote and challenging places anywhere. As will be seen later on, this would take Morrison overseas to build in such places as war zones, the Falkland Islands, the Caucasus and Antarctica. Summer visitors might be seduced by mild weather and light nights, but in the winter things could be different. Fraser's memories of the weather are kind: 'I think we get a bad rap as far as the climate is concerned… the climate on the east coast of Scotland is relatively temperate… we are used to working outside in the rain'.[3] Those working on sites often offered contrasting opinions to this. The primary response to weather was by programming works to take account of these challenges. Ron McGraw, in his role as estimating engineer, had to 'allow for weather in estimates, but if you have exceptional conditions, a severe winter or a wet spring, that could disrupt' the programme, leading to reducing working capacity in winter months, despite contingency for weather.[4] This would only get so far: Allan Russell remembers building the Eastgate Shopping Centre in Inverness in 1979:

> Snow and frost are always a problem… it was so cold that year that the frost was probably a good eighteen inches/two feet into

the ground. Excavating was like concrete. You could not hand-dig anything. When you are working amongst existing utilities, you can't afford to put a machine bucket anywhere near it… In Civil Engineering you are up against it in the winter… if you are not snowed off, you are rained off; we never liked to be rained off, we tended to just work away.

Yet just as in theatre, the show must go on. Allan Russell added that it 'has to be really bad' for work to stop.⁵ Certain steps could be taken to mitigate against the risk of weather disrupting schedules. Firstly, as Dan MacDonald points out, the customary practice of programming a fortnight's leave at Christmas offered not only a rest but avoided two of the worst weeks of the year. Investment in equipment could help: 'It gets dark here [Inverness] about 3 o'clock, never mind Orkney or Shetland. You had to work or go home', so for Donald MacLennan, lighting was essential.⁶ Hugh England remembers that the company invested in technologies and materials. For many jobs, where:

Dry Dock for HMS *Discovery*, Dundee.

> the foundation is muck, it is the most weather-susceptible of material… you can make it an awful lot worse: you have to know when to say stop… Sometimes you have to spend more on material of whatever sort which is not so weather-susceptible. Then you lean towards… pre-fabrication – you do what you can in factory conditions.⁷

Working with a consulting engineer, one innovation developed in response to this was for bridge construction:

> a lot of bridges are steel beams with a concrete deck [and with] what we call a cantilever, the edge bit. It is out of all proportion of spend because it is so awkward. We developed a system with a particular innovative engineer of pre-casting this, and basically doing it Lego style.

This technique has provided popular, and Hugh says that 'every bridge I see [uses this system of pre-casting] and I smile'.⁸

If the weather presented challenges, rising to meet these helped the company build up expertise. Ken Gillespie suggests that when it comes to the weather, 'Morrison learned quite early… [that] in an extreme location… you need people who know' how to choose the correct materials and programme realistically. This was valuable expertise, because 'if you have not got it, you make a lot of mistakes until you get it. That is what made Morrison so successful

The first rig at Nigg Dock under construction, early 1970s.

in North Scotland and the Islands'.[9] If building in remote areas presented logistical challenges, if harsher climates demanded higher specifications, all of this could be turned to the company's advantage. The accumulation of this intellectual capital by the company continued across its history, so giving it a competitive edge over new entrants.

In 1980, the company moved its head office to Inverness. To many this was a momentous day. Alex was still prominent in the business and Michael Martin remembers: 'the first time I came into the head office was the day that the Inverness office opened… and met Alex Morrison, as he was still pretty much in charge of things… I can distinctly remember Alex saying what an important day it was for Morrison to move to the Capital of the Highlands'.[10] This move signalled the company's ambitions: Tain was simply too far north and remote to serve as a centre of a company now operating across Scotland, and even Inverness was a long way from work in the Borders. A strategy of opening regional offices to offer services across Scotland was implemented in the early 1980s. By April 1981, there were offices in Inverness, Aberdeen, Perth and Glasgow. A map in the corporate newsletter showed civil and building works. North of Tain, in the sparsely populated northern Highlands, the focus was on civil engineering works, where regional expertise, such as in coping with the weather, was clearly paying dividends. Many of these related to the oil industry, in particular developments at Nigg in Easter Ross.[11]

In August 1983, the company opened an office in Edinburgh, serving as a further regional base. The heart of the business remained in the Highlands. The idea was that this Edinburgh office was simply part of the network of offices, arranged around a principle of 'decentralising control in order to offer a specialised local service to key regional centres of the Scottish economy'. The inclusion of a map replete with boundaries made it very clear to customers and prospective customers that the company was in a position to offer services, right down to the English border.[12] The opening of each office was supported by publicity. When the firm moved to new Glasgow offices, a reception was held at the Holiday Inn hotel.[13] This provided an opportunity to showcase the various projects and capabilities the company offered. Another party was held to celebrate this launch, with a mixture of representatives from 'Government Departments, Local Authorities, [and] a host of professional firms in the region'.[14]

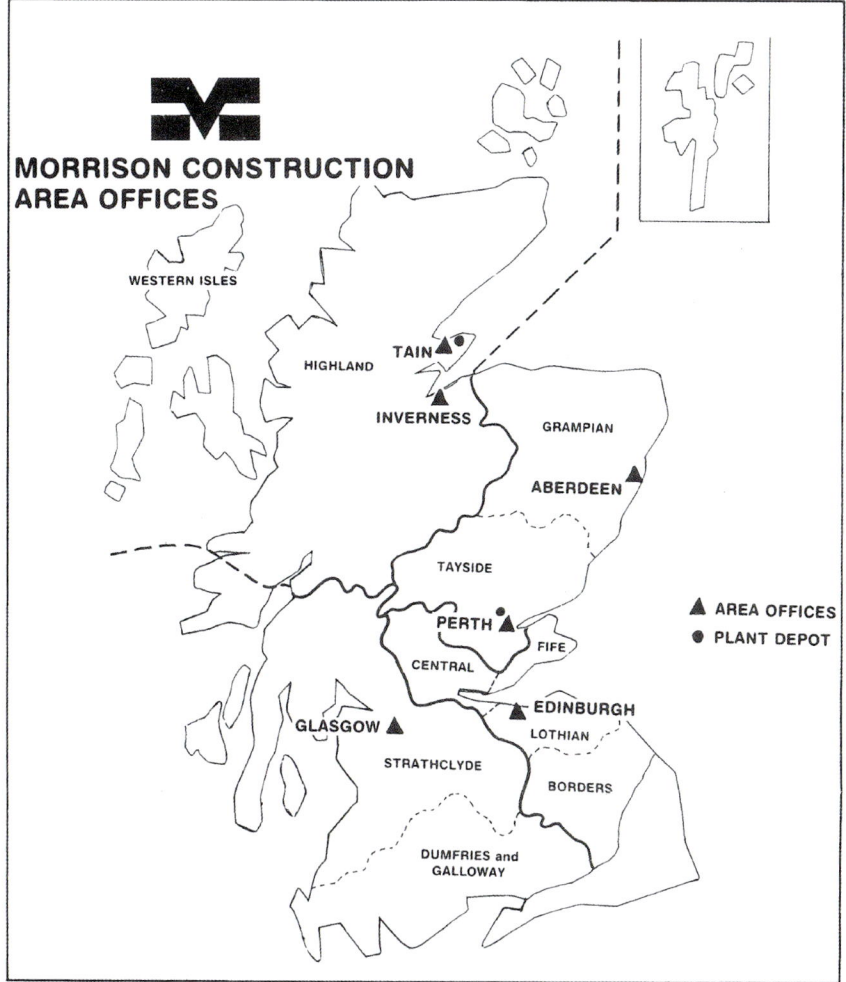

A map from *Morrison News* showing the company's main offices, 1983.

This was a time when Morrison was expanding beyond being 'a Highland building and construction company'. As John Morrison recollected, it was 'really exciting time to join as Company Secretary', because whilst the company 'had ventured into the central belt' it was only just 'preparing to expand'.[15] For a young board, comprised of men roughly Gordon and Fraser's age, this was indeed an exciting time. The ambition and excitement were matched by a strategy of opening a network of regional offices. This structure allowed for entrepreneurship in winning business locally and to draw on networks, whilst allowing the company to be a national one. Creativity lay at the heart of the company's ambitions, as Stewart MacLeod saw it:

> One was not reined in in terms of coming up with good ideas or trying to be creative… to promote the company's standing and to come up with creative ideas… to go into new areas of contracting.[16]

Receptions and other high-profile celebrations which accompanied the opening of new offices helped build up the networks which had served the company well in Tain and its immediate Highland hinterland with their strategic guest lists.

Links might also come with employees joining the company. Stewart MacLeod recalls that he:

> fortunately had quite a number of connections with senior engineers in the Scottish Office and through my relationships with them, and with the Institution of Highways and Transportation, I was able to introduce Morrison staff to quite a number of senior engineers at the Scottish Office, and therefore was able to develop what I think was a very worthwhile relationship… for contracts throughout the whole of Scotland. That developed and the contracts in which we were successful in obtaining simply grew and grew.

It was not just contracts which were won through networks of contacts. Staff at all levels were recruited often through these links. Stewart MacLeod remembers the Dundee-Forfar road stretching the civil engineering capacity of the firm:

> [There was] a very substantial job on the Dundee-Forfar road, called Parkford. We had to recruit quite a number of staff, and I was very fortunate in being able to 'poach' quite a number of good and competent engineers.[17]

Much as in the case of the Invergordon Warehouses contract discussed in chapter three, nearly twenty years earlier, the company recruited a number of staff, for the Dundee–Forfar road making this an important job in helping build corporate capacity. The company moved out of the Highlands by having a network of regional offices providing different services to clients locally, whilst offering a comprehensive national service. As will be shown, Morrison developed new capacities in engineering, civil engineering and property development.

## Oil onshore: engineering capacity

The spirit of innovation and seizing opportunities led the company to try to meet some of the engineering needs of the oil industry. Britain had produced oil domestically before, during World War Two. British Petroleum had a number of small-scale, expensive onshore wells, but this production ceased in 1964 because they had only been viable due to tariffs which were abolished when the UK joined the European Free Trade Area.[18] Oil produced a range of positives and negatives. Undoubtedly, in the short and medium term it provided a valuable injection to regional economies especially the Highlands and Grampian, but this new industry was vulnerable to the volatility of commodity prices. The industry's success has always rested on simple arithmetic: identifying which reserves are economically recoverable based on lifting costs, so that when prices rise, more is worth extracting and when they fall, some of the oil and gas becomes too expensive to bring to the surface. Technological innovations, taxation set by the government and global prices also had a major impact. Certainly, the boom in the North Sea generated employment, but created relatively few jobs compared to the level of capital investment required.[19] All the same, this was a boost to the regional economy. In 1974, British Petroleum's expenditure on exploration more than doubled, more than half of this within Europe, especially the North Sea.[20] Those jobs that the industry did bring commanded high salaries. Between the early and late 1970s adult male wages had been 70 per cent of the national average in Aberdeen; by the end of the decade, the oil industry had driven this figure to 115 per cent.[21]

Even if the direct benefits fell on a relatively small proportion of the Scottish population, in the 1970s oil lubricated a cultural and political renaissance in Scotland and promised much for an economy marked elsewhere by stagnation and decline.[22] More directly, the SNP was able to set this lucrative natural resource within their sights. It made for an effective election slogan: 'It's Scotland's Oil'.[23] Perhaps this harked after an experience more like the Norwegian model of harnessing the value of oil and gas for the common good: when leveraged for long-term benefit, the results have been remarkable, with a sovereign wealth fund driven by the proceeds of the industry worth some $1 trillion.[24] In contrast, the British approach was more short-term: prompt economic development was encouraged by selling rights to encourage free market and tax proceeds were used to defray general government spending, rather than being set aside as a special asset. The British Government's policy sought to encourage development of the industry along free market lines. The gold-rush atmosphere of the early 1970s must be understood in this context.

Oil was not a crucial area of Morrison's development: it would have been a successful company without the contracts it won. But the offshore industry shaped the Scottish economy generally, especially in those areas where Morrison were well-established, such as the Moray and Cromarty Firths and Aberdeen. Building new houses, for example, was driven by the needs of the industry. As Dan MacDonald put it, 'the uplift that Alex got from the oil industry in Easter Ross' was of great value.[25] For Gordon:

> There was a major blow-out on the Piper Alpha Platform, owned by a consortium of oil companies, and we were working for a number of these oil companies at the time. And unknown to us, they decided to give us work to create structures that would lie on the seabed and cover important valves to protect them against blow-out in the future. We supplied that work very successfully. One of the supervising engineers from I think Marathon was a student with me at Edinburgh… then we started looking for replacement work, and could not win any… They had given a very clear instruction to their procurement departments that no other work must go into our yard… we were devoted one hundred per cent to this Piper Alpha project.[26]

This was a source of passing frustration to the company's ambitions in this sector, but again shows the importance of networks.

Morrison's house building operations continued to expand, and their quarry business did well: the demand which CAST had anticipated in making a bid for Morrison had materialised. The demand from the oil industry meant many were looking for homes in the area: 'only with the advent of the oil-related developments that the housing position became very difficult' in terms of supply.[27] Winning contracts for the fabrication yards in which offshore structures would be built, there was increasing need for aggregates and concrete. So brisk was business that Lawrence Allan remembers they had a hard time keeping up with the paperwork, such was the number of deliveries made from quarries to the yards and Nigg:

> The sand and gravel quarry and the concrete block manufacture was very much in demand, to such an extent that lorries were running from the quarry at Kildary down to Nigg more or less non-stop. As one lorry was leaving the sand pit, another was waiting to get its load.[28]

This was a context in which logistics were crucial. The development of the Sullom Voe Oil Terminal in Shetland provided considerable demand for sand. Gordon won a contract to supply sand to the terminal. To achieve this Gordon purchased a conveyor belt system to help with loading the ships. When Philip Bathurst from Selection Trust came to inspect, he asked about the new system. 'I was somewhat economical with the truth as the Capex system was rather slow, so I said it was on hire.'[29] The entrepreneurial approach here was successful as a large volume of sand was supplied using this equipment.

With such opportunities came risk, as was shown when a company called AQS, with whom Morrison had a contract to supply British Petroleum (BP), went bankrupt. AQS had neglected to take out insurance against demurrage and so Morrison lost the considerable sums they were due. They were, however, given more contracts direct from British Petroleum, which enabled the money lost to be made back. Another challenge was arranging transport, as ships were held up unloading. BP secured an open top dredger at over four times the going rate for shipping, which arrived and was duly filled at Invergordon, but 'by the time it got to Sullom Voe it was contaminated by sea water'.[30] This shows that know-how was important and simply throwing money at a problem would not solve everything. More importantly, it shows the fever pitch which the rush for this 'black gold' had reached. This kind of demand was in sharp contrast to everything else in the area. The company got a chance to participate in the oil industry when 'there were yards at Nigg', which Fraser describes as 'a great opportunity for the quarry business'.[31]

In 1984, Morrison acquired Cromarty Firth Engineering (CFE), in what the *Financial Times* described as a 'move into the North Sea service industry'.[32] As Gordon recalls, 'CFE was a steel fabrication business and all their work was related to offshore structures. We supplied steel substructures to Highland Fabricators and McDermott, the two rig fabricators in the area. We also did a lot of work servicing floating oil platforms in the Firth and the specifications were very taxing and the clients were very taxing'.[33] Alongside various workshops, CFE included 18,000 ft² of fabrication bays.[34] A year later, corporate promotion boasted of extensive refurbishment and a 20 per cent increase in CFE's workforce.[35] Ultimately, it was one of the less successful of the company's ventures. John Morrison suggests that CFE was 'quite different from the other parts of our business'.[36] One of the major reasons for this contrast was, as Gordon notes, that this was the first time Morrison was dealing with non-government contractors on major projects and found them 'commercially difficult'.[37] For Fraser, whilst the company had been bought 'because of the steel work associated with the oil industry', and the venture 'was not a success… we had to close that down eventually', the opportunity was still valuable: 'it is all those experiences of things you try going wrong that give you the ability to make more sensible decisions going forward.'[38]

This direct contact with the oil industry sat uncomfortably with the corporate ethos, too. It was not just for the Morrisons that the company was a family business: the partners and families of many employees made contributions to the success of Morrison. Pam MacKay, Alasdair MacKay's wife, remembers unease at the arrival of a very different culture. When oil took off, there were expectations of 'gifts to people and so on… Americans would say my garage door is open – you can drop off a case of Dom Pérignon any time you like – they were blatant about it [but] they did not always get [what they wanted]'. Some of this was before Alasdair joined Morrison, but the imperative of winning the deal came up against ethical standards.[39] This indicates just what a culture shock the oil industry presented to quiet Highland communities.

One of the first things which happened when the oil industry arrived in the Highlands was the building of fabrication yards in which a range of engineering products could be produced for offshore use. Partly to support the sector and also encourage development, the government supported the planning and construction of these facilities. The yards at Nigg and Ardersier were successful in part because American companies were keen not to deal with the heavily unionised Clydeside dock yards. They also had the advantage of being deep-water ports and, therefore, able to accommodate very large vessels.[40] Morrison's work was largely concerned with making it possible for clients to build, or as Donald MacLennan puts it 'mostly our contracts were work we did for them so they could do their job'.[41] At Nigg, this included 'quayside ground consolidation… together with the installation of undersea barge support strips'. Indeed, the limited work done for the industry was often one step removed from either exploration or production. For example, in 1981 the company completed a 27,000 ft² pipe-coating factory.[42] These were technically demanding jobs and proved that the company was increasingly competent to build anything. In 1982, a new engineering division was established with Angus Christie recruited to manage it. From Morayshire originally, he arrived with broad experience including at a Toronto metal foundry before returning to the UK as project manager at the Invergordon Smelter. This new division offered 'a comprehensive service to industry' in mechanical and electrical engineering, which included:

- Process plant maintenance
- Plant installation
- Plant commissioning
- Instrument and control engineering
- Waste management
- Manpower services.[43]

The move into engineering was important for several reasons. If demand for engineering had originally been triggered by the oil industry, the potential to offer it more broadly was seized upon promptly. The notion of offering the most comprehensive service – the idea of the 'one stop shop' with a wide range of activities – was becoming an imperative for the business. Oil companies were trying to reduce the number of interfaces with contracts which they had to managed. Finally, this was also expansion aimed firmly at private sector work. The civils division, which was thriving too, relied on government contracts, vulnerable to policy decisions or cuts in spending.

In a sense, oil was a stalking horse for the broader economic context of the period. In 1975, Margaret Thatcher became leader of the Conservative Party and, in 1979, Prime Minister. In Britain at large, contractors generally were supportive of Thatcher, but the reaction in Scotland was very different.[44] Deeply unpopular policies such as the Poll Tax, led to a collapse in the broad backing the Tories had enjoyed in Scotland before this period, most especially from the working classes. In 1970, 38 per cent of the Scottish electorate had voted Conservative; in 1979 this fell to 31.4 per cent; by 1987 and 1992, it was reduced further to some quarter of votes cast.[45]

Efforts continued to stimulate the economy through the HIDB which became the HIE (Highlands and Islands Enterprise).[46] Moreover, the continued influence of the oil industry meant that the Highlands and Grampian regions had a very different economic experience compared with the south of Scotland. The key thing was that the regional nature of the Scottish economy was reinforced, underscoring the logic of the regional structure adopted by Morrison. The Scottish economy had its own dynamics, and its own problems: housing was more likely to be public sector than in England, local businesses were set-up at a lower rate, whilst foreign investment was less likely to be attracted, tending to be focused on the South-East of England, rather than in Scotland, especially for research and development.[47]

The final thing to be said on Thatcher is that, for all the pronouncements of the state being rolled back, historians have increasingly challenged this view, on the grounds that overall, most cuts were modest.[48] Far more significant, and especially for Morrison, was how the state would spend money, as will be seen in the next chapter, through the management of risk and the role of the private sector in pursuing this agenda under New Public Management.

## On a road to success: civil engineering

By the middle of the 1970s, the pressure of high inflation was taking its toll on the construction industry. Inflation between 1972 and 1980 averaged 16 per cent. For civil engineering jobs, which frequently took place over a number of years, it was increasingly difficult to quote realistically for work and remain competitive with high inflation rates. Fixed-priced orders could pose an existential threat to some firms. Some attempt was introduced when these rates peaked in the middle of the decade, some action was being taken, with the advent of Price Fluctuation contracts using 'Baxter and Osborne adjustments were used for civil engineering works'.[49] These were named after National Economic Development Organisation committees chaired by J. W. Baxter and J. G. Osborne which produced monthly prices for various types of inflation. Roger Croson suggests 'brought great stability to the construction industry at a time of widespread economic instability'.[50]

In 1977, Morrison acquired Alexander Sutherland of Golspie (ASG) whilst they were trading in receivership. In civil engineering, ASG 'dominated Sutherland', and had expertise and equipment. It might be remembered that both Fraser and Gordon had read civil engineering at Edinburgh, but Morrison did not get involved in this discipline. ASG presented the capacity that would be needed to make Morrison a one-stop shop for construction including civil engineering abilities. The most famous project they had completed was a crossing at the Kyle of Tongue which included a causeway and bridge, saving a twelve-mile detour.[51]

The company was a good fit for Morrison. Selection Trust, which had bought 80 per cent of Morrison from Alex in 1974, acquired a 90 per cent

A painting of the Kyle of Tongue crossing by Morrison Director Roger Croson, 1972.

Painting by Grant Boyd of Kylesku Bridge.

stake in Lehane, McKenzie and Shand in 1976 and the remaining ten per cent in 1977.[52] In the acquisition of Alexander Sutherland, the parent company was signalling a serious intention to enter the Scottish civil engineering market. A good number of the individuals who joined Morrison in this way, such as Ian Keith, Donald McLennan, Roger Croson and Hugh England, would continue to have long, successful careers within the new company, with strong senses of loyalty and pride.[53] The companies were a good fit, as Fraser suggests:

> Shand was a very similar family business. They were very much bigger than Morrison… but they had similar cultures, they could understand the family culture, they equally thought my father's role was important as the non-executive chairman, and that helped us develop the business in a disciplined way, but in a way that did not destroy the culture of the business… Alexander Sutherland was a business one county up, which would have been very similar in its history… run by a chap called Bertie Sutherland.[54]

Civil engineering was integral to the corporate regional structure outlined above. The range and number of jobs which were undertaken are far too great to catalogue, but a sense of the diversity and difficulty attendant upon these major engineering works gives a sense of the demanding tasks which faced the company. Much of civil engineering involves pushing against, diverting or otherwise controlling elemental forces. Where water is involved, 'little problems very quickly become big problems in terms of cost', as Hugh England puts it. In 1980, the company won contracts on the Caledonian Canal – a Thomas Telford project – with work worth £1.2 million, requiring upgrades to swing bridges, and more permanent steel decks replacing timber ones.[55] *Morrison News* noted the pleasure of being 'associated with… one of the great Telford's most significant engineering landmarks'.[56] In 1983, a further contract for £300,000 suggests that British Waterways were happy with the quality of work done in this sensitive project.[57]

Works often included water. The company's first contract for Grampian Regional Council within Aberdeen saw a reservoir metres constructed at Bridge of Don.[58] At Fort George, 600 metres of coastal protections were provided, requiring 18,000 tonnes of rock, broken up into tight specifications of size, hardness and resistance to abrasion. This presented a logistical challenge to ensure enough material in a given time-frame in remote locations. Against the harsh tides of the North Sea, work was programmed in one continuous period.⁵⁹ In Banff, in 1983, the company excavated 130 metres of beach and erected a sea wall, requiring 1000 cubic metres of concrete.⁶⁰ In many cases, the scale of the task was astonishing, compounded by an environment which allowed little margin for error.

Another way of thinking about civil engineering is that it provides links between people. In Morrison's order books this included airports, roads, and bridges. The need for roads in the Highlands was self-evident. In rugged, sparsely populated terrain, almost an unlimited amount of money might be spent building and upgrading roads to make them safer and faster. Some of this reflected the needs of rural communities, but roads, and particularly motorways, represented something more significant. Gleaming modernity and personal autonomy in the motorcar, along with international air travel, remained relatively glamorous and for most people unusual.

Auldearn Bypass A96.

Aberdeen Airport was another example of the far-reaching consequences of the oil industry, as demand soared for passenger travel to and from the city for business, as well as a very busy heliport serving the rigs in the North Sea. Between 1972 and 1977, passenger numbers increased from 15,000 to 226,000; where there had been 135,000 helicopter passengers, by 1974 this had increased to 450,000. This led to the construction of a new £3.5m terminal in 1977.⁶¹ In 1984, Morrison had several contracts at the airport underway or recently completed: providing access roads and services to Cordyce View for the expansion of airports; providing a Hangar for Hawk Aviation, which was quickly leased by Brymon Aviation for De Havilland Dash 7s; and some hard-standing for Peregrine Aviation.⁶² The second two contracts were negotiated whilst the first was underway. This is reflective of the importance of maintaining a good reputation and suggests that this goal was achieved and maintained.

The runway work was the most critical, where Morrison was providing drainage and resurfacing. Failure to meet high specifications might have fatal consequences. These works were done at night so as not to interrupt flights, with inspection at 6:15 am before the runway re-opened at 6:30 am, having ensured that 'any potential aircraft hazards are delethalised [sic.]'. Even in the context of the light-hearted confidence of the corporate newsletter, the anxieties about mistakes here are reflected in the language used.⁶³

More mundane but even more essential to living well, was the provision of sewage treatment works. The scale of these varied, but towards the end of the period with which this chapter is concerned, they included a large number of new or upgraded contracts at sewage treatment facilities.

Crieff Sewage Treatment Works.

Table 5.1 Morrison Sewage Contracts 1981–1984

| Place (year awarded) | £ nominal | £ real 2017 by share of GDP |
| --- | --- | --- |
| Dalbeattie (1983) | 68,000 | 394,600 |
| Ochiltree (1983) | 270,000 | 866,000 |
| Elgin (1981) | 300,000 | 1,093,000 |
| Dornoch (1984) | 300,000 | 916,500 |
| Pitlochry (1981) | 400,000 | 2,812,000 |
| Carbans (1982) | 1,000,000 | 3,354,000 |
| Crieff (1982) | 1,200,000 | 4,025,000 |
| Total | 3,538,000 | 13,461,100 |

Sources: based on information in *Morrison News*. Dalbeattie, Ochiltree, 'Report on Other Works in Hand', *Morrison News*, 9 (December 1983), p.4; 'Crieff Town Sewage', ibid, p.3; 'Pitlochry Sewage Works', *Morrison News*, 8 (August 1983), p.4; Elgin, 'Morrison Move into North East Scotland', *Morrison News*, 2 (April 1981), p.3; Carbans, 'Motherwell on Target', *Morrison News*, 9 (December 1983), p.4; Dornoch, 'Building is Buoyant', *Morrison News*, 12 (November 1984), p.2. Calculated using Officer and Williamson, per share of GDP to 2017.

The award of these clusters of contracts shows that local authorities at this time held shared priorities about treatment works. It seems likely that Morrison won these further contracts as its reputation spread.

Elsewhere, a range of road building projects in the Highlands provided a steady stream of work. These were all government contracts, and subject to various tests of the risk to the taxpayer – the same principles which were ordinarily applied to loans and grants, but from which the HIDB had permission to derogate. The HIDB, as discussed in the previous chapter, was a government response to concerns about the Highland economy and sought to boost the economy by offering loans and grants to offset the relatively high costs of doing business in a remote region. Reputation and confidence were important in this context as Alexander Sutherland of Golspie found out just before Morrison took them over. The A894 from Geisgeuil to Dartmore project was in the late stages of the tender process when ASG entered receivership:

> There was a question raised by the Scottish Development Department, who was the paymaster, should a small company in receivership be awarded a contract? Was it not a risk to the public purse? A fair question. We were obviously concerned… we would fold, we would have no work. So a colleague invited a local MP to our house, and I explained the dire position it would leave us in. We had priced and were cheapest and had won it fair and square and it was a natural concern in the Scottish Office could we do it? Could we survive?… [Caithness and Sutherland MP] Robert MacLennan made representations, and the job came our way. Somewhere along the way Morrison acquired us and it was all go then.[64]

This underscores the importance of reputation, local networks and the broader significance of these civil engineering projects to small, local economies.

With Alexander Sutherland, Morrison inherited work on the A9 road north of Inverness. As Roger Croson explained, it was a good example of the challenges faced by engineers in this northern zone.

> Sutherland's won that job, and whilst that was underway, Morrison acquired Sutherland's… Over on the Black Isle, the soil on this job was clay, and very susceptible. The first winter was very wet, and working was difficult. There were times you just could not work, and the job got behind schedule, and that obviously impacts on the financial position. It was looking a bit worrying for a time… but it picked up… made a profit, and traffic still runs over it today.[65]

From the flurry of road projects that followed, certain themes emerged in what the company aimed to do, and how it sought to capitalise on opportunities. The company started making a real selling point of finishing projects ahead of schedule. A large banner by the side of the road announcing that it was 'another early completion by Morrison' offered good advertising. For example, several sections of the A94, between Perth and Aberdeen, were completed substantially ahead of schedule: 'the Balnabriech stretch… [was] completed by Morrison… a full 18 weeks ahead of schedule', and 'the Stracathro section', *Morrison News* boasted, 'will be open by the time you read this, 13 weeks ahead of the contract finishing date'.[66]

The company was keen to emphasise that this was not a result of cutting corners. Work on a previous section of the A94, at Parkford, constituted 'major and difficult roadworks and completing them to a very high standard indeed'.

It is hard to prove or disprove this claim however, Morrison continued to establish a reputation centred on these two leitmotifs: quality, and completion ahead of schedule. Further evidence is offered from the fact that these road contracts were awarded in relatively small increments by the government agencies and that Morrison received repeat contracts on the same projects.[67] Another project at the same time for the Scottish Development Department was the Elgin Relief Road to divert 'through traffic away from the bottleneck of Elgin's busy High Street'. This again was measured for its success in terms of 'the quality of finished work and the speed with which it has been accomplished'.[68] In March 1984, work began on the Perth Western Bypass, a £3 million contract awarded by Tayside Regional Council on behalf of the Scottish Development Department, to build 4 km of new dual carriageway.[69] In terms of road building, Morrison's expansion was successful, with a throughput of valuable contracts which did not generally stretch the resources of the company overall. They served to establish Morrison's reputation as a very competent Highland building company.

## Morrison on the map: Kylesku Bridge

Few projects completed by Morrison were more challenging than Kylesku Bridge and none did more to promote the company's reputation. The over-used word 'iconic' is one of the few to describe its remarkable status. Many interviewees, even those working outside the civil engineering division, suggested this was the most important or even their favourite project. The graceful geometric curve of the bridge offers a deceptive simplicity, as it is a technically advanced and demanding structure which blends perfectly into the Highland landscape. Completing this job on time and to exacting standards put Morrison firmly on the map. Morrison was only eligible to tender because Shand, by then Morrison's parent company, had a large enough balance sheet to absorb the risk. The project turned out to be challenging due to its complexity and location but, executed on time and to a high standard, financial settlement was reached, and after a royal opening by the Queen, the company was left with a valuable addition to its portfolio. The bridge was designed by Ove Arup, one of the foremost architectural practices. The contract was worth around £2.75m and the bridge due to open in 1984. The technology used was innovative: 'post-tensioned, concrete box beam bridge, supported on inclined vertical legs, and vertical reinforced concrete abutments'.[70]

After a successful tender, Michael Martin, then a young civil engineer, remembers Hugh England saying to him: 'Well done, lad, but now you've got to build it... and I got a cold shiver running up my spine'.[71] Martin suggests 'It is a beautiful bridge... but my God it was difficult to build'.[72] For this, he suggests, there were three reasons: firstly, it is a three-dimensional structure with complex geometry, making the plans very hard to read because they were projections rather than true drawings. 'I had to understand the geometry and explain how the dimensions presented on paper could be resolved into true dimensions'. Secondly, 'sheer complexity, particularly in the reinforcement', made 'it very difficult to visualize'. Finally, stability during construction was precarious: 'whilst it was being built, the [various structural] elements could fall down at any particular time in any particular direction... what stopped them falling down was the strength of temporary works, which is relatively unusual.'[73]

The job was becoming risky. Morrison was reliant on the larger size and value of the Shand company in order to qualify for the job anyway, but as it ran over budget, it started to cause concern from directors. Michael Martin remembers:

> The Shand directors must have got uppity about the fact Morrison had taken on this job and were losing a fortune. I remember one senior director visiting, and I had to accompany him to the site. I had the feeling he was coming to tell us what to do, what we were doing wrong... we walked north along the approach road. You don't see the bridge until the last minute when it all opens out in front of you. We were reasonably well on, and we got to the point where you could see the temporary works and he said, 'fucking hell' and that was it – after that he did not make any criticism whatsoever.[74]

The point may have been somewhat forcefully made, but many might well have had that reaction to it. If the company ever had a reputation for coping in tough weather conditions, it was surely earned at Kylesku, where the tower cranes were exposed regularly to force nine gales – Stewart MacLeod recalls 'The general foreman we had on site at the time was six foot four, and very broad shouldered and I remember him being flung against a fence by [the wind] – it was exceedingly difficult'.[75] The corporate line on this was rather more prosaic: 'Visitors to the site don't believe how hard the wind can blow, as they're almost invariably greeted by calm, sunny conditions.'[76]

The financial realities of the project were challenging, too. It was a big project, and it 'was losing a lot of money and Morrison on their own would not have been able to fund that project, but Charter Consolidated supported us'.⁷⁷ Roger Croson was able to make a case for a commercial settlement with the Highland Regional Council, which meant that the Council paid Morrison the cost of building the bridge, rather than the lower amount agreed in the original contract. The company's estimate had been similar to other tenders and, due to concerns from an early stage, consultants had inspected the site. Ultimately, it hinged on Arup's somewhat optimistic claim that 'a wonderful piece of information given to tenderers by the consultant… said "This bridge was designed with ease of construction in mind"'. Expert advice from Dr Olag Currentzski, a contact of Stewart MacLeod, suggested that it was, in fact, a difficult structure.⁷⁸ Ultimately, as Michael Martin puts it: 'We got paid for Kylesku because we did a quality job finished on time'.⁷⁹ Kylesku was not only successful in engineering terms, but also financial ones: and this is remarkable. Given that such jobs are rarely profitable, David Jeffs took a pragmatic view:

> If anybody ever came in to me and said this is a prestigious project, I would say we are not pricing it, because generally, prestigious projects do not make big money.⁸⁰

The completed Kylesku Bridge on the day of its Royal Opening, with the ferry it replaced in the foreground and, in the background, the Royal Yacht *Britannia* on which HM the Queen and Royal party arrived for the ceremony.

BUILDING CAPACITIES

HM the Queen attends the opening of Kylesku Bridge, here with Stewart and Fraser, 8 August 1984.

This may be somewhat tongue-in-cheek, but it underscores the success of Kylesku and perhaps the naivety of the company in having bid for it in the first place.

In many ways, Kylesku was the Morrison job *par excellence*. The company was punching well above its weight. But the job was finished on time, a commercial settlement was reached, and the complex bridge built in an exceptionally difficult environment. All of the company's resources were mobilised, including a huge amount of directorial attention and energy. As Hugh England put it: 'There came a time when… anyone who the job needed was cherry-picked from the company'.[81] But what really made it a triumph was the way it became almost a kind of blueprint for how the company would capitalise on future jobs: happy clients, early completion, industry and specialist awards, teamwork. And in amongst it, there seems a dash of luck. Indeed, the corporate history might have finished here. As Fraser puts it: 'We were making £200,000 a year at the time and at one stage it was losing £2 million'.[82] In the final reckoning, the project cost £4.75m instead of the original £2.75m. Had this happened, it would have been a financial disaster which Morrison alone could not have withstood and would have placed severe strains on the Shand group's finances had commerical settlement not been reached. It had not been an easy project but, in the end, the company had a serious marketing tool at its disposal. The bridge had a special commemorative issue of *Morrison News* devoted to it on its opening, and featured in all sorts of advertisements throughout Scotland, not just Morrison publicity.[83] Combined with the apparently timeless landscape scenery, it is surely a masterpiece and very different to what is typically shown in representations of the Highlands.[84] But the old Highlands never went away either: the bridge was used to decorate promotional bottles of whisky which the company distributed to clients and staff.

The technical complexity of the structure has warranted numerous technical publications, but when the Queen came to open the bridge Roger Croson was required to describe the process of pre-stressing concrete. He remembers clearly her response: when half-way through his explanation she interjected: '"Oh so it is plenty strong" – she wanted to move on to something more interesting'.[85] Various presentations were made to the Queen, including 'Mr James Nicol of Rogart, the longest serving member of Morrison's workforce'.[86] The celebrations when the bridge was opened with a royal visit and under the media spotlight provided valuable publicity for Morrison. For Roger Croson, it was this project which:

> promoted the company image beyond any other... Kylesku put us on a different footing. The image of the company changed very significantly between starting Kylesku and finishing Kyleksu. I can't think

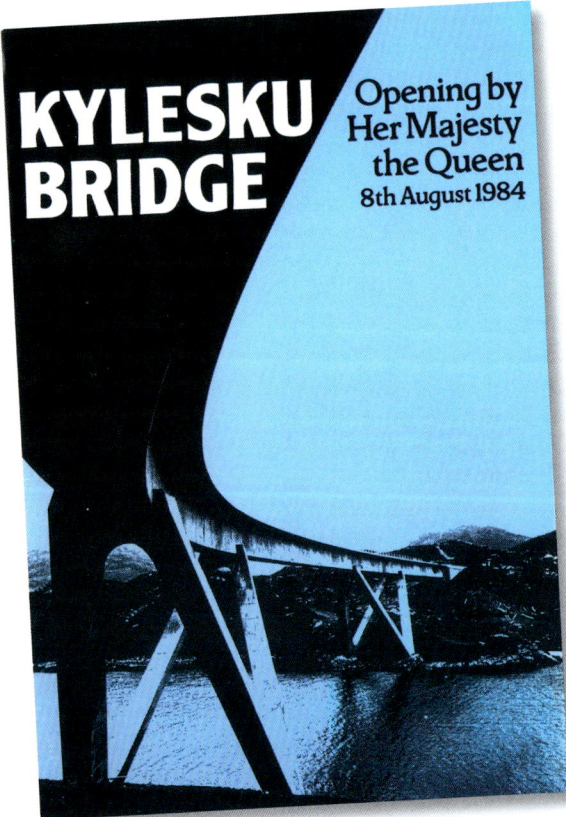

The official programme for the Kylesku Bridge Royal Opening ceremony.

of anything which did more… got our losses back, but we never made any profit on it… It gave the team there, and the division I suppose, [the confidence] that we could face up to a challenge, and stick with it, and come through it… Kylesku would be the most important project the civils ever did.[87]

The Kylesku Bridge has received many accolades for its design and execution but perhaps the most significant came in January 2019, when Historic Environment Scotland designated it as a Category A, the highest listing:

> It is one of Scotland's most architecturally distinguished bridges of the second half of the twentieth century and is among the most outstanding of its type in the country. This is now reflected in the bridge s growing status as tourist attraction along the North Coast 500 route, and in its use in a number of high-profile international advertisements.[88]

## Highland at heart

The reality is that the majority of the jobs which the company undertook were mundane and quotidian. High volume and high number of areas of activity were important. One of the ways the company innovated to sustain this was the concept of minor works, which Morrison developed to challenge the idea 'that small private contracts should go to small private contractors, since they necessarily have fewer overheads, and are able to offer a more competitive scale of costs'. The 'Minor Works Division', was 'to offer an instantaneous, mobile and flexible service, unique for a major construction company, at highly competitive rates', with whatever contracts were held to be managed under this single heading. An example contract was '[t]wo cattle grids and fencing at Lochinver for Highland Regional Council'. With this approach, a familiar Morrison mantra was repeated: there would be 'no question of trading quality for cheapness'.[89] The emphasis on quality would dominate the company's approach for the next few decades and would become synonymous with the night.

Innovations could be technical, too: from Wight construction, a company purchased by Morrison in 1981, the Wight Ring Pile System was adapted to the 'Vacuum Kentledge Pile Load System', designed to offer 'a substantial reduction in the cost of proof testing the bearing pile element of a project', as only one, rather than nine lorry-loads of equipment were needed for this method.⁹⁰ In 1981, the company started offering 'MORESPACE' modular accommodation units, much like 'portacabins', which were transportable and flexible, with stock ready to be fitted up, so offering 'instant accommodation'.⁹¹ Another version of the experimentation in pre-fabricated technology were Morrison "A" Frame Chalets. A pilot project funded by the Scottish Tourist Board was cited to suggest that there were 'handsome benefits' available in providing this kind of pre-fabricated accommodation. The two bedroom 'Morangie' cost a total of £14,000 including '[s]uperior [f]ittings and [f]urnishings', and there was prospect of help from the HIDB, with a 35 per cent grant and 15 per cent loan potentially available. The average income promised was £3,750 per chalet, plus capital appreciation: these were being sold as an investment.⁹² These brought together a number of themes: the company's experiments in factory-based production of buildings, and the role of HIDB in stimulating the Highland economy. The willingness to innovate and take risks in the pursuit of new business is striking here.

A modest volume of housing remained part of the balance of the business. The two aspects of this which are demonstrative of the corporate approach developing in this period are of partnership and marketing. Firstly, if not quite a specialism, the company did a lot of work for housing associations and sheltered housing organisations, that required a collaborative. Work for Langstane Housing Association in Aberdeen highlights this well. After completing a first project on Bloomfield Road building new flats and renovating an existing tenement, ahead of schedule in 1981, Morrison won repeat business in 1983 on Seaforth Road, boasting of 'close co-operation at all stages'.⁹³

Likewise, specialist attention was required in sheltered housing built for the Kirk Care Housing Association in Portree on Skye. This used the

These Morrison 'A' frame chalets were marketed to investors as the Highland tourism market boomed, 1980.

company's experience in working in remote locations to produce 'the means to an independent life style… incorporating safety aids such as hand rails next to bath and lavatory, warning pressure pads located at bathroom doors, and individual unit-to-warden communication systems'.[94] This was the company responding to demographic changes in society: an ageing population in the early 1980s gave a taste of the demand that would come as the baby boomers generation aged with unprecedented means and life expectancy. The company did other specialist housing work. In July 1984, Garnett Hill was one of 'five sheltered housing contracts currently being carried out by Morrison Building Strathclyde'.[95] Partnership and quality appear to have appealed to housing associations.

The company continued to build private houses, including in central Scotland where the economy was performing strongly. Marketing became increasingly important. This meant show homes as standard, and some television advertisements, too.[96] In August 1983, potential buyers were encouraged to visit the opening of a Dunfermline show home with 'champagne for grown-up visitors and ice cream for the kids', whilst the Old Edinburgh Road, Inverness, show flat was opened with a champagne reception and a donation to Christian Aid.[97] The opening ceremony for a 1983 Kirkwall housing project was combined with a Christmas tree lights switching on ceremony, so maximising the audience: even those not in the market for a new home would get to know the name Morrison.[98]

Even as the company moved into southern Scotland, the Highlands came with them. At the launch of the Polmont Bank scheme near Falkirk, the company offered a '[t]aste of the Highlands'. This involved '[t]he sales team, in their new uniforms of blue kilts, pink blouses and "Morrison" scarves' and a competition to guess the length of the River Findhorn, with 'prizes of hampers containing smoked salmon, malt whisky, pheasant and other Highland Fare'.[99] By March 1984, the company had housing projects in Glasgow, Edinburgh, Falkirk, Pitlochry and Dunkeld. Morrison was becoming a name across the central belt and so a national rather than a regional company as it filled in the grid structure introduced above.[100] The flair shown around the publicity for the Kylesku Bridge was transformative for the company, as lessons were clearly learned about how to promote business.

The company's commercial building business continued to diversify. Contracts included Bellahouston Hotel, Glasgow. A prestigious hotel contract invariably involves tight schedules, but despite 'considerable delays due to bad weather' the hotel was completed ahead of schedule by three weeks, and opened in September 1981 by Alan Devereux, Chairman of the Scottish Tourist Board.[101] Commercial contracts reflected other changing consumer

THE MORRISON STORY

Co-op Inverness.

behaviours. Increased demand for single malt whisky led to contracts to build extensive bonded warehouses for Glenmorangie.¹⁰² Building some of these large commercial buildings was fun for the men, simply because steel frames with some cladding and brick were quick to erect. Donald MacLennan points to a number of units built for the Co-op as an example here.¹⁰³

One such job was for the Co-operative Wholesale Society (CWS), building the new Inverness Co-op superstore. In 1982, the advent of a supermarket was an exciting one: 'opening up an exciting new dimension in shopping facilities for the Highland area', with much media attention. Fraser presented D. M. Landau, Chairman of the CWS, with a fancy commemorative silver trowel at a ceremony to mark the laying of the foundation stone. With the Provost of Inverness in attendance, it had many of the features of a grand civic occasion.¹⁰⁴ The 50,000 ft² building was 'on programme for an early opening' in April 1983.¹⁰⁵ This was important for a number of reasons. In the publicity around it, the company repeated the persistent leitmotifs: quality and early completion. But it was also important because Morrison sold CWS 'a development, design and build package', which was indicative of the kind of contracting arrangements which would become increasingly common in the later 1980s and 1990s. Again, this was part of a new, modern way of presenting retail to consumers: much larger shops with a bigger range of products, brilliantly lit, with self-selection of goods. The 'new concept in convenient, town outskirts shopping' was reliant on private car usage.¹⁰⁶ The CWS Superstores Group had drawn its inspiration from the United States and was more ambitious in what it did in Scotland than England, with large stores in Inverness and Paisley replacing a number of local ones.¹⁰⁷

For the public sector, the company built recreational facilities: a sports centre in Invergordon and an all-weather centre in Fort William.¹⁰⁸ Local Authorities were offering expanded leisure facilities, and this provided work in the Highlands especially, where good links had been formed with government agencies by the company. Government work was not limited to the Highlands, however, as evidenced by a contract for the Strathclyde Development Agency which was awarded in 1984 to build a £340,000 factory at Linwood.[109] The company continued to build a number of schools.[110] This included Culloden Academy, with a £3.25m contract to build a 10,500 m² building.[111] The Scottish Arts Council supported and financed a £2,000 commission for artwork for the new academy, which was awarded to Jim Cathcart.[112] Donald MacLennan remembers this project as a favourite. Schools presented challenges because they have to withstand the exuberance of successive generations of children:

> They were interesting, but with all due respect to them, they were all different – a high degree of difficulty… schools are very bitty and [need] a fine finish.

Getting to some of the more remote sites could be a logistical challenge. When building Barra Community School, workers arrived by helicopter, landing on the beach. Over the Highland landscape, this could be little short of a spectacular flight. Donald MacLennan has not forgotten the sight of a golden eagle flying below the helicopter on one occasion.[113] This highlights not only the logistical challenges of remote projects, but at only 2000 m², was much smaller than Culloden Academy. The weather made life difficult, with force eight or nine gales common during the winter months.[114]

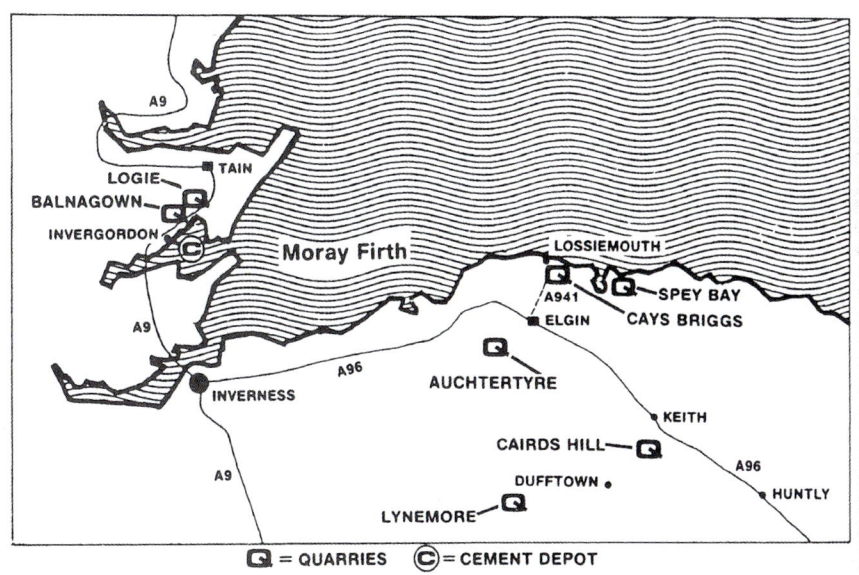

The quarries business was always an important ingredient in the Morrison success story. This map shows the quarries network in 1983.

Logistical considerations also included the growth of the plant and transport division that provided important services within the company. In 1981, this had a turnover of £1m and machinery valued at £3m, suggesting equipment was put to hard work. The 150 vehicles owned included the Steelfield 60 mobile concrete batching plant, capable of producing 45 m$^3$ per hour.[115] The internal tendering process between divisions to hire this equipment could give rise to tensions. David Jeffs suggested that builders do not necessarily have a good view of any plant departments: 'the general view of construction people is that they overcharge and the machines are pretty bad' and when done internally any disagreements required careful management.[116]

The aggregate side of the business was still important, with sales to the oil industry continuing. Rising Sterling prices had made sales to Germany uncompetitive. This area of the business was highly sensitive to external pressures: fluctuating prices and foreign exchange rates. A weaker pound would 'put Morrison Quarries back on the competitive basis on the continent', as Alasdair MacKay put it in *Morrison News*, and for oil sales:

> business prospects in this area depend to quite a large extent on the scale of the proposed developments at Nigg and on the pretty massive infrastructure which will have to be built up in association with it. This could mean very substantial increases in our own operations.[117]

By 1983, the company was taking advantage of currency rates to import cement to their Invergordon base on the Moray Firth, bagging 1.5 tonne 'Euro bags' into 50 kg customer packs.[118] Later that year, the company boasted a network of quarries.[119] In May 1984, the company began selling aggregates by shipping to London. The currency situation had improved sufficiently for a shipment to Holland, with more negotiations for Hamburg sales, too.[120]

## Property Development

The final new discipline added to the business in this period was the property development division. The company's entry to this market was triggered by demand from the offshore sector for quality office accommodation.[121] In 1979, Morrison Developments Limited was formed, to pursue 'speculative, self-motivated projects involving new and refurbished office blocks, shops, warehouses, factories and other commercial and industrial projects'. The business was not necessarily capital intensive, if developments could be sold quickly, but it did require expertise, with projects requiring 'a professional team which includes an architect, a structural engineer, letting and selling agents and solicitors', usually appointed locally.[122] The first sale had been the supermarket in Inverness to CWS, drawing on local expertise within the company.

Another area of the company's business, which developed rapidly in response to commercial opportunities was the provision of office accommodations in Aberdeen, specifically tailored to meet the expectations of American oil companies. As was by now usual, the approach was led by quality. One of the first projects was 22 Rubislaw Terrace in the west end of Aberdeen. A small development offering 3,500 ft$^2$ of offices was sold to the Northern Ireland Electricity Board Pension Fund.[123] Another Aberdeen development at 16 Carden Place was billed as 'making going to the office a pleasure', when it was launched with a reception for local solicitors and estate agents. The sensitive restoration aimed to preserve 'the original, attractive, architectural style'.[124] This was swiftly let on a 25 year lease at £27,000 to a firm of accountants, whilst ownership of the building itself was sold to an investment company.[125] The model was to lease the building to tenants, making it easier to sell the asset to an investor, often pension funds seeking long-term income. Increasingly, the company was becoming an established force beyond the Highlands. Dan MacDonald, responsible for this division, remembers the buoyant market in Aberdeen as being central:

> We saw the opportunity in Aberdeen to take residential property at the west side, buy it, convert it to offices, rent it to oil-related industry and sell on the investment. That was a massive breakthrough, because that was a market we did not have in the Highlands – it still does not exist. Aberdeen became a focus for investment – so pension funds and property investors would pay attention to what was happening to Aberdeen… It was almost by accident. It gave us construction work but opened up a whole new area of expertise… you have got to spot the opportunity… take it through the system, take it through planning, get change of use. I learned, and the Morrison Company learned a whole new culture. That was part of the fuse that was lit that drew attention much further south.[126]

After Aberdeen, Glasgow was an important early market for the property development part of the business. For example, Byres Road in the fashionable West End, saw the company provide offices and retail units, all done to a high standard of finish. 2 Queens Gardens offered '"up-market" appeal'.[127]

An emphasis was placed on the right location. Byres Road was situated immediately above the Glasgow underground railway.[128] Dan MacDonald recollects:

> The market was so buoyant because of incoming prospective tenants – and they were good tenants – it would be easy to say we could not go wrong… I think we had the right attitude with the planning office too… it taught me always to work with planners.

Expansion in Glasgow encompassed different types of property development:

> An industrial development out at Baillieston – it was quite daring looking back at it, perhaps we did not realize quite how daring it was. Then we did some shops over Byres road underground. And we did a big office scheme in the centre of Glasgow in Bath Street. 25,000 ft$^2$… it was big at the time for what we were doing, but it let [without difficulty, so] we got it right. It had car parking underneath, which is of course always the secret. [129]

By March 1984, there were also industrial projects in Oxford, Leicester and London, but the focus was on office refurbishment in Aberdeen and Glasgow, as well as in Inverness.[130] This division would continue to grow and, as will be shown in the next chapter, take on some major projects.

## Stepping up and stepping down: the evolution of a corporate culture

During the late 1970s and early 1980s, a new kind of corporate culture was established in Morrison. A regional and divisional structure created smaller, agile sub-companies, responsive to local conditions, with directors in charge of them, empowered to take advantage of opportunities. At this highest level, other changes occurred over the period, both in companies owned by Morrison and those companies acquired by the company. At this point it is worth restating that the Morrison company was made up of a number of subsidiaries, often acquired: Alexander Sutherland of Golspie in 1977; some of Wight Holdings Ltd's construction interests in 1981; and Cromarty Firth Engineering, 1983. Each time, the purpose was to add a new capacity to the business. As described in the previous chapter, Morrison was bought by CAST, who were acquired by Selection Trust. In 1976 it bought most, and in 1979 the remainder of Alexander Shand. Morrison was transferred to be a subsidiary of Shand in 1977. Operationally, this had limited consequences, except in the case of Kylesku Bridge, when the balance sheet helped keep operations running.

In July 1980, a record £400 million takeover saw Selection Trust acquired by British Petroleum. A press release at the time stated that

> It is, however, possible that the Shand Group's future will not lie within the [Selection Trust] Group. As a result of discussions between the directors of Shand and Charter Consolidated it has been agreed that Charter will negotiate with ST for the possible acquisition of Shand following the completion of the offer.[131]

It was perhaps not a surprise that in 1981 Shand, and therefore Morrison, were duly sold to Charter Consolidated, when British Petroleum divested these interests.[132]

The fine detail of this is not especially significant to the Morrison story: capacities were added, and parent companies changed. What was remarkable was the extent to which a strong culture persisted – thrived even – despite sales between transnational corporations. In a sense, it was still a family business, but it might be more properly suggested it had a family *feel*. Alex had largely stepped back to allow his sons to take over the business shortly after purchase by CAST in 1974. In 1984, he retired, and Fraser became Chairman. From a small

To mark Alex's retirement in 1985, he was presented with a painting of Achiltibuie, the Wester Ross village where Connie's family had originally come from. Left to right: Johnny Morrison, Donnie MacRae, Ian Ross, John Fisher Ross, Alex Morrison, Sandy Duff, Alec Semple, Billy Lowden, Jimmy Thomson, Alex MacAngus.

amount of savings Alex had built up a company employing 1,250 people with a turnover in excess of £40m.[133] Donald MacLennan recollects of Alex, 'we got on well, he did not interfere very much. By the time I came on the scene, Fraser was pretty much in charge'. Donald also noted that 'you have to admire the father because he made sure Fraser was educated to do the job'.[134] The transfer of leadership from one generation to the next is a crucial moment in the story of any family business. Where a founder has dominated a business, succession can present a real challenge in any number of ways: family members may not have the skills or the desire to take over from a parent or may hold back from taking control whilst the founder is still active. One academic has characterised this as the 'lengthening shadow of one [person]'.[135]

In the case of Morrison, whilst Alex certainly cast a long shadow, the transition was very smooth. He ensured his sons had gained technical qualifications and diverse practical experience to position them to take key leadership roles. He provided space for them to take important jobs within the company. Fraser took a major role in 1974 when the company was first sold. Gordon was a director with responsibilities quite separate. It might be posited that, because of this, it was able to be a company which was managed successfully and professionally, as well as retaining the characteristic of being a family business. Not necessarily on the most intimate of terms, nevertheless it was still possible to have some familiarity with the Morrison employees; over time as the company grew, this would become impossible.

As the company grew, becoming ever more complex and part of a large international group, it became more challenging to maintain this 'family feel'. The loyalty and sense of belonging for the longest-serving members was maintained through the continuing Twenty-Five Year Club discussed in the previous chapter, with an exclusive party once a year.[136] New members got a watch and a tie, but further down the line some employees accrued 40 years' service and were presented with claret jugs.[137] Roger Croson recollects golf outings at Gleneagles. As the company spread through the UK, especially with the Shand side, individuals had to travel further. After a few missed trains, these day outings started being held at hotels so that people could spend the night.[138]

Shand also had a Twenty-Five Year Club, and the two held joint events. Roger remembers one amusing incident:

> We were having a joint Twenty-Five Club with Shand at Matlock. So the Highland boys in the Twenty-Five Club jumped in a plane that Fraser had hired, and enjoyed themselves. I had to go down and back in the same plane on business – I was not in the Twenty-Five Club. These boys were in a minibus on their way back from Matlock

to East Midlands Airport. We stopped at a supermarket somewhere because a couple of boys wanted to get a bottle of whisky… the driver of this minibus was persuaded to pull across the road in front of the supermarket, so they could get out directly onto the pavement, which they did; they disappeared into the supermarket. We had not been there long before this policewoman came across and said, 'you cannot park here you know.' … The driver explained to her about these two guys they had been celebrating and had parked… as they had gone to get a little refreshment. She said 'I'll go and get them'… in a few minutes she appeared out in between the two of them, and they had their arms around her neck.

On the flight home,

> Someone said, 'I fancy a drive at this thing' and walked up the aisle to get to the pilots. Fraser or someone stopped them. They were good times. We worked hard, we played hard.[139]

The company had expanded enormously, and the Twenty-Five Club became too big. Smaller events took place instead within divisions.[140] One was the Morrison Old Boys, another was the annual meeting of senior managers of the old civils board – about sixteen of them – meet up and celebrate old times and jobs done.[141] The ethos of working hard and playing hard has endured into retirement.

The company had not only expanded, but things within it had changed: things had stepped up a gear. Accounting had moved a long way since calculation on the Morrison family dining table.[142] A much more professional system had been required when CAST had bought the company, a transition which was already on the cards. Eventually this would result in a system of modern management accounting.

Success was growing. Restructuring continued within the company to ensure directors were empowered to make local decisions. With increased demand for new kinds of contract, such as Design and Build, Morrison was well placed towards '[t]his total package approach to new projects'.[143] Some of the leitmotifs running through the story such as quality and client satisfaction, an entrepreneurial culture, a persistent 'family feel' have already been identified. Two other important ones would come to be crucial: a culture of training, from apprentices to board level, and an increasing emphasis on safety.[144] These priorities would be crucial as the company looked not only to the rest of the UK but also overseas to expand.

No 12 Atholl Crescent, Edinburgh.

CHAPTER SIX

# Opportunities beyond the Highlands: a new era 1984–1994

A DECADE AFTER IT had been taken over, Morrison had expanded beyond all recognition. It had added capacities in engineering, civil engineering and property development, with successful, prominent projects demonstrating not only that it could find alternative ways to create new business, but that it was amongst the most capable civil engineering companies in Scotland. Various threads run through the company's history, around quality and corporate promotion, as well as an enduring sense of being a family business, despite being much larger. Despite a period of sustained growth and mergers and acquisitions, fundamentally the company still had maintained something of its own characteristics and personality. If the scale and type of operations had become so much larger, it is remarkable that much of the corporate ethos and spirit had been maintained, and that the workplace culture withstood these considerable transformations.

The next decade saw some extraordinary work done as the company repositioned itself yet again. Expansion saw work overseas in some of the most difficult contexts in which to do business: namely Soviet Russia and Kuwait immediately after the First Gulf War. Yet there was a real sense in which the company retained the feel of a small family business. This was a result of the fact that Fraser and Gordon were running the company, the regional structure of the business and the fact that people typically worked at the company for a long time.

In this period, in addition to the expansion, there were two crucial changes in the ownership. In one of the most thrilling episodes in this history, the family bought back the business from Charter Consolidated in 1989. In 1995, just a few years later, the company would be successfully floated on the stockmarket. Whilst the IPO (Initial Public Offering – the first time shares are made available to the public) is dealt with in the next chapter, the

Morrison people checking out drawings in front of St Basil's Cathedral in Red Square, Russia.

company was positioned for this well in advance, with smart annual reports, an emphasis on quality and a move to an Edinburgh headquarters. The first experiments in partnering and non-traditional contracting would put the company in an excellent position to grow its orders when the PFI (Private Finance Initiative) became the dominant mode of financing infrastructure in the 1990s, as contracts transferred risk and responsibility to the contractors and financiers. Morrison was well-placed to take advantage of these changes.

## Moving south again: Edinburgh becomes HQ

The May 1986 issue of the corporate newsletter excitedly announced the group had opened an additional Edinburgh office. This was tactical rather than strategic, as it 'will involve only a handful of key Morrison directors and personnel, led by [C]hairman and [M]anaging [D]irector Fraser Morrison'.[1] Taking stock, Fraser reckoned it was 'a logical move', given 'rapid growth from a small Highland building and contracting concern to one of the leading Scottish construction companies, employing around 1,000 people'.[2] Fraser again approached marketing consultant Michael Fraser, to advise on how to promote the company as it sought to establish itself as a major player in the industry. One of his suggestions was to embark on a high-profile artistic sponsorship scheme. This resulted in Morrison supporting the 1987 exhibition 'The Queen's Image' to mark the 1986 move of their corporate headquarters from Inverness to Atholl Crescent, Edinburgh.'[3] In return for financial support, the company could use the exhibition for corporate entertainment.[4]

Pam MacKay remembers that as a wife of a director, she was expected to host one such event, which she rather enjoyed doing – it appealed to her own cultural interests, even if that still involved work.

> I have always loved art, and I had the privilege of attending two dinners in the Portrait Gallery… the first time we were hosted so we could learn about the exhibition; the second time… we had a very enthusiastic architect and his wife [to host for the evening]… I loved it [but] I do remember one wife being totally mumped [sic] about the whole thing and not getting it, but she was the only one; everyone else seemed to apply themselves automatically to that role of entertaining people – because that's the Highland thing.[5]

Hosting like this was a particular kind of labour and is another example of the contribution made by families to the company. Whilst many obviously did this with good grace and charm, some may have been less than thrilled, as Pam noted.

This initial foray into arts sponsorship was successful and was followed up by a more ambitious programme. A few months after the exhibition closed, in February 1988 overtures were made by Michael Fraser about the possibility of Morrison sponsoring a national portrait competition, under which:

> Morrison would negotiate a series of dinners [and/or] private views within the Galleries; this arrangement to be structured along similar lines.[6]

The prize for the winner was £5,000, and there were five consolation prizes of £100. The first prize was awarded to Joyce Cairns from Aberdeen, by Ian Lang Minister of State for Scotland and Minister responsible for the Arts. There had been considerable interest in the competition, which attracted 214 entries, over 70 of which were exhibited.[7] Sir Roy Strong a prominent art historian and curator was the guest speaker at the dinner.[8] In true Scottish self-deprecation, Cairns replied to news of her acknowledgement accepting the invitation but with a block capitals post-script 'P.S. ARE YOU SURE YOU HAVE NOT MADE A MISTAKE'.[9] Michael Fraser had successfully engineered a sufficiently high-profile competition that a Minister of State and prominent figures in the art world had been attracted. It had not been a cheap exercise: the prizes totalled £5,500, and expenses added £3,488 to the cost. If it were designed to announce Morrison had not only arrived in the capital, but were entering the major leagues, the sponsorship had been highly successful. The winner also painted a portrait of Alex.

The prize ran again in 1991, with Alexander 'Sandy' Fraser winning the prize, presented by Sir Alan Peacock, Chair of the Scottish Arts Council.[10] Fraser was unable to judge due to pressure of work, so sent Stewart MacLeod instead.[11] Stewart remembers:

> Michael Fraser, who was our PR consultant had a heavy hand in it, Trish Morrison, Fraser Morrison's wife, had an interest in it, and when it came to the selection committee, Trish, Michael Fraser and myself sat on the board to decide who was going to be the winner… that was a very good example promoting the company's image.[12]

It cost Morrison £6000 in addition to any prize money.[13] Again in 1993, Trish Morrison became actively involved in arrangements as well as the judging of the competition.[14] A selection of works from the competition were displayed

THE MORRISON STORY

at the Caledonian Club in London in December, helping take the Morrison name yet further.[15]

The competition was repeated every two years: in 1995 Joe Fan won the award; in 1997 David M. Sinclair received it.[16] In 1999, the prize was split between Vincent Butler for sculpture and Jennifer McRae for painting, with £2750 each, and £250 to three runners up.[17] McRae had been a runner up in 1991. She wrote:

> I also appreciated the interest shown by Sir Fraser Morrison in the story behind the portrait itself as it made me realise that the sponsors of the arts are genuinely fascinated by this area in life which can only result positively for myself and others.[18]

By the time the next competition was due to take place, Anglian Water Group had bought Morrison. The competition continues to this day with different sponsorship and is an important part of the Scottish art scene.

For Morrison, patronage of the arts offered positive promotion, demonstrated good corporate citizenship and provided some good entertaining opportunities. More than anything, it had aimed to provide a meaningful connection for the company with some of the cultural institutions in Edinburgh.

> Michael Fraser came up with the idea, it was as we moved to Edinburgh as I recall, this was a sort of landing in Edinburgh with no connections whatsoever. We looked for something to do that would help connect us to the community in Edinburgh.[19]

New offices continued to open as the company's structure was fleshed out. In 1991, the Shand North Thames business became stronger and a larger order book included some quite substantial projects, necessitating a new office. It reflected a similar sort of profile in terms of range as the Morrison works in Scotland, with warehousing and offices, a driving range, work at a sewage plant and refurbishing a factory and offices, together worth £2.2m.[20]

In 1987, Charter Consolidated owned Shand; Shand owned Morrison Construction Group Ltd. The group, referred to here as Morrison or simply the company, was comprised of four sub-divisions. The building and civil engineering divisions had Highland, North-East and Central Scotland divisions; the property development business was non-geographical, and Engineering was arranged thematically: Plant, Quarries and Cromarty Firth Engineering.[21] In 1990–1991, Property Development was integrated into

# THE THREE FAMILY COMPANIES BEFORE THEY CAME TOGETHER IN 1989

## Shand

Hyde Park Underpass built in 1962 looks little different today.

Plant and equipment was always a major interest of the Shand business. This is an early mobile crane nicknamed 'Old Faithfull' purchased in 1938.

Baslow Bridge is over the River Derwent in the Peak District National Park. It was originally built in the seventeenth century and refurbished by Shand in the twentieth century.

Shand successfully completed this section of the Leeds inner relief road in the mid 1960s, but it was another 40 years before this complex infrastructure project was finished in its entirety.

In 1977 opencast coal mining was a major activity of the Shand business. It was sold within ten years by Charter Consolidated when they decided to focus on construction. Some of the heavy machinery can be seen in this photograph of the Shand Rowsley Yard from 1977.

This reservoir was built within a short distance of Matlock and was completed in 1938 at a cost of £480,000.

The Head Office sat in the same grounds as the main administration and operational headquarters of the company.

Shand Head Office, Matlock.

Staff hard at work, Shand, 1975. From left to right: Chris Benbow, Director of Shand Midlands; Simon, Graduate/Sandwich Course Engineer; ???; Richard Ready, Contracts Manager; Ken Tallant, Commerical Manager.

# Biggs Wall

Biggs Wall was established in 1884. They originally manufactured pipe fittings for the water industry. When Biggs Wall moved to their headquarters in Arlesey in Bedfordshire in 1967, they named the office building Hampden House after their manufacturing base in Muswell Hill.

Laying of underground pipework had always been a major activity of Biggs Wall, working for the water and gas industries. Attention to safety has significantly improved since those early days.

Colne Valley Water.

Colchester deep pipe laying.

This picture of the Board of Biggs Wall is believed to have been published in the early twentieth century showing representatives from both the Biggs and the Wall families.

Emergency repairs.

Contract for Eastern Gas.

# Morrison

Blue Circle Depot, Inverness, was built in the early 1970s and the photograph was taken in 1995. These reinforced concrete silos stored cement delivered by rail.

Cumbernauld Airfield was Morrison's first entry into civil engineering in Central Scotland.

In the 1970s the construction of council housing was a major activity for Morrison, with large schemes getting built in Maryburgh (above), Alness, Invergordon (opposite) and Tain (opposite lower).

In 1943, the North of Scotland Hydro Electric Board was formed in order to manage the water resource of the Highlands for the production of electricity. Securing work from this company at this facility in Evanton, near Dingwall, was a major breakthrough for Morrison.

Alex Morrison had to be extremely entrepreneurial to get his business established and he saw bespoke private housing as the way forward. This house for Mr and Mrs Sutherland was the first such project and the purchasers remained life-long friends of Alex and Connie.

Invergordon warehouses.

Teannich Distillery, Alness.

Houses, Invergordon.

In 1970 Morrison secured its first minor road contract in Fearn, near Tain. This photograph taken in 1995 suggests a lack of maintenance over the previous 25 years.

Connie Morrison's family all went to Hilton School which was replaced in 1960 by this new building. Alex Morrison was always very proud to be given the opportunity to rebuild a school where his wife was educated.

Mansfield Housing, Tain.

building division, whilst housing was a separate division.[22] This restructuring reflected a move southward. 1986 had seen 'substantial growth' across Scotland, but a growing focus on the central belt. 'Increasingly, and wherever our far[-]flung contracts were actually carried out, our work was beginning from Scotland's central belt.'[23] Even as the centre of gravity was shifting south, the network of regional offices preserved a small, local feel to the business.

## Risk management

One of the key aspects which emerged from interviews conducted for this history was the way risk was perceived and managed in the company. Ultimately, construction is a low-margin business but particularly with the move to civil engineering, risks increased. As the group had expanded in the geographical and disciplinary ways outlined above, the implicit underpinning was the low barriers to entry into each new market and place; none of these required rounds of capital funding or debt. In effect, the business was still drawing on the original capital. Jim Arnold considers that times when contracts lose money are often when a company is, 'moving into new markets and going a bit too quick', suggesting that the crucial thing 'is how you limit the damage and mitigate it… [and] understand the risks when you start those contracts'.[24]

New types of contract sought to move risk away from the client and towards the contractor. This was true both for private and public sector clients, especially under the Private Finance Initiative (PFI). Many of these were very large contracts and were won in joint ventures to spread the risk. Hugh England was struck by several things in relation to PFI. Firstly, the risks involved were considerable in their scale and complexity was considerable:

> The risk profile… was wide, and it was potentially pretty massive as well… [therefore] you tend to think slightly differently. My mindset was we price this to do it, and we have enough money to do it.

The efficiencies of this collaborative way of working were identified as valuable by a number of interviewees:

> To me it was wonderful… for the first time in my career, we could sit down and work out how much it would cost us to build… lots of innovation, which was in our own hands because we are designing

it… so we can drive innovation, but you have enough money. I'd never worked with multi-million-pound money for risk… Then you get the opportunity to discuss that with your client… the whole thing is much more open. As a contractor, the ultimate in openness.[25]

The other change where risk became important for the company was overseas transactions. Even if contracts were priced in Sterling or US Dollars, international business entailed risks which required careful management. Ian Cusden suggests that on occasion it could be 'quite hard to get money back out of those countries'.[26] The scope to mitigate such risks was relatively limited.

Risk management would continue to be a central concern. Peter Heathershaw remembered Fraser making a deliberate choice to focus on risk.

> He wanted to us to understand the risks we were taking and get better at risk management – that was the one thing which stood out for me more than anything. When you are working day to day, you get to the point where you lose focus at times on the risks you are taking.[27]

This is also an area where management has tightened up over time.

> We did use to keep a generic risk register for the business, but it probably had about a dozen items on it – not as structured as it is nowadays… we [even] have a risk committee here.[28]

None of this was unique to Morrison, but the range and reach of work added to the complexity of implementation.

## Total Quality Morrison

If attitudes to risk defined the sector and, indeed, business generally, Morrison sought to establish a unique selling point which meant the company did not try to compete on the bottom line, or even necessarily total cost of ownership. From the mid-1980s, the company focused on selling its services as being high-quality. Tendering was traditionally concentrated on competition in pursuit of the lowest price, leading some contractors to cut corners to meet their contractual obligations, rather than focusing on satisfying clients. In sharp contrast to this, Morrison sold itself as providing a quality product. Whilst this approach is quite mainstream now, when it was launched in the company, it was much more radical. 'Quality Built In', became a widely

recognised slogan attached to the Morrison name, sitting alongside the distinctive red M logo.

There were two origins for the quality agenda which was developed by Morrison. Firstly, it drew on Quality Assurance, where it was already in vogue in Cromarty Firth Engineering (CFE), the engineering company acquired by the group. However whilst it was, as Stewart MacLeod noted, 'probably the most important feature of that business', its impact was limited to the work undertaken for the offshore industry.[29] A much more comprehensive quality agenda stemmed from a book read by Fraser during one Christmas break about Total Quality Management (TQM), by Barry Popplewell and Alan Wildsmith.[30] Systems were soon adopted in the company to communicate ideas about quality to employees and to customers, with considerable investment was made into this across the company. For example, Stewart MacLeod spent three weeks studying it at CFE in order to apply elsewhere in the business.

Like many innovations ahead of their time which come to be mainstream, TQM may seem less remarkable today. It was first adopted in Japanese manufacturing, especially the automotive industry in the 1980s, it placed an emphasis on 'company-wide quality control'.[31] The key task was to ensure that each employee internalised a commitment to quality: that is to say, individuals were expected to hold their own work to account. It might be thought of as self-certification rather than a regulatory regime. In that sense, a close association between TQM and the prevailing ideas about Health and Safety, discussed in chapter four, can be seen.

Rather than looking at quality in objective terms measured against a specification, the Morrison view of this was that it was a subjective thing, defined as 'what the customer says it is – not what the contractor thinks it should be', which the company assessed through customer satisfaction surveys.[32] Such surveys are ubiquitous now for everything from online shopping to railway journeys, but in the construction sector, they were rare then. As Ken Gillespie remembers, customer satisfaction was regularly gauged. I had never heard of [them] before Morrison... the concept was... if we did that we would make a better return.[33]

Detailed explanations of Total Quality Management are found elsewhere.[34] For Morrison, it followed earlier experimentations around ways to ensure quality.[35] The most relevant features of TQM included the need for leadership, encouraging education, dialogue and to restore 'pride of workmanship', all requiring comprehensive, long-term cultural realignment in the workforce. In an academic analysis, Kanji identifies fourteen characteristics of TQM, of which the most crucial was a move away from 'the practice of awarding business solely on the basis of price tag'. The company did not generally tender on the basis of offering the lowest price. Roger Croson explained what was meant by 'quality' in a circular sent to staff on 30 July 1987.[36] Ken Tallant recollects:

> at the outset, when people talked about quality, it had to be explained to them what we meant, because to me quality meant something that was expensive… but now… it has come to mean a measure of how good something was… [but then] you would never put value for money in the same sentence as quality.[37]

Ultimately it came to a question of reputation. A common theme was the idea that Morrison's Quality agenda was ahead of its time. Ian MacKay felt that 'we were a bit different then… we were fairly early doing that'.[38]

Quality was secured through the commitment of people, but this was not always immediate, as Stewart MacLeod put it:

> This word quality pervaded across many, many aspects of the business, and apart from… building whatever contract we were doing, it was always done to the very, very highest standard. On reflection, being able to achieve that speaks very highly of the quality of the staff we had.[39]

In 1993, the 'Quality People' device was designed to embed the Investors in People scheme across the business, with an emphasis on training and internal communications.[40] For Charles Morrison, it served the purpose, that 'after a time, it definitely created a team'.[41] It was described in almost religious terms by Norman MacLennan in the 1991 Annual Report 'much more than buzzword, it becomes an attitude to life as well as work'.[42]

In the 1990 Annual Report, Fraser announced the company was committed to 'deliver[ing] a product of consistent quality – a quality which we are determined to mirror in our approach to customer service'.[43] A year later, he claimed: 'we are very definitely seeing the practical benefits… in the quality of the products and services which we are supplying to our clients – as well as a real reduction in the waste which has been a hallmark of the industry in general'.[44] The approach was successful. Awards followed for many aspects, perhaps the most prestigious of which was the Digital Scottish Quality Award in 1994 for the TQM programme.[45]

THE MORRISON STORY

How the message was communicated was important. 'Quality. Built in.' was one slogan sitting alongside the famous logo. It accompanied other projects, such as a new bypass, with the slogan 'And Auldearn got its street party', where Donald MacPherson, the contracts manager for the project, was pictured next to a company hallmark: 'Auldearn Bypass – Another Early Opening by Morrison'.[46] In 1988, these were part of a Quality Improvement Programme. Stewart MacLeod was appointed director responsible for this programme, which 'embraces everything from customer satisfaction and operational safety and efficiency, through to job satisfaction for our own people'.[47] The breadth of the concept was astonishing, and it was firmly established within the corporate culture at Morrison

Communicating this new mode of working required various communication strategies. One, Fraser remembers, was:

> A series of cartoons… they were quite important. Teamwork was the other important thing. I remember we used a rowing boat analogy to make the point that if you have people who are co-ordinated you will move forward much more quickly. We used a whole range of analogies.[48]

One analogy, of motor racing, was as adopted as a result of sponsoring the Jackie Stewart racing team:

This cartoon highlights that if you are well organised and work as a team you win the race.

We sponsored Jackie for various reasons – one of them was Jackie's focus on quality… and really the whole formula one industry: how tiny, tiny improvements make a difference over time… it was an interesting sponsorship because it said what we were trying to explain to our people.[49]

Another way of promoting the quality agenda was the Five-Star Site programme. If a worksite was up to scratch it could fly the Five-Star flag, 'providing they met [certain] criteria'.[50] In 1988, following pilots, Quality Circles were introduced across the company: 'small groups of employees who meet voluntarily and regularly to discuss and solve their own work-related problems. The focus was on 'how could they be better as a team', working around any number of topics, such as health and safety, accident rates, site cleanliness or providing better customer service.[51] Morrison supported these circles by providing 'facilities and a [f]acilitator', and this was rolled out across the business after it had been piloted.[52] Over time this was developed into a virtual Quality College with its own in-house manager, Hamish Robertson, although there was no porticoed building as indicated in the cartoon. Instead, it was:

> a virtual college… an umbrella concept for TQM initially… and it was very much about innovation, quality circles, internal customers

The red 'M' on the Jackie Stewart racing team's car can be seen prominently. Jackie Stewart on far left, and his son, sitting on the car, are pictured with Morrison people.

The drive for quality: Total Quality Morrison was an innovative tool used to inspire staff to ever greater quality in their work. TQM was later illustrated graphically with a range of specially commissioned cartoons, published in a popular booklet, highlighting the benefits of such things as teamwork, eliminating waste, maintaining tidy sites and sharing good ideas. This cartoon highlights that ISO 9000 and TQM are part of the same process.

This cartoon shows the virtual quality college and through that keep reducing waste.

This cartoon invites all employees to join the quality journey.

This cartoon highlights that working in a well planned manner increases profits.

This cartoon asks employees to be proud of profitability.

This cartoon highlights waste on construction sites.

This cartoon highlights that if Morrison cut its waste we could save one house per year.

This cartoon invites all employees to be heard.

This cartoon highlights that confrontation with clients costs money.

This cartoon invites employees to stay ahead of the competition.

This cartoon asks employees to communicate professionally and not to rely on smoke signals.

This cartoon highlights that quality is a continuous process.

This cartoon reminds employees not to ignore the customer.

This cartoon illustrates that working in partnership results in everyone winning.

as well as external, about creating a culture within the business of doing the right thing... one of the underpinning principles was around reducing waste... construction materials and time and effort.[53]

One of the main ways in which staff were motivated was internal recognition for their quality efforts. All employees were given a specially commisioned model of a Morrison wheelbarrow being pushed by a workman, made especially by Border Fine Arts. Whilst initally given a wheelbarrow with square wheels, staff were promised they would receive one with round wheels if they made an exceptional contribution to quality. The round-wheeled models in particular were highly prized.

Andrew Aldred received one with round wheels for his work on TQM and a process flowchart system he devised to assure quality across all areas, including health and safety, environment, people management and bidding.[54] These remained popular and many still have them, but likely due to expense and difficulty, they were replaced with mugs eventually. Many interviewees still proudly own either their mugs or square-wheeled wheelbarrows.

In 1995, the company added a 'scorecard' in the pursuit of 'a holistic approach... and [this element of] TQM offered us a quantum improvement'.[55] Ken Gillespie explained that this took 'an academic quality system [and]

This was the most famous cartoon and illustrates that if our predecessors had not listened to new ideas the square wheel would still be in use.

converted it into a golf course. The nine holes are KPIs [Key Performance Indicators at a time] when nobody talked about KPIs.' Communication with the workforce was successful because 'Everyone understood a golf course [and it was a] concept easily communicated… each [person] had a target' to achieve, and a range of things were measured, including health and safety and risk management.[56]

Communicating this outside the company was crucial: if clients were to buy quality and value rather than simply lowest-price competitive tendering, the benefits had to be articulated. One way was the 'job finished early' signs.[57] Supply-side quality was important, too, and in late 1991 and early 1992, the company held information evenings where suppliers could learn about what TQM was all about, as the company looked at 'stronger working relationships with fewer suppliers who would provide the highest level of quality, service and value for money'.[58] Embraced and supported by the management and staff, quality would serve as the company's organising principle for further expansion.

A project which emphasises this high-quality approach was the Exchange Plaza office development in Edinburgh. In 1994, the company announced that this joint venture with CALA had been 'prefunded by the Railway Pension Fund Trustees' and planning permission had been secured. Phase one would provide 96,000 ft$^2$ of office space over seven floors, a restaurant

The Total Quality Morrison square-wheeled wheelbarrow ornament showed people how not to do a job and was highly prized by staff who received one from Morrison's TQM College.

Clydesdale Bank Plaza, Lothian Road, Edinburgh.

on the ground floor and a stylish atrium.⁵⁹ The quality of the building work and the prestige of the site were sufficient for the top floor and naming rights to the building to be sold to the Clydesdale Bank. Dan MacDonald remains enthusiastic about this project. He remembers asking the Chairman of CALA 'if he'd be interested in doing the best joint venture you' will ever see. He said I agree with you – that is the best site in Scotland.'⁶⁰

The project itself was designed to 'form the gateway to the overall new district of Edinburgh to be known as the Exchange'.⁶¹ At £55m in 1994, or £139m in 2017 money, the project was a major development for the city and the company.⁶² This was a prestigious contract in an important area which sent a very confident signal to financial markets as well as further building a reputation for prestigious work of the very quality which the company was promoting through its TQM strategy.⁶³ With investors buying the building before it had been built, this was a very successful project. A second phase followed in 1999, also in joint venture with CALA and was sold easily, this time to Standard Life, adding 11,000 ft² to the development.⁶⁴ The original project itself was commemorated on a £20 Clydesdale Bank note.⁶⁵

## Morrison international

Several international projects demonstrated the company's ambition and resolve, but doing business abroad presented certain challenges. Where networking had been central to establishing the company in the Highlands, this was not immediately replicable overseas. One attempt which the company made at using personal networks to win business overseas was employing consultant, Bill Polk. By any account, his life has been interesting: a distinguished scholar of foreign policy, connected socially to elites in governments and royal families across the world and he even crossed the Arabian Desert by camel – so surpassing Lawrence of Arabia – at least in one sense.⁶⁶ Morrison engaged him as a consultant and arranged meetings with the Russian Prime Minister, Yevgeny Primakov, as well as other Middle East contacts. Even after a number of visits to Russia, however, no business came out of these meetings. A joint venture agreement with an Azerbaijani company likewise did not lead to any business.⁶⁷ It could be argued, however, that this gave Morrison confidence to bid for contracts in relatively unlikely places. Another unsuccessful effort was in Bogotá, Colombia, in an effort to win work to provide expertise in integrated bus systems. Michael Martin 'even got inoculated', but the job did not materialise.⁶⁸ The frustrations of trying to do business in different cultures where networks were less certain and more tentative ought not to be forgotten. The company could lean upwards on Shand, which had an existing international division including some Middle Eastern interests.[69] Just as when the Kylesku Bridge project put cashflow pressures on the company, being a part of the Shand group of companies for these projects proved a valuable resource on which to draw.

### Russia

Perhaps one of the most surprising areas of work was in Russia in the late 1980s and 1990s. Some initial efforts had been made during the final days of the USSR. Somehow three Morrison men, Roger Croson, Andrew Aldred and Fraser, found themselves in Moscow to discuss putting out oil fires started by Saddam Hussain in Kuwait. Fraser and Roger had to leave early. Andrew remained in Moscow and, to support him there, Fraser and Roger emptied their pockets of cash – not being readily obtainable when overseas in those days. The negotiations came to nothing because the USSR then collapsed before anything was concluded. This was doing business in a very different world: 'You had to have a protocol man with you all the time', said Andrew. Things were very different: 'I remember the meetings... everyone you met seemed to be a deputy minister, but you never met a minister'. One symbol of what was to come in Russia was this: 'they had just opened the first McDonalds in Moscow... there was a queue'.[70]

The unfamiliarity of this business environment is not hard to imagine. As Dan MacDonald puts it, this was 'immature capitalism' – a period of what economists would term transition from a centrally planned or command economy to a market one.[71] Perhaps the fact that the company did work in Russia in this context is more significant than the type it did. It signals ambition and ability. 'We went from a village in the Highlands to being the first ever to do commercial property development in St Petersburg'.[72]

Over time, Russia became increasingly open to business, new opportunities became available:

> The School for Political Enlightenment in the ancient Russian capital of St Petersburg, which once played an important part in the lives of the Communist apparatchiks, and is now being converted into the International Centre for Business Co-operation.[73]

If the former communist state wanted to demonstrate a commitment to moving towards a market economy, then bringing in an international company

# THE MORRISON STORY

to fulfil this £20m contract represented both symbol and praxis. As to how well 'Quality Built In' translated to Russian it is harder to know; certainly the picture on the front page of the newsletter would have impressed upon readers that anything was possible. No less potent symbol was the opening of first Russian Subway sandwich shop in St Petersburg, which was celebrated with the special Kylesku Bridge commemorative whisky.[74]

One other project in Russia was of acute cultural sensitivity and significance, when the company completed work on a building contained a room in which 'Dostoyevsky had written, and we had to show we held it in high regard'.[75] In Moscow work refurbishing the Saudi Arabian Embassy was doubtless a result of the reputation established out of the work in Kuwait.[76]

The tact and finesse which was needed in Russia was also helpful elsewhere in Central and Eastern Europe. The company sought projects in these areas, too, but often long negotiations came to very little business. As Norman MacLennan wrote in the 1993 Annual Report '[i]n what are evolving market economies, these projects do, of course, take time to come together.'[77] A joint venture set up with Infrastructure and Technology Communications to 'pursue technology/business park and major infrastructure projects in Eastern Europe', is an example of the type of initiative which despite it being 'a region of great potential' did not lead to very much business.[78] Many of these international opportunities were driven by geopolitics. After the fall of the Berlin Wall, the company did

A sign of expansion: the Morrison brand – and the famous 'Quality Built In' strapline – feature on a construction site in Russia, a long way from Tain!

some small work building houses on the East side. Ian Smith remembers, however, that their own accommodation during the contract was in the former West part of the city, which had enjoyed a higher material standard of living during partition.[79]

Two contexts in which Morrison did business or attempted to do business were not easy ones: the aftermath of the First Gulf War in 1991 and during the transition towards a market economy during the breakup of the USSR. Ken Tallant remembers asking Roger Croson and Fraser 'Why do only you want me to go to godforsaken places'?[80] There was one occasion during a contract building a Marriott hotel in Georgia when he remembers being threatened because he declined to give more money, being told 'Mr Tallant, I know where your children go to school'.[81] As he had only one son at school, he was not unduly worried, but this does highlight how difficult managing and adapting to different social and contracting norms could be when doing business internationally.

In Ghana, whilst work for the government generally went off without a hitch, on one occasion Roger Croson was taking a photograph of the bare site on which a multi-storey mixed development was to be built in Accra.

> My abiding memory of being there was standing on one corner of the site before we started work and taking a photograph of it as a bare site... and suddenly the traffic all stopped going into a crossroads. The policeman who was on points duty marched over and asked why I had taken his photograph... The conversation went on and I was not impressing him. At the vital moment, my mate Ken Tallant and our two sponsors, a government minister and the chief of police, came along in a car and saw me being challenged, and I didn't go to prison, in short.[82]

The work Morrison did initially in Azerbaijan was for British Petroleum (BP). It will be recollected that British Petroleum had owned Selection Trust, which owned CAST, which in turn owned Morrison. As was often the case, further work in the area followed, but when random tax demands appeared for other contracts which did not benefit from the preferential tax treatment which BP had negotiated, the deals became unmanageable.[83]

Former company secretary, John Morrison, recollects that overseas work would require 'a lot more in terms of bonds and guarantees... a lot more are on demand bonds, so I would be involved at bid stage'.[84] Contracts were in dollars rather than local currencies, so eliminating the risk of changes in the value of local currency, although the risk of goods or services based in local currencies remained. Ultimately the whole business of overseas work presented a series of potential transactional problems. As Ken Tallant remembers:

> One of my sleepless nights was in Azerbaijan, where we had a Turkish sub-contractor. The norm for international contracting was that you had an advance payment, and you put up a bank bond against that payment. So that you would get say £250,000 – we got a payment from BP and we went to a Turkish M&E [mechanical and electrical] sub-contractor to buy all the kit for the M&E in the building. He wanted £250,000 upfront so he could buy the kit, and have it shipped.

Things then went wrong: 'The guy did not perform, he did not buy the kit, you cannot find him anywhere'. In theory, all that was required was 'a letter saying he had not delivered the goods' and the bank would pay. When Ken took the bond down to the corresponding bank in London, he had 'this awful sinking feeling' during discussions with a clerk. After several telephone calls, 'he comes back again and points out the bond was issued by Bank of Ankara, but the money we paid was into the Ankara Bank.' They saw neither equipment nor money. Ultimately, this is part of the risk of 'international business – you must make sure you have the right [International Bank Account Number]… which is why the profit margins for international should be higher, because eventually you will have something like that' occur.[85]

### Kuwait

One of the most exceptional contracts completed by Morrison was a civil engineering project for the United States Army Corp of Engineers to restore water to Kuwait City after the First Gulf War in February 1991. The original contract was a 90-day emergency project to fix water mains and sewerage, but was subsequently extended in value and time, but reduced to water supply only, reflecting the difficulties of the job and extent of the damage done by the War.[86] By October 1991, Morrison had won work worth $24m, including $7.9m to rebuild damaged hangers at Kuwait airport and $6.28m for repairs on 'Failaka Island and Ra's Al Ardh – the first part of Kuwait to be liberated'.[87]

There was a British expectation of 'a commensurate return' and that some companies would win shares of the reconstruction work.[88] Morrison was the only British company to win reconstruction work, after a late, anxious night writing a bid: the central requirement was for all boots to be on the ground quickly.[89] The company was prompted to bid after an approach through the Scottish Office. 'We had to put together a team of people to go and engineer the reconstruction' willing and ready to go immediately, 'like tomorrow'.[90]

Arriving in Kuwait as part of a military convoy saw the men camped in a hotel with emergency generators. The scenes were hellish. In his account, the well-known ITN broadcaster, Sandy Gall suggested with 780 of 900 oil wells giving off thick, acrid smoke it presented 'an inferno which only Hieronymus Bosch could have done'.[91] At first, they simply had to get on and establish themselves in no small part by to the generosity of the US Army providing necessities such as a spare torches. Amidst 'six weeks of camel meat and mushy peas', invitations to dine at the mess were gratefully accepted.[92] Ultimately, the first few weeks were about 'understanding what the rules were: [but] there were not any'.[93] The risks of the situation were particular: landmines and discarded ordnance presented threats to life and limb. Ken Tallant warned the men: 'we didn't want any heroes', and instead the risk was managed through a 'permit to work system'. Passive Barriers was an Aberdeen company specialising in clearing sites ahead of reconstruction work.[94] Ken remembers many of the men being 'quite tense the night before because they were going into a war zone'. They went 'to join this army convoy, and when we got there the majority of the other passengers that were going up there were middle-aged American ladies who were wages clerks… we were feeling quite heroic until we actually got there… so I did not feel quite so bad sending these guys'.[95] The key focus was 'emergency repair work to the water supply and sewage systems in the war-torn state of Kuwait'.[96] Soon pipe breaks were reported and they could get to work.[97]

The risks were considerable and could not be entirely removed: 'nobody would insure that because it was still technically a war zone; [Saddam Hussein's troops] had mined the areas and set fire to oil wells'.[98] However payment for work, providing it was certified, was prompt.[99] In the 1991 Annual Report, Fraser noted it as a 'landmark achievement'.[100] Yet for all the unusual circumstances, much was the same, it was a standard job: it led to various bits of ongoing work 'with a local partner'[101] and with typical flair, the handsome dual-language book *A Year in Kuwait*, written by Sandy Gall, made for effective publicity. Fraser reckoned Kuwait 'put us on the map in terms of UK construction companies'.[102]

The management of risk in this context was strategic: 'short-term construction contracts which establish a presence', while more significant property development projects are progressed mainly in joint venture with local partners and western financial institutions.[103] These two strands provided business in some extremely difficult and challenging environments. For all

THE MORRISON STORY

Morrison working in Kuwait with the raging oil field fires in the background.

OPPORTUNITIES BEYOND THE HIGHLANDS

Above, devastation and fires in Kuwait and far left, more devastation on Mutla Ridge. Left, broken water mains – their repair was a Morrison priority.

# THE MORRISON STORY

the strains, a sense of business as usual remained. Even in the war-ravaged desert the 'Quality Built In' flag was flown on site.[104]

## Housing

Portlethen Housing, Aberdeen, 1990.

For all the broadening scope of the international business, there were areas of continuity for Morrison. Housing remained one such area, where the company completed between 83 and 302 units annually. The difference here is that these were *private* homes. Just as with the New Public Management, an explicitly ideological view was taken to reduce the role of the state in the provision of housing. Rather than seeing it as a public good benefitting all of society, it became a private commodity. Building houses for a mass private market was very different from either public housing contracts, or the small private market with which much of the company's business had started.

Table 6.1 Morrison private house completions 1986–1994

| Year to March | Completions |
| --- | --- |
| 1986 | 114 |
| 1987 | 98 |
| 1988 | 86 |
| 1989 | 113 |
| 1990 | 83 |
| 1991 | 216 |
| 1992 | 189 |
| 1993 | 212 |
| 1994 | 302 |

Notes: 1986 figures are for 15 months; 1991 includes Morrison Lema Homes; 1992 excludes 280 homes built under contract. Source: derived from the Fred Wellings, *Private House Builders Annual*, prepared for Credit Suisse, and extracts kindly provided by the author.

In December 1984, housing sales started to improve after 'one of the leanest years experienced by the Scottish housing industry'. The approach was the same as the quality agenda elsewhere: not necessarily low cost, but rather 'quality building and value for money'.[105] The Scottish economy operated on a different track, at least in part due to the oil industry.[106] The demand for private house building was fundamentally different to council housing, being driven by cyclical activity and prevailing economic circumstances. Changes in mortgage rates for example could encourage or discourage potential buyers. Developments all required show homes through which to sell the houses. One example of a development was at Udny in Aberdeen aimed at 'executives with oil-related companies' concentrated in Bridge of Don or Dyce. The homes offered a high material standard of living:

> The development will comprise 30 three and four bedroom detached houses with lounge, dining room and large family kitchen giving total floor areas of from 1300 to 1800 square feet. Most will have double garages, at least one stone fireplace and two bathrooms. The top of the range house will include one bathroom, two ensuite bath/shower rooms and a cloakroom.[107]

Some eye-catching promotional material was produced to market the homes, including some Rupert Bear cut-outs and custom cartoons. In one, Rupert pointed to tracks in the snow: 'At times like this Rupert is glad he's going back to a Morrison Home with double glazing and central heating.'[108]

The logic of the cartoon character is not immediately apparent, but the idea was simply that the cartoons were 'appealing' and 'visually exciting', designed to grab attention, and help assert 'space and quality' Morrison Homes offered.[109] The houses were aimed at very particular socio-economic groups, with sufficient disposable income seeking a high material standard of living, but not necessarily aiming for the most luxurious end of the market. The approach taken 'our strongly held philosophy that low-priced housing can still be high-quality housing'.[110]

In 1990 Morrison acquired Lema Homes, which continued to trade under the name Morrison Lema Homes.[111] This acquisition supported the increase in volumes shown in the table of completions above. Some Local Authority housing continued to provide work and in 1987 some projects were finished with 'a series of high standard small housing projects for local authorities in Dingwall, Strathpeffer and Nairn'.[112] In 1993, the company was completing 11 housing contracts across Scotland for various government bodies, Scottish Homes-subsidised projects, and local enterprises, 'to allow access to the housing ladder [for] people who would not otherwise get on it'.[113]

By the end of this period, housing was doing a reasonable turnover, with 212 units sold in 1993, with a turnover of £12.6m and £512,000 of profit.[114] In 1994, a further increase to selling 302 houses represented a 'modest but patchy recovery', but concentrated in the lower end of the market, with

# THE MORRISON STORY

New approaches were always encouraged at Morrison. Here, Rupert Bear points the way to a new Morrison home in a 1986 advertisement.

65 per cent of the homes sold in the lowest end. The focus was, however, on partnerships with Local Authorities and housing associations. In housing, a number of continuities can be seen: quality, working with a range of clients both government, other public or charitable sector and private clients. Housing was never a dominant area of activity for the company but was nevertheless important in promoting the Morrison brand to a wider audience.

## Chester City

A willingness to seize opportunities wherever and whenever they arose did not always mean major contracts or overseas developments. A singular episode in the history of Morrison was the slightly unexpected acquisition of Chester City Football Club. In 1990, Morrison Developments entered into an agreement with the Club to develop a major shopping centre on their old ground at Sealand Road and to build a new stadium at Bumpers Lane. The idea was that this would move the Club from an expensive site to a cheaper one, so freeing up capital. So grave was the financial threat the Club faced, there was a chance it might not be able to continue playing football, but by swapping sites, Norman MacLennan argued, '[t]his deal will enable the club to ensure a soccer future'.[115] The first plans were drawn up in 1988, but refused planning permission in 1989; the hope was that Morrison, with its established expertise, would have more success than the Club. There were all sorts of problems within the Club, and 'an awful feeling now that this could be the end', as Ray Crofts, the football Club's Managing Director, put it.[116]

The agreement signed saw the old ground sold to Morrison: £2m was to be set aside for the new ground, £1.7m to pay creditors, and half of the rest for profit. However, problems were discovered with methane on the new ground which was an old 'tip site'.[117] Eventually, the new ground was built to a modern high standard: it was 'the first such built to comply with the requirements of the Taylor Report', in response to the disaster at Hillsborough in April 1989 which saw 96 fans crushed to death. The principal recommendations were around reducing the amount of standing accommodation, adjustments to perimeter fencing, the signposting of emergency exits and other strategies designed to reduce the risk presented by large numbers of spectators.[118] The new stadium was designed to allow expansion in the future: firstly, to provide the minimum necessary for operation with 3,000 seats and 6,256 standing places; a second phase to convert to 6,800 seats, and a third to 10,380.[119] Fraser recollects:

> We decided that Chester City had a very poor ground and a good location which would have worked well as a supermarket site. Chester City Football Club were struggling financially... [we] developed a proposal to them that we acquire their ground, we build a new ground to all the latest standards, and that we move them to the new ground, and develop a supermarket on the site... The Board accepted this. We bought the Club... [and] saved them from financial ruin.[120]

The £14m shopping centre development built on the old site included 730 car parking spaces 'in a heavily landscaped environment' with 145,000 ft$^2$ of retail, a fast food outlet, and a petrol station. All the units had tenants waiting in advance and the development was sold on to institutional investors.[121] Whilst Morrison had only fairly limited involvement with the Club and no intervention on the sporting side, the example is indicative of the company's approach of sticking with a project through to resolution, rather than cutting losses and moving on to other work. Whilst it may have landed up being

Chester City Football ground and Retail Park.

a more complex, drawn-out process than had originally been imagined, ultimately the clients were happy, and the project was a commercial success.

## Continuities in civil engineering

The civil engineering division continued to grow. Undoubtedly, this was still partly on the back of the successful Kylesku Bridge project. In 1985, it was featured in *Cemento*, a specialist Italian journal.[122] The company also had an exhibition, which was shown alongside a lecture given by Fraser at Heriot Watt University.[123] The portable displays were an example of how the technical capital produced by the building of the bridge was used by the company. Awards continued to follow, with one from the Civic Trust in 1985 in addition to the previous Saltire Society award.[124]

## OPPORTUNITIES BEYOND THE HIGHLANDS

*Crossing the Dornoch Firth*

Since the mid-1960s, there had been plans to cross the Three Firths north of Inverness to support regional development and economic growth. Some local opposition had advocated more direct routes than the one designed by the Jack Holmes group.[125] In March 1988, Morrison won the contract to build a bridge across the Dornoch Firth, in a joint venture with Christiani and Nielsen.[126] The contract reflected many of the Morrison themes: partnership, technical innovation, completion on time, difficult northern environment and a royal opening. The partnership aimed to 'combine Morrison's construction expertise and local resources – including the group's quarry operations... with Christiani's world-wide experience in Marine construction'.[127] Reputationally, Fraser suggested it followed 'the Kylesku bridge... [and] puts the group very much at the forefront of Scottish bridge construction'.[128]

The innovative design of the bridge was technically demanding.[129] At 800 m long, it required some major equipment, including a 400-tonne barge to carry the 'C120 Eiger crane, [which] is capable of operating in water depths of up to 24 metres'. An array of 42 piles, 20 piers and 21 spans would witness a ground-breaking innovation: 'incremental launching':

> As each half section of the deck is completed it will be launched over the piers, like squeezing toothpaste from a tube.[130]

The concrete itself had to be 'high-specification', due to the demands placed upon it.[131] Stuart Higgins remembers the temporary works being particularly challenging:

> We had to construct large steel tube piles, launching them from fabrication yard on land, float them out and lifting them into the piling gates on the jack-up barge, then drive them through the seabed using a diesel impact hammer to a specified level and set. The inside piles where excavated and dewatered to allow the construct a concrete pier inside it. [132]

He worked on the Dornoch bridge as a consultant on the marine element. Michael Martin was responsible for planning the push and launch part of the bridge's construction, which was cutting edge:

> I went to the ICE [Institute of Civil Engineers] Library in London and got out... technical papers on incremental launching and read

how to do it. There was a job underway in Amsterdam, the Zeebrugge Bridge... I went over there, watched what they were doing; we [subsequently] bought their kit.[133]

In March 1991, the two Lord Lieutenants – of Ross and Cromarty and of Sutherland – shook hands across the bridge, shortly after '15,000 tonnes of concrete slid gently for the final 6 metres'.[134] The theatrical nature of the occasion was striking, but just as impressive was the realisation that the bridge would open three months ahead of schedule.[135]

The Queen Mother opened the bridge on 27 August 1991. The royal opening of projects was not uncommon for Morrison, and with Michael Fraser's help, these opportunities were always capitalised upon effectively to showcase the company's work. Coverage on television news offered free advertising and when the story was a positive one, of completion of time and technical innovation, the reputational benefits were considerable. However, this did entail work. Liz Urquhart remembers:

> One of the biggest highlights was the opening of Dornoch Firth Bridge... because the Queen Mother was opening it, everything had to be just so.

Working with Stewart MacLeod, Liz had the usual invitations to send out, but also to recce the route from the helicopter and check all the arrangements.[136] The project had been a major one, providing a considerable boost to the local economy during construction. In the local press, a poem from 'Grant the baker and paper shop', appeared, saying 'Thank you lads for your custom each day.'[137] This highlights a perhaps neglected aspect of major construction projects, particularly in less densely populated area the immediate boost they provide to the local economy.

The reputational benefits from it were considerable. The company's 1993 Annual Report noted that the bridge had won both the British Construction Industry Award and the Saltire Award for Excellence in Design and Construction'.[138] It received technical coverage – the *New Civil Engineer* referred to it as 'one of the most impressive performances of bridge building in Scotland' before explaining the detail of the '"cast-push" incrementally launched bridge'.[139]

Yet for all of this, one of the important aspects of the project was that it was completed as a joint venture. In the following chapters, it will be seen that new collaborative ways of working became important to civil engineering, construction and utilities services divisions of the company. Indeed, this

OPPORTUNITIES BEYOND THE HIGHLANDS

Dornoch Bridge painted by Donald M. Shearer.

HM the Queen Mother performs the opening ceremony of the Dornoch Bridge. August 1991.

THE MORRISON STORY

Two Morrison bridges were celebrated on whisky bottles.

The Dornoch Crossing which transformed road travel around the estuary.

approach would become the dominant paradigm, spreading risk and finding more efficient ways of working, by reducing the burdens of competitive practices. Collaborative working also featured in engineering. The oil industry's CRINE (Cost Reduction Initiative for North Sea Engineering), saw a concerted move towards much more collaborative working practices and contracting to cut operating and capital costs by 30 per cent by 1998.[140] Undoubtedly, the oil industry suffered from periods of lower oil prices, when it seemed that it might not be possible to extract oil profitably. Accordingly, Cromarty Firth Engineering's success fluctuated. One collaboration was with Howard Doris Cromarty Firth Ltd to offer 'repairs, modifications and conversions of semi-submersibles for the exploration and production of oil and gas'.[141] The reality was, however, that through the 1980s this was neither a particularly stable nor a core element of the group's activities.[142]

In the case of the Dornoch Bridge, the general division of labour was that Christiani and Nielsen did the work below the water and Morrison worked on the structure above it. Ian MacKay has very positive recollections of the project, naming it as one of his favourites:

> On that job we were doing 900 metres of deck in 20-metre segments, so we did the same thing every week for a lot of weeks, and usually you can get 25 per cent quicker... it took weeks to get the first pour... then down to five days. So we got a production line... the last pour was done in [only] four days.[143]

## Other continuities

Many of the items in the group's order books were similar to those which had gone before. For example, in 1985 the company won a £4 million contract to build phase one of '[a] magnificent new leisure complex' in Paisley.[144] Similar stories, too, were found in the early opening of the Perth Western Bypass, five months ahead of schedule on 17 September 1985.[145] The quarries business continued to look for new markets. In 1985 this included the export of a new product – "Moraystone" cobbles – to Bristol and Holland.[146] The Small Works Division continued to prosper. In the 18 months to November 1986, contracts worth £750,000 had been won by this unit, showing the benefits of the approach of being willing 'to tackle the smallest of jobs'.[147]

Another area in which there was continuity was building for 'the Co-op' – or more properly CWS. After the success of the Inverness superstore,

THE MORRISON STORY

The Dornoch Crossing from the air: the new bridge marked a major improvement in the local trunk road network.

OPPORTUNITIES BEYOND THE HIGHLANDS

more developments followed as part of the alliance. Work on a smaller shop in Thurso began in January 1985 – 15,000 ft² against the 55,000 ft² of the Inverness one, as well as another in Castlebay on Barra.[148] Later that year, a further contract followed to build a new shop in Forres. This had taken some negotiation as it was in a conservation area and required special permissions. Dan MacDonald noted that '[e]very effort is being made to ensure the new supermarket will retain the character of Forres High Street'. This was even smaller at 7,000 ft² and reflects repeat custom as well as reflecting the company's willingness to take on small tasks.[149] Yet another followed in 1986, but this time it was back in home territory – Tain.[150] The original superstore at Inshes in Inverness was extended in 1989 to add a further 87,000 ft², and included 'DIY, home furnishings and a garden centre', alongside improved car parking reflecting the continued growth of a new style of out-of-town shopping centre.[151]

## The minnow eats the shark

One of the most dramatic episodes in the company's history was when the Morrison family regained control of the business. In 1989, the family bought Charter Consolidated's construction interests: not only the Morrison business, but also Shand, Morrison's parent company, and its Biggs Wall subsidiary, combined in a group with a turnover of £125 million per year. It meant Fraser had fulfilled 'my long term ambition to achieve this independence and control'.[152] This deal to acquire several businesses was possible because Charter Consolidated wished to divest itself of loss-making enterprises, and Morrison, whilst profitable, perhaps no longer fitted with their ambitions.

Biggs Wall, like Morrison and like Alexander Sutherland of Golspie, had also started as a family business in 1884 and over time had become focused on 'mains and service laying, both replacement and new work, for the gas and water authorities'. Its activities included a small works division and Biggs Walls Fabricators Limited making steel tanks and fittings.[153] In late 1988, Gordon arrived in Arlesey, not even entirely sure what the company did 'apart from it having something to do with pipes'. He had inherited a very difficult position:

> Arriving at Biggs among nobody I had ever met before, in a market I did not understand, delivering a service I was not familiar with and working in a geographical region I did not know was going to be a major challenge.[154]

Early 1980s: a line-up of Biggs Wall Transit vans painted in their corporate mustard colour which would later become red when the name was changed to Morrison Biggs Wall.

Gordon took on responsibility for the following four divisions:

    Biggs Wall Utilities    Biggs Wall Small Works
    Biggs Wall Pipelines    Biggs Wall Plant

This was not a happy workplace, not least because Charter Consolidated had changed the name to Shand (Southern); Gordon soon brought the employees onside by announcing that he would revert the name to Biggs Wall again making a surprise announcement at the Christmas party to 'a great cheer'. In the fullness of time, the name would become Morrison Biggs Wall, and eventually Morrison Utility Services. The changes in branding were done with more sensitivity than by Charter Consolidated, and one or two of those interviewed started with Biggs Wall, but their loyalty was carried along. Two family companies with long histories understood the value of reputation and name. The branding was switched quite quickly to standard Morrison red rather than '"lavatorial" yellow' which was used previously.

The office in Stevenage.

THE MORRISON STORY

Client entertaining at Madame Tussaud's. One of many between 1990 and 2000.

Another reason the staff was miserable was that they had been placed under notice of redundancy. Business was in a poor state, and external consultants engaged by Charter Consolidated recommended 'that Utilities be closed down'.[155] It had only two small contracts, for British Gas Eastern and Three Valleys Water, and with no estimator there was little hope of winning new business. Gordon quickly secured an estimator for the business and presided over a continued period of remarkable growth. In order to win new business and retain clients, some very upmarket and black-tie events were held, at places such as Goldsmiths' Hall, Hampton Court, Wimpole Hall near Royston, Hanbury Manor near Ware, Harewood House near Leeds, and Madame Tussauds.

The success of this network-building is apparent from the numbers, which speak for themselves: Morrison bought Biggs Wall for £1; in 2018, M Group Services, as the company is now known, had a turnover in excess of £1 billion.[156] This remarkable success stemmed in a large part to innovations in the contracting through collaborative approaches and a number of partnership contracts, discussed in the next chapter.

## Far from Tain

By 1994, Morrison had come very far from Tain, both in geography and in every other sense, and the previous decade in particular had been a formative one. The company had established its thorough competency and capability in many ways. Firstly, it had not only adopted management techniques of a kind unimaginable in 1948 but did so in ways which took the company to the cutting edge of the industry, with – the quality agenda helping establish the company's reputation as a very serious competitor. Secondly, connected to this was a focus on partnerships and collaborative working, which not only offered efficiency, but placed the company ahead of the competition. Thirdly, successive major projects built on the reputation won through the success of Kylesku, most obviously the Dornoch Crossing. In the same line, overseas work proved that work could be done to a high standard anywhere. Fourthly, a series of astute moves, such as moving headquarters to Edinburgh had placed the company to be a major competitor. It had pivoted from being a Highland firm with outside interests to something much more adaptable. Finally, the company was back in private hands, and the family also controlled a utilities division, adding yet more capacities. Just a few short years after this, the company was preparing for Initial Public Offering and flotation on the London Stock Exchange.

A portrait of Alex by Alexander Fraser. This painting of the founder was specially commissioned to celebrate the success of the company. The insert shows Dornoch Bridge and the artist.

CHAPTER SEVEN

# The Morrison Approach: trading on reputation 1995–2000

IN THE RELATIVELY SHORT period that Morrison was to be on the stock market, a great deal happened within the company. The years 1995 to 2000 were fundamentally a period of great success. Shortly after seeing the company he had founded with only some saved wartime pay become a publicly listed company, Alex passed away. He must surely have been happy as he left a thriving business behind. The company had been floated at the right time, as it raised the extra capital needed at a time when the Morrison Approach of high-quality work done in longer term partnerships was in vogue. The company was amongst the vanguard of the contractors meeting the collaborative intentions of the government's Private Finance Initiative. The New Public Management agenda, of which Private Finance Initiative was a point of continuity in both the Conservative governments until 1997, and under Blair's centrist New Labour after this. Similar logics seeking to find more efficient ways of working which avoided onerous costs of competition became increasingly popular in the private sector, too. In both cases, the co-operative approach which had been found under the Quality agenda positioned Morrison to take advantage of these opportunities. Quality also positioned the company ahead of the curve in its commitment to Health and Safety as well as technically demanding and sensitive work.

## Endings and beginnings

On 13 November 1998 Alex died at the age of 79. The company he had started with very little had become a major construction company with broad development interests, with shares trading at 309.5p, valuing the company at over £200m.[1] He had formally stepped down some years earlier but maintained a keen interest in what was going on at his company. Few interviewees knew Alex very well, but those who had even a passing acquaintance with him spoke fondly. Charles Morrison said he would drop by for a cup of tea at CFE and was 'charismatic, down to earth and impressive'.[2] Allan Russell remembers Alex visiting projects regularly and that 'he was always interested in what was happening'.[3] Dan MacDonald knew him quite well, meeting him in 1972 for the first time: 'I liked him enormously because he was very straightforward… I would have done anything for him'.[4] Stewart MacLeod also has very fond memories of Alex:

> Alex Morrison was a delightful gentleman… and his wife equally… Alex came down to Perth for annual dinners on at least two occasions, so that describes the interest that the man had in how the business was being developed. When I was in the Inverness Office, which I went to in 1982, Alex sat on the board of that meeting, and I detected… that Alex would ask some fairly direct questions in terms of the business, and that showed his tremendous business acumen. At the same time, he was a very, very humble man.[5]

Pam MacKay offered one fond memory with nothing to do with the company, but which showed how he got on with anyone. The MacKays had just moved to Edinburgh and were staying in Gordon's flat until the entry date for their own home:

> [Alex] came to the door and said "I need your help, I need your boys". His grandson David's birthday was coming up… "I think I'd like to buy David a skateboard, but could I take the boys? Where would we go? We would want to build the best skateboard ever for David", and of course money was no object, so my boys were thrilled to go off and have free rein to get the best trucks, the best wheels, the best board – they had a ball.[6]

When they came back, having had a great deal of fun, Alex thanked them profusely.

Towards the end, Alex was very discreet about his illness, showing much concern for others suffering. David Henderson, who had grown up friends with Gordon and Fraser, remembers Alex disguising his own health problems at the end when he was dying from cancer because he knew David had concerns of his own.[7] It was not just Alex's friends who had great affection for him, many of his employees did too:

# THE MORRISON APPROACH

Alex filming the central lift at Kylesku Bridge.

Asked to carry his coffin from the church to the hearse… six of them were approached… Sandy Duff, who was a great character, an old Morrison man, who had a sense of humour, said "We've been carrying him the last twenty years, we may as well carry him that distance out of the church."[8]

## Successful flotation

On Friday, 6 October 1995, Morrison Construction was successfully listed on the LSE becoming Morrison Construction Group Plc. On the first day of trading, shares started at 115p, hit 120p and closed at 118p, valuing the group at £78.8m.[9] The company launched a share save scheme for staff which 'was

THE MORRISON STORY

**Morrison float to bolster builders**

Rebel shareholders attempt Signet coup

Morrison set for 115p float

**Building up their strength**

**Morrison float bid**

**Morrison motoring to market**

Life's a pitch in Chester

Morrison float aims to raise £30m

**Softly, softly for Morrison**

Group builds up a bright future

**Upbeat Morrison defies pessimists**

Morrison flotation will buck the trend

Morrison motoring to market

**£77m float value pinned to Morrison**

Morrison heads for £77m market debut

Morrison target

Giant goes public

**Morrison keeps its date with market**

**Float values Morrison Construction at £77m**

£20m for 'quango link' boss

**Morrison group seeks Stock Exchange listing**

Morrison tests the perils of floating in a stormy sea

Flotation values Morrison at £76.8m

Float forecast

Morrison seeking £18.75m

Morrison offer

**Morrison's tough task ahead**

Confident Morrison plans share flotation

Construction contraction

Morrison to market with £70m tag

Hitting the headlines: stories about the flotation from a family cuttings book.

THE MORRISON APPROACH

**From a clapped out van to luxury lifestyle**

Morrison seeks £20m with promise of half-year fillip

A BUILDING boss who was accused of winning contracts through "insider knowledge" yesterday saw his personal fortune rocket to £21 million

MORRISON AT 115P

**Morrison to raise £30m on market**

AGAINST THE FLOW

£65m Morrison float hope

**Gems firm in mystery move**

Morrison does pick its moments

**Morrison to float for £70m**

Morrison predicts £3m halfway

Morrison offer 91% taken up

**Brother, that's £40m**

**BROTHERS SET TO CASH IN... WITH £40M**

Morrison Construction heads for exchange

**Morrison to go for a quote**

**Morrison shares to start trading**

Morrisons seek funds by going to market

193

heavily oversubscribed and in addition nearly 150 employees bought shares under the intermediaries offer' indicating a commitment to the business from a number of workers willing to invest their own money in the business.[10] Before flotation, the family still controlled 80 per cent of the company's value, and other directors the remaining 20 per cent. The flotation raised some £20m, so that the majority of shares and therefore control, were retained in the family, with extra funds now raised being earmarked for expansion. This was the first time, after nearly 50 years of business that the company was raising major external finance, with a particular view to expanding internationally, and to 'increase its size and enable it to compete for larger projects, including joint ventures, particularly of the kind that may become available under the government's [P]rivate [F]inance [I]nitiative'.[11] On paper at least the family had profited, which led to what the *Daily Mail* described as 'that peculiar Scottish suspicion towards success'; the newspaper defended the family as having 'made money by the old fashioned and honest means of hard work and quick thinking'.[12]

It was the company's approaches which had persuaded institutional investors at least in part. In 1995:

> We had a good spread across the business. We had made it a feature of our approach that we worked in partnership with our clients where we could. We looked at adding value for them as well as for ourselves and developed a very nice approach in the construction business, which was a very… traditional sector, and by the mid-1990s, we decided it was a good time to float the business, maintaining a significant shareholding ourselves… we went through the process of appointing advisors, Noble Grossart in Edinburgh, and worked through the flotation process, which is a quite time-consuming and comprehensive process of reviewing the business, preparing a prospectus, then going through all the shareholder presentations, which Norman MacLennan [a senior director, who subsequently became Group Managing Director in 1996 and Group Finance Director Keith Howell] and I did, and eventually getting it away by the skin of our teeth: it wasn't oversubscribed, [but we got] the investment we were looking for…[13]

Unusually for a construction company, Morrison often combined the roles of property developer and building contractor on the same job in sometimes elaborate schemes.[14] Indeed in May 2000, the company renamed itself simply

Morrison, in part reflecting the much broader scope of corporate activities and services.[15]

Whilst normally the changes in governance and probity for a listed company would present challenges, as Fraser put it, the fact that '[w]e had managed the business as a public company for a number of years, so we were used to it', meant that this burden was much reduced.[16] There were new tasks for the Company Secretary, John Morrison:

> From my perspective it was great, because what every company secretary wants to do at some point is a flotation, and be a quoted plc secretary – I was delighted with that. It was a great process for me, professionally.

One governance challenge was to be found in bringing in appropriate oversight:

> We had to bring non-executive directors onto the board… we got three really good heavyweights on board… Alistair Hamilton an eminent lawyer, had been president of the Law Society in Scotland… Nelson Robertson… had been Chief Executive of the General Accident Group worldwide… we were a Scottish company floating in Scotland… the third one was Lord Sanderson of Bowden.[17]

Lord Sanderson was an ex-Minister of State at the Scottish Office and a prominent businessman. The reorganisation and structuring continued, and the main imperative behind this seems to have been constant repositioning to expand and win new business. What might be termed a culture of entrepreneurial risk was established, where a large number of directors and managers were able to go off and win work. The reorganisation of Building and Civil Engineering divisions in 1998 set up new Management Boards for England and Wales and for Scotland, which it was hoped 'will enable us to retain a sharp focus in each region and improve customer service whilst continuing to expand the business'.[18]

THE MORRISON STORY

A flow chart showing organisation in the building division into regional divisions and some specialist areas

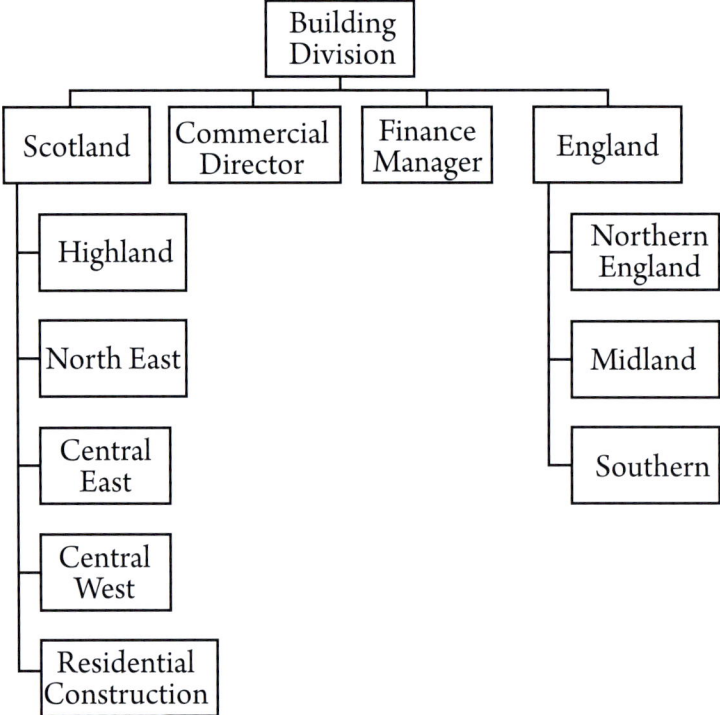

## Partnering for success I: Private Finance Initiative

What had persuaded the stockmarkets to invest was the company's approach and prospects for considerable future expansion. The fundamental approach, as we have seen, was of *collaboration*: joint ventures for both public and private sector contracts were focused on a more co-operative and less competitive approach. The 1999 Annual Report offers a neat description of this:

> The "Morrison Approach" has progressively moved the Group away from the traditional, competitive tendering in which the industry was generally rooted towards innovative project development.[19]

The Private Finance Initiative (PFI) was one of the most significant experiments in the delivery of public services in the UK. . During the 1980s, considerable needs emerged relating to construction and infrastructure: the roads, hospitals and schools built after the Second World War required renewal. The state was not willing to commit to major infrastructure projects in the same way as it had when Alex was starting his business. In the late 1980s and 1990s, government policy sought to achieve efficiency and reduce levels of state spending though the greater participation of the private sector. In other words, the answer to the question of how to provide public services at a lower cost, it was reckoned, was to use private companies. The term New Public Management describes efforts to drive down the cost of public services by making services more efficient and accountable, driven by an ideological conviction that the private sector would provide better value.[20] Government authorities used private companies or consortia of companies to design, build, finance and operate facilities. A key advantage perceived was that the government bore no risk, as these new PFI contracts transferred all risks to the contractors.

On paper, the system appears much more efficient and certainly it allowed a new generation of roads, schools, and hospitals to be built sooner than if they had been financed traditionally. However, whilst keeping obligations off the national balance sheet may have pleased the Treasury, the reality was that costs were high because governments are usually able to borrow money at much lower rates than anyone else. The policy was reformed considerably to produce PF2 in 2012. Ultimately however, in response to criticisms that it was too expensive to finance and inflexible as needs changed, the October 2018 budget announced that Private Finance policy had ended.[21] The point here is not to present either critique or rebuttal, but rather describe this alternative view on delivering government projects. Interviewees have provided a construction perspective on PFI, and this provides an important dimension which has been overlooked elsewhere.

Morrison was in the vanguard of PFI. By 1996 it was clear that this would become the dominant process through which major infrastructure projects would be financed.[22] It was a natural fit for Morrison, with its considerable experience and expertise of collaborative approaches. Fraser asked Michael Martin to take up a new role as director pursuing PFI contracts: 'I moved to an office in Atholl Crescent… all I had in front of me was a desk and clean sheet of paper'.[23] This saw Michael set off into terra nullius, as the concept was very new. Fraser notes Morrison was an early adopter and was:

> enthused about PFI and saw it as an opportunity to develop our approach by working with our clients. [We] took a bit of a lead in the early days… we were certainly in the leading group [of PFI contractors].[24]

The A69 heading east towards Newcastle and bypassing Haltwhistle. (© Copyright J. Thomas)

The point of continuity with the infrastructure upgrades which followed the Second World War, work on which the company had cut its teeth, ought not be ignored, but the way of tendering and financing was quite different. It was again a reflection of the company's great ambition.

Michael Martin enjoyed considerable success in his new role, and won the smallest of the five contracts in 'tranche one of the government's DBFO roads programme', where the contract winner would design, build, finance and operate a road scheme. Risk framed the approach: 'we set up a big joint venture to spread the risk'. As winners of the first PFI contract, Michael 'signed it with the Minister for Transport… on the national one o'clock news'.[25]

A consistent and not unreasonable response from interviewees was that contractors were only doing what government policy required. As Michael Martin puts it: 'The construction industry is a service industry. We are not here to create government policy.'[26] Not bidding for PFI work would have meant the company would have precluded most major construction and engineering projects.

Fraser argues that it was designed to be more efficient than traditional contracting:

> PFI has created a framework for professionals and contractors to work together, to devise creative solutions. So far as the country is concerned, infrastructure… has been built, and is being run effectively. If your perspective is that the public sector can and should do it on its own, then you are not going to be for [PFI]… But it does in my view create very effective solutions to providing infrastructure and it does so in a commercially sensible way.[27]

As the name suggests, the private sector provides the finance and it is, therefore, not a charge on the national accounts, despite contractual obligations to buy services over a prolonged period, typically decades. Construction companies themselves, which are not generally capital-intensive by nature, therefore turned to banks and other institutional investors to raise the necessary finance. Just as in the case of the Exchange Plaza project in Edinburgh and other property developments, these were sold on to investors. The process of financialisation, of creating tradeable securities based on underlying assets fundamentally shaped the story here. Many interviewees complained PFI got an unfair press, as it was driven by the retreat of the state and by the financiers seeking a return on the risk which they had taken on. In reality, for the main part as David Jeffs put it: 'Did these things make a fortune? They did not', even if some of those who sold on did better.[28] It was meant to save money but as part of the tendering process, several parties, including the unsuccessful ones, carried substantial bidding costs. All in, it is perhaps unsurprising, as Liz Urquhart contends, 'PFI to begin with was considered a great way forward; in hindsight, I am not altogether supportive.'[29]

Peter Heathershaw suggests we might take a longer view: 'under a PFI model, basically the risk was transferred out of the client's pocket into the contractor's.' In his view, it is still too soon to tell how well the scheme work: 'I am still waiting to see, after thirty years, when the project is handed back to the client'.[30] What will Local Authorities and the NHS make of these assets when they are handed over, in a good state, and do not have to pay more? Morrison participated in the first PFI infrastructure consortium, Road Link. On 1 April 1996, Road Link took over control of the A69 from Newcastle to Carlisle for thirty years, with the task also including building a bypass at Haltwhistle.[31] This was awarded after a complex and competitive tendering process which Michael Martin likened to 'waiting for Samuel Becket's Godot' when announcing the development in *Morrison News*.[32]

Even at this early stage, as the first contracts were coming to the start of their lifecycles, Martin noted than many commentators were already questioning it, with 'talk... about the cost of making it happen and whether or not it will last'.[33] If the value offered by PFI is unclear, what is certain is that it was one of the most important developments in Morrison's history. As will be shown in the next chapter, 'the Morrison Approach' sought to avoid competitive tendering and work in partnership with clients to remove wasteful repeat tendering processes and overly onerous accounting practices and instead pursue efficiency.

The new Royal Infirmary for Edinburgh, a major teaching hospital and another Morrison PFI, opened in 2002. Ian Smith is very proud of this:

> It was an excellent job... the largest project of its kind in Scotland, 126,000 $m^2$ of new building... 4,400 rooms... it was built to a very high standard, to budget – [c.] £230m... – and finished and handed over six months ahead of programme.

For Ian, collaboration was central to the success of the project: 'We worked so well together – it was a pleasure working with Balfour and Hayden'. Hayden were a specialist mechanical and engineering company, brought in because, as Ian puts it, a hospital might be thought of as 'a building wrapped around complicated services... and we on the building side did not have to manage it'. Morrison was brought in because 'you do things differently, you are always looking for better ways... innovation was the main reason for Morrison's involvement'. An efficiency achieved was that 'the car parks et cetera were all completed at an early stage whilst the steel work was being completed, and we were able to put the site huts and park'. As well as making deliveries much easier, this helped keep out mud from the new building.[34]

Gordon explains that the idea was that dialogue and co-operation would lead to savings. 'We saw [partnering] as an enormous opportunity. One of the negatives about searching for construction efficiency is when the interface between client and contractor is not working efficiently.' PFI was designed to solve this:

> where the contractor took the initiative, usually in a joint venture scenario, we would employ the engineers and cost engineers as part of the consortium, and that allowed the input from the contractor to be maximized. Some of the big PFI projects in the UK which have been heavily criticized have been hospital projects. Building a hospital is as close to a nightmare in the industry as you can get. They are always late. There are always serious cost overruns.

In the case of Royal Infirmary of Edinburgh, 'everyone was delighted with the project'. The costs might seem expensive, because the contractor must borrow money and factor in maintenance costs, which are considerable over the lifespan of the project 'during which time windows and heating systems, for example, will have to be replaced'. Gordon suggests that the evaluation must come when the building is handed over:

> It looks very expensive when you look at the monthly charge... but I don't think it is... After 25 years... the investor has to hand the building back to the original client, probably for the notional figure of a pound, but that building must be in first-class order.[35]

The scale of the job was considerable. When operating the hospital would have 5,000 staff, '900 beds, 24 operating theatres and 25 wards'.[36] In order to reduce the cost of the project, the valuable site of the previous Infirmary in the Old Town of Edinburgh was to be redeveloped by Morrison, on which 400 homes were built, so offsetting the cost of the new hospital.[37]

Certainly, these projects have been controversial.[38] In the final analysis, these early PFI contracts in particular may turn out to have been expensive for the public purse. Perhaps what has been missing from the general discussion is the efficiency of the construction process they were designed to achieve,

The new Edinburgh Royal Infirmary hospital was a pioneering PFI project and a major success for Morrison.

which interviewees for this history fully appreciated based on first-hand experience. Moreover, part of the reason for the expense was the absolute transfer of risk. As the business case for Edinburgh Royal Infirmary made clear 'it is an essential requirement of the PFI process to be able to demonstrate a substantial transfer of risk from the public to the private sector'.[39]

Following these first contracts there were other projects. Facilities management was another area where Morrison offered services. The CityCare Service in Norwich was established in the late 1990s to offer facilities services. As Ian Cusden recollects:

> Basically, we took over the services for the Council in Norwich, that was a facilities services business… we were doing dustbin lorries [and many other services]… That was extremely complicated' with large numbers of employees transferred over to us.

A similar service was made available to the private sector through facilities management services. This new way of maintaining various premises, services and facilities was becoming increasingly popular not just for the public sector, but also private clients. Part of the appeal lay in controlled costs, but also in not having to worry about engaging a variety of maintenance contracts. Ian considers that 'it was challenging, as we were expanding into a new universe'.[40] Adam Gosnold credits Gordon for facilities management:

## Ode to CityCare

In the year 1998
Norwich City Council decided its fate
Its DLO to be externalised
Its services to be privatised.

And so the long saga began
The government said you can
The consultants came to advise
And the bills started to rise!

A specification was written
A contract was prepared
And so we went into battle
To see how we fared.

We embarked upon our mission
To submit our submission
Three hopefuls put in a bid
The others? Went and hid

The winner was announced
The others were denounced
We were put in reserve
However we kept our nerve

The negotiations commenced
The preferred bidder, they fenced
Then discussions came to an end
And Norwich City, for us they did send.

Of course we were never in doubt
That we would be back in with a shout
We only needed to wait
For the preferred bidder to meet their fate!

The lawyers were brought on board
The costs? They just soared
The teams were brought together
The negotiations went on for ever

Richard headed the bid team
Andy caught all the own goals
Ian looked for the savings
Ably assisted by Killingback Bowles

Jim was captain of Citycare
Mike Boult made sure we didn't fail
Mike Reed thought of the pensions
While Graham questioned the sale.

Our facilitator was Peter the sailor
His laptop ever in use
He struggled for all the solutions
And took a lot of abuse

Deadline dates came and went
Our energies, they were spent
Night and day we did battle
Our nerve ends they did rattle

April the first was looming fast
When all the talk had to be past
We were getting weary, getting sad
Some of us thought we were all going mad!

The grand finale was about to begin
Three days, one night we all put in
The deal was signed, the ink was dry
CityCare was ours, we did cry!

A MD they required to make
And as Roy was the only one awake
He found himself in the role
The alternative would have been on the dole!

We got to know each other well
What side we were on they couldn't tell
We now have ten long years to reign
Until we do it all over again!

To Anne and Paul and Charles as well
We hope you'll listen when we tell
Of the great pains we had to give birth
To CityCare, Here on earth.

And so this ode is to CityCare
With Robert now firmly in the chair
To wish it luck and weather fair
And we'll remember the wear and tear!
And now it's time to say adieu
As off I go to pastures new.

Roy (McGonagall) Davidson
1 November 2000

He saw going into facilities services as something we should be doing, in terms of high-volume repairs maintenance activity; we normally focused on utilities, underground assets, but Gordon saw an opportunity for us to move into facilities services… fixing heating systems and windows and doors and air conditioning units.[41]

This kind of experiment paid dividends, even if it was not always a roaring success. 'We got some traction there and did some good stuff', as Adam puts it.[42]

A joint venture with Bechtel was the first in its sector too. In December 1996 the North of Scotland Water Authority awarded Morrison a £45m 25-year contract which one of the consultants was reported as asserting 'was likely to serve as a reference deal for other PFI deals in Scotland'.[43] Working with an American company with very different norms in management style presented some challenges. Bechtel were a company of some antiquity.[44] Hugh England recollects this partnership. 'was a different ball game' as the American company 'had a way of working which was just different'. Meetings were much larger and 'they had this risk process – the Monte Carlo analysis', measuring by statistics, taking you away from the 'nitty gritty' of a project.[45] In short, Morrison had a distinctive attitude to risk and so did Bechtel.[46] For example, there was also doubling-up on accounting standards.[47] With negotiation, and a willingness to innovate, these barriers were overcome, and the venture was successful.

## Partnering for success II: collaboration in the private sector

The same collaborative logics were applied to the private sector, too. The fundamental idea is that if jobs are sufficiently complex relative to the size of the award, the cost of tendering becomes burdensome. Bidding costs are considerable and unrecoverable, and in competitive processes the majority are unsuccessful. Even if only three or four companies tendered, this meant considerable costs. Companies would have to meet the costs of all the jobs they tendered when contracts were successful, including from those bids which failed. Clients, too, incurred costs in the bidding process. In the case of sectors which had repeat contracts of broadly consistent nature, such as utilities, this process was especially onerous, and the argument could be made that it was inefficient and wasteful.

The nomenclature used varied: partnering, framework and alliances, as the idea of collaborating evolved. It might mean something with little more force than a memorandum of understanding, or could be a full contract, but it avoids repetitive competitive tendering. This was an area in which Gordon took the initiative, based on what he had observed in the oil industry:

> Through our links with the oil industry, we got a good understanding of what happened in partnerships there, where the oil company and contractor were working on high-risk projects and working together for a common goal. So we launched our own partnering concept; primarily it was in the utility industry. We pitched very hard to a number of clients. The problem with partnering is that by client and contractor working together you will save costs, but at tender stage you cannot prove that saving, so therefore clients become nervous about it.[48]

One company to which Gordon pitched in the early days of partnering was Anglian Water. A change of personnel in pitching to Anglian Water meant that a potential partnership did not immediately materialise. This contract was eventually awarded and ran very successfully for a number of years with considerable savings. It was the Chief Executive of Anglian Water, John Simpson, who drove the concept within his company.[49]

Gordon remembers winning a contract with Thames Water after other lower bidders had proved unable to deliver what they had promised within six months: 'We got a phone call saying they would like to award us a contract in central London on a partnering basis'. He gives a practical example:

> There is a valve to be replaced in central London. It may cost £1,000 to travel across London install the valve, and then come back again; but if the client identifies three valves in that location, cost savings can be substantial.[50]

In this scenario, the incremental cost increase might be very little, but it is the challenge for the accounts to find 'ways to capture savings'.[51]

This leads to other efficiencies too. 'We both got rid of our commercial teams… I think our savings were 25% on that project'.[52] This kind of practice has become much more ordinary especially in the utilities sector and would go on to be an enormous success story, as discussed in the next chapter, leaving a remarkable legacy. These new kinds of contracts offered more stability and were ostensibly less wasteful by avoiding repeat competitive tendering. However, one of the fundamental tensions for both public and private-sector collaborative working practices comes in the requirements of probity. It is hard to document and demonstrate specific savings which have occurred as a result of non-combative working practices and streamlined tendering.[53] These innovative forms of working required ways of accounting which included open-booking accounting.[54]

These challenges notwithstanding, a number of government reports advocated changes to working and tendering practices in the construction sector that were broadly in line with what Morrison had already been doing. From the perspective of purchasing, too, Zoe Gentle notes that longer-term contracts make all sorts of accounting and invoicing easier.[55] Partnerships required open-book accounting, and Ian Cusden never had any significant problems providing this.[56]

The *Latham Report*, the first of these Government reports, was published in 1994, and Hugh England suggests that this was 'in many ways it was a development of what we had been doing... getting a mutual respect with your client'.[57] The *Report* presented a series of strategies for making construction contracting more collaborative and less inefficient: rather than 'endlessly refining existing conditions', '[a] set of basic principles is required on which modern contracts can be based', proposing refinements of the New Engineering Contract (NEC), and to use standard terms wherever possible.[58] In 1998, the *Egan Report* followed, which argued that the British building industry should look to the Japanese car industry's TQM system to achieve quality and efficiency. The fundamental drivers of change, the *Egan Report* asserted, are:

- 'committed leadership'
- 'a focus on the customer'
- 'integrate the process and team around the product'
- 'a quality driven agenda'
- 'commitment to people'.[59]

In effect, corporate policies had become government policy. Or, as Fraser noted in the 1999 Annual Report, it was 'very much in line with our own established philosophy'.[60]

Partnerships were important for Morrison's success and, indeed, an investment tip in *The Times* recommended readers to buy shares in the company because of '5 per cent plus' profit margins. This return was achieved by the partnership model where Morrison 'gets involved with the design and development of idea and suggests the most appropriate construction methods', which 'not only add value, but also protect Morrison from the zero or near zero profits game of tendering'.[61] In the 1999 Annual Report, Group Managing Director, Keith Howell observed that, 60 per cent of the group's business came from partnership and joint ventures.[62] The next development of this approach was alliancing: 'now partnering is no longer the word, alliancing is the word', 'partnering got to the stage where they thought it was just a little bit too cosy and sent the wrong signals', whereas alliancing 'still has a contractual edge to it'.[63]

The first major contract Utilities Services won using this model was with Thames Water. Looking back, Thames water's Andy Hall suggested the model had been adopted in an effort to 'squeeze out waste'.[64] To establish the savings, joint performance objectives were measured, around job completion, service levels and repair time. The relationship has been an enduring and beneficial one, as evidence by the signing of the Thames Water Agility Alliance, an extension to the original contract. In 1994, the turnover on this project was £5m per annum, rising to £18m by 2000. Jim Arnold identified some typical steps taken on contracts, by looking on a total cost basis and identifying inefficiencies. Just as with the Quality agenda, it requires effort from all employees, as well as leadership, to achieve these goals: Morrison received international recognition to their approach through a speech delivered by Bill Alexander in Naples, Florida in 1996. Just as with the Quality agenda, it requires effort from all employees, as well as leadership, to achieve these goals:

> we took the decision ten or twelve years ago [around 2007] we brought in some business process engineers in the way that our competitors

The relationship continued, with the signing of the Thames Water Agility Alliance contract being signed here, with Charles Morrison on the left and Adam Gomold third from left.

**An extract from an article in *Utility Weekly***
In a different area, Thames has formed another alliance in the hole-digging business with contractor Morrison Biggs Wall. [T]he logic here was that, in Alexander's words, 'my company digs a lot of holes in the street – rather more than any other utility in London.

'Traditionally we have used our own direct labour, supplemented by streetworks contractors. But the quality of work undertaken by contractors was often poor, while the cost of work by in-house teams was often very high. The image and perceived impact on customers was very poor.

'This time, instead of forming a partnership with a "management-rich" organisation like Andersens we were trying to build a partnership with existing suppliers to correct the problems in our existing relationships. With Andersens we were building on success, with streetworks contractors we were building on failure'.

So Thames and Morrison Biggs Wall got together and combined their management teams. The alliance has, says Alexander cut work backlogs by 70 per cent, reduced customer complaints by 80 per cent and produced annual cost savings to Thames Water of 10 per cent.

did not. [We were] starting to map processes. We did not call it Six Sigma [a popular management technique] at the time, but… it is one of the reasons I think we have upper quartile margins…We pay our people a little bit more, but we expect a little more out of them as a result, a little more thinking, a little more worry.'[65]

Collaborative working fundamentally informed the corporate approach. Ian Smith recollects with some pleasure the work he did with Sainsbury supermarkets which he considers 'a good example of working with the client', when they built a £21m store at Garthdee Road in Aberdeen.[66]

The company's advertisement feature in the local newspaper suggested that 'a close relationship with the client enabled its staff to tackle head-on any problems or challenges'.[67] The fundamental assertion underpinning the partnership model is that it is more efficient. The board of any potential client had to be persuaded that the savings and other benefits would outweigh the lack of audit trail available with traditional, competitive tendering and working practices.

Urquhart Castle on the banks of Loch Ness painted by Donald M. Shearer.

## Demanding and sensitive work

Older sites with heritage value required particularly sensitive handling. Morrison's refurbishment of the scheduled Bridge of Oich at Aberchalder in 1997 was awarded the Saltire Society Award in 1998. The bridge is a '[d]ouble cantilever chain suspension bridge', of sufficient importance to be considered of national significance.[68] The bridge is the oldest surviving one by James Dredge, an early Scottish suspension bridge engineer.[69] Another site of historical concern was the world-famous Urquhart Castle on Loch Ness, where Morrison had to deal with Historic Scotland whilst building a new visitor centre which would be sensitive to the historic fabric of the castle. There was strong opposition to the project during the planning application stage.[70] This indicates the kind of problems which could arise. Liz Urquhart remembers that the Urquhart Castle visitor centre involved 'a huge sewage problem', which 'we managed to overcome'.[71] Heritage contracts were one area where lowest-price tenders might not always be imperative.

Another example of sensitive work which drew on corporate reputation and where bid evaluation criteria might take account of quality, were works on Kirkstall Lock, where in 1995 Morrison build new student accommodation

THE MORRISON APPROACH

blocks for Leeds Metropolitan University around a disused brewery. The site had been painted by J. W. M. Turner so was of considerable heritage value and posed environmental challenges because of bulrushes and natural springs. Beyond site-specific issues, ecological considerations became Morrison's 'very strict environmental policy' and meant they chose to use 'pressure-impregnated New Zealand softwood instead of hardwood'.[72] This kind of policy was bound up in the broad notion of Quality, and here it was paying dividends in terms of the kind of work which could be done. In 2019, these kinds of procurement and environmental policies are entirely normal, but in 1995 this was forward-looking for a construction company.

The TQM programme had been partly promoted by sponsorship of Jackie Stewart's motor-racing team. Morrison had also done some work for the team by building their factory in Milton Keynes.[73] Morrison built the Rockingham Speedway between 1999 and 2001. This is an example of where safety was incredibly important, especially the specifics of barrier design. Peter Heathershaw thought it was '[d]ifficult at times because of the requirements of NASCAR [racing], but a thoroughly enjoyable project.' The challenges came because 'It was an old open cast site… [which required] ground compaction and consolidation, and ensuring that the running surface

A striking aerial view of the nearly complete Rockingham Speedway in Northamptonshire.

was in tolerance', was vital. An example of something which had to be modified was when 'we put all the safety barrier up around the track… the posts stuck up an inch over the barrier, and the client said you cannot have that in case the car goes over'.[74]

## What's the worst thing that could happen to you? Embedding safety cultures

Many of the risks present in construction are physical ones to the person. The seriousness of this issue cannot be overstated: relatively small mistakes could have major repercussions – in the worst cases imaginable, the loss of life. One of the ways which Morrison sought to embed in its corporate culture an attitude where safety was taken very seriously by everyone was to ask exactly that question of those working on sites: what is the worst thing which could happen to you? Answered honestly, this might be expected to have a sobering effect. Fatal or even serious accidents were very rare. One interviewee recollected a project where a fatality occurred when a worker fell into trench which had been excavated, and his head struck an abutment which proved fatal. The interviewee explained that this was not because the health and safety procedures were poor, but because the individual was in the wrong place at the wrong time: '[t]he system was good; he should not have been there'. This highlights one of the biggest challenges: that the best systems could be in place, but these cannot preclude human error or disregard for the rules. Corners might be cut at any time, in a very human way, perhaps in a rush to get home, with fatal consequences. On another occasion, – a more fortunate one – a worker failed to stabilise a tower and fell off a trestle. Whilst the worker survived the accident, he was promptly dismissed.[75]

The solutions to this problem lay in individual responsibility. Much like the internalisation of quality, which included health and safety, the idea was to make individuals responsible. As one interviewee put it: what was needed was a 'cultural change about taking responsibility – you will have the right tools, and proper training; but if you knowingly put yourself or others at risk, you are out the door'.[76] Jim Arnold identifies the key thing as being having the 'confidence to tell someone to stop. We want everyone in the business and affected by our business to be safe.' Where once it was a distinguishing feature, Morrison's competitors have now caught up in this regard, which is surely a good thing.[77]

Even if there were no moral and legal imperative, clear business cases can be established to take health and safety seriously. As Charles Morrison puts it: 'I've never known a contract yet [with poor] safety performance and everything else is good'.[78] Like every other interviewee, Charles said he was entirely committed to health and safety. He suggests that if someone were not convinced of its importance, their attitude would change on 'meeting [someone's] wife and family' at their funeral.[79] The company adopted different ways to internalise safety culture. Much of the TQM initiatives featured safety prominently, but there were specific campaigns, too. David Jeffs was director responsible for safety for a number of years, and remembers:

> The company was quite forward thinking… for our size, for the market, we had the best statistics, but "larger companies had large offices [which] tend to offset onsite accidents."

David recollected that,

> Morrison had a reputation for health and safety: we were well-respected in the sector; in Scotland we were seen by the Health and Safety Executive as one of the leaders in standards. They expected a lot from us, it did not stop us having fatalities.

David offered the example of a fatality in Edinburgh: 'the site manager said it really came home to him at eleven o'clock at night when everybody had gone, the Health and Safety Executive had left, and he went to lock the compound up and there was one car left there… that always stuck in my mind'.[80]

Strategic Safety Conversations were one way in which Morrison tried to improve health and safety under David's leadership:

> I spent a lot of time and money on the idea of the worker saying what he thought was wrong. For example, whenever I went around a construction site… we had a requirement you had to go and speak to three of the workforce when you did a visit… and ask, "how is the site looking after you?"… nine times out of ten, the work force was co-operative and sensible in their answers.

Then there was the introduction of 'NAB [No Accident Behaviour]… where the workforce were actually encouraged to comment on each other's performance at a meeting'. Through these different initiatives, David suggests that in the 1990s, the company 'was right up there' in terms of its health and safety culture.[81] Approaches included different ways of talking about safety. Julie Brinkley reports that this tradition has continued and that 'we poke fun at our health and safety with our Morris and Son... the little cartoon that we have got... Morris does everything correctly, and his son [who does not] – they are just hilarious and go to prove that there is a right way and a wrong way to do things... showing people without lecturing them'.[82]

The important thing was to get staff to think about health and safety for themselves. Safe behaviour discussions have focused on asking the question: *what is the worst thing which could happen to you?*[83] On a construction site, the answer is might give cause for reflection:

> Instead of bawling and shouting at operatives/people/guys and telling them not to be so effing stupid, I would instead treat them with respect, explain who I am, so starting the conversation in a hugely different way. At first, this was seen as daft. I would ask them what they are doing and have a Safe Behaviour Discussion. What is the worst thing which could happen? This would encourage them to understand risks to them and those around them. I always used to say: what is the worst thing which could happen to you? Conceptually the answer was you could die.

The No Accident Behaviour regime lasted for perhaps ten years, Ian MacKay suggested.[84] This has now evolved into CBAB (Challenging Beliefs, Affecting Behaviour).[85] Liz Urquhart remembers the Safety First and Stop the Job initiatives, designed to make safety and absolute priority.[86] Alan Russell recollects safety nights with presentations and discussion about various issues over 'sausage rolls', so providing an informal environment.[87]

Ultimately, this was successful, and a clear reputation was established. Stewart MacLeod notes the reputation in Scotland was very strong:

> The senior Health and Safety Executive manager had a reputation like some wild animal – he was feared by everybody. He particularly appreciated efforts we went to ensure Health and Safety was given the high standard that it rightly deserved... He used to come to our seminars and give us a talk, so it was constructive, as well as signifying a very good relationship that we had with the Health and Safety Executive.[88]

In particular, Morrison Utilities Services, had market-leading accident frequency rates. Safety was a measurable element of the company's performance and reputation, and ultimately was the most important thing – both for those working on site and in the boardroom.

THE MORRISON APPROACH

## Conclusion

The story here is of two things. Firstly, success borne of having the right approach and being in the right position at the right time. The company had raised capital through flotation which meant it could take advantage of opportunities which arose in the public and private sectors with approaches to quality, collaboration and safety which struck a chord with clients. The collaborative approach would continue to pay great dividends, especially in the utilities sector which Gordon led. Biggs Wall would eventually become M Group Services, which is a major player in the industry with a 2018 turnover of over £1 billion.[89] The reputation for winning work through the Morrison Approach and for completing it to a high quality had resonated with the stock market as much as it had with clients. Floating on the stock market had served Morrison well, but also exposed the company to the risk of takeover. In the buoyant years which followed deregulation and privatisation of utilities companies, Morrison became an attractive takeover target. Secondly, intersecting with the first, was the persistence of a distinctive corporate culture. This culture fostered a sense of belonging, of friendship and simple satisfaction in your work which attracted, retained and motivated talented people. The ethos also created leading safety and quality cultures. And it is this culture which is explored in more detail in the final chapter.

Handle with care: safety cartoons were printed on mugs.

THE MORRISON STORY

# CHAPTER EIGHT
# Afterlives 2000–2019

## Takeover

IN 2000, ANGLIAN WATER GROUP bought Morrison for £262.5m having made an offer of 385p per share.[1] Gordon, Fraser, and many employees received cash settlements and shares in the new business and Morrison plc ceased to exist. From the mid-1990s, a combination of deregulation and privatisation saw many utilities businesses pursue much more diverse portfolios of activities. Anglian Water had a substantial international division with interests in geographically diverse places including the Cayman Islands, Norway, Finland, the Czech Republic, China, South Korea, India, New Zealand, Argentina, Brazil and Chile.[2] Reflecting its ambitions beyond the water sector, the company renamed itself AWG (Anglian Water Group), with two plans for the two parts of their activity – the water business which was regulated, and their other activities, which were not:

> Our goal is straightforward: outperformance in the UK regulated business and growth in our non-regulated business, and our culture is to be competitive, responsible, responsive and friendly.[3]

On paper, the companies were a good fit, as Morrison's business fitted AWG's strategic goals. And in terms of the bottom line, the takeover had done much to add to AWG's balance sheet: in 2000, £12.9m of profits on £363.2m of turnover, with orders worth £1.6bn. Both in value and capacity, Morrison made a clear contribution which it was hoped would 'improve our ability to market our skills and expertise to a broad base of industrial customers, a core strategic goal for AWG'. Whilst the acquisition went smoothly, as Robin Gourlay, Anglian Water's Chairman, put it, the takeover was 'not without its difficulties'.[4] The issues with some contracts were resolved through £60m of impairment charges and £39.3m of exceptional charges being recorded in AWG's accounts, which Elliott Mannis, the group's financial director noted as being 'primarily in the Developments and Commercial Services division', and an out of court settlement under confidential terms.[5] Amidst these problems Gordon resigned from the board in May 2001.[6]

Indeed, whatever problems there had been with the takeover, Annual Reports reveal the value Morrison brought.

> In commercial developments, Morrison Developments' further expansion of Strathclyde Business Park, along with our enterprise zone office development in Motherwell, were highlights of an excellent year.[7]

Despite suffering major institutional shock due to the takeover, the Morrison story does not end at this point.

## Institutional shock

In contrast to the purchase by CAST, where Alex, Gordon and Fraser were left to get on with running the business, Morrison experienced substantial restructuring and integration under AWG. In 2002, AWG reported it had been a 'management challenge… to resolve the problems found within Morrison after acquisition and put these firmly behind us and to integrate the parts of Morrison essential to our growth strategy'.[8] This was a more complicated union and certainly there were a series of major adjustments for Morrison employees. By 2005, there were still 7,500 of them, with a focus on PFI business, support services and construction work. Some things persisted: '85 per cent of the current order book is under long-term framework agreements, which considerably enhances contract visibility and reduces risk'.[9] The Morrison Approach, had proved compatible to a very different attitude towards risk. This key shift was to a much more conservative approach termed as being more 'prudent': '[s]ince purchasing Morrison, AWG has adopted a more prudent financial approach and changed its strategy to focus on lower risk, higher margin work within its core competencies.[10]

It is perhaps unsurprising that, amongst all this flux, the name of the company was important: just as Biggs Wall had kept its name rather than becoming Shand, so retaining the Morrison name was essential, not only for the sense of belonging fostered in employees, but for fact that the name was recognised and respected in the marketplace. Adam Gosnold suggests that 'Charles Morrison has defended the red M [logo] and the brand, almost to the extent of it nearly costing him his job, I think, particularly under the AWG ownership, and it stands for something.'[11] In a sense, the name was the reputation.

Yet by 2006, after a protracted process of integration, AWG had started selling off parts of Morrison. The company had been restructured as three areas of activity under the AWG business: property management, utilities and construction. Whilst the property management division remained in AWG ownership, AWG itself was bought by Osprey, 'a consortium of four investment funds' in June 2006.[12] AWG Property manages 1.2 million ft$^2$ of office, retail and industrial space across '34 projects with a portfolio of £170 million'.[13]

The other two divisions were sold to new buyers: the construction concern was sold to Galliford Try in 2006, where trading continues largely in Scotland under the Morrison name. In 2008, Morrison Utilities Services was sold to a pair of private equity investors, then to First Reserve in 2016. By this time, the company was of sufficient size to require approval from the EU Commission for the acquisition partly mirroring the way Morrison built up its capacities to include civil engineering, engineering and property development, resulting in a comprehensive service. Morrison Utility services forms the major share of a new Group, called M Group Services which has continued to develop its offering under private ownership. M Group Services made five acquisitions under First reserve ownership and is structured around four divisions: Utilities, telecoms, data and transport. Morrison Utility Services making up the Utility division and a large part of the telecoms division. In July 2018, PAI Partners, a third private equity firm, bought M Group Services.[14] The sale from private equity was part of the normal investment pattern and in a press release, Jim Arnold explained that the move:

> allowed First Reserve to realise the benefits of their investment to date and for us to introduce PAI, as a new long-term investor to sit alongside the existing senior management and to actively support the future development of the group.[15]

Keeping the name was important to many interviewees. Charles Morrison, responsible for Morrison Utility Services saw the value in the name:

> I nearly lost my job over it: AWG wanted to drop the Morrison name… they did not appreciate what a strong brand it was… they

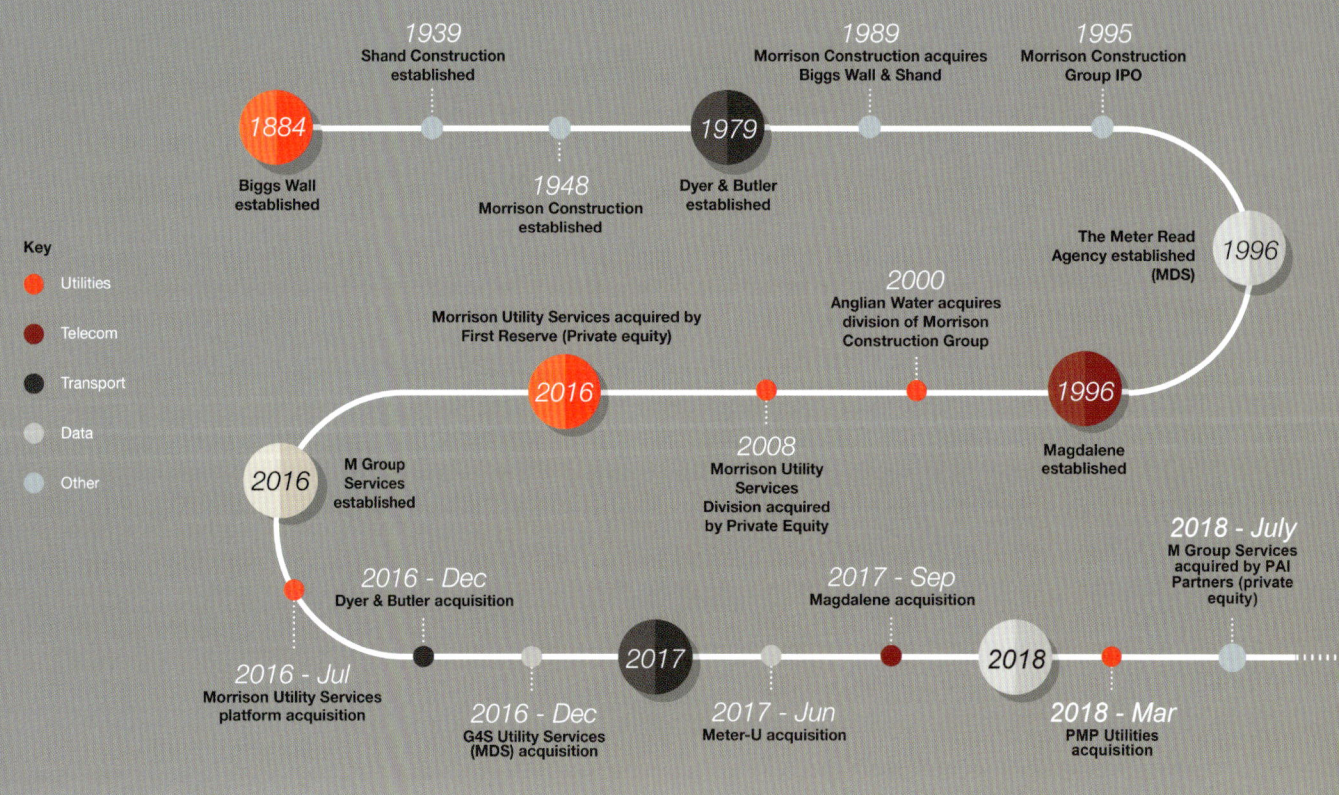

came to me and said we want to drop the Morrison name... I said we cannot do that... you will destroy the business... Morrison is eternally a strong brand, everybody has pride in the business.[16]

The construction business keeps this name in Scotland too, which Ken Gillespie had to defend too:

> I can talk about Morrison today, because Morrison is still real in construction in Scotland, and I am hugely proud of that fact that I have managed to do that... through a number of boards, which was pretty tough... and the fact that we still have a Morrison Construction business in Scotland says all it needs to say about the quality of that business... I retained the brand because it was a strength in the market and for the people.[17]

For both construction and utilities the name survives, the reputation reflected in it has proved enduring. The continued expansion of the Utilities division under Gordon, then Charles Morrison, and now Jim Arnold reflects the prescience of the collaborative approach. The reputation for safety established by Morrison Utility Services has helped this, as the company has received, and continues to receive a remarkable number of awards, in particular

AFTERLIVES 2000–2019

High-visibility safety: a jacket carries the slogan 'Zero Harm: You can make a difference'.

Morrison Utility Services.

THE MORRISON STORY

from the Royal Society for the Prevention of Accidents, including several Construction Sector Awards, the President's Award for over nine years of Gold Awards in 2017 and in 2013 the Sir George Earle Trophy, which the Society describes as 'internationally recognised as the premier performance award for occupational health and safety'.[18] These are collectively considerable accomplishments and fit entirely with the long-established corporate tradition.

## Taking risks: business as usual

### Falkirk Wheel

Whatever drama was taking place in the boardroom, the work of winning contracts and completing them continued, including some of the most important civil engineering and construction projects completed in the UK since 2000, as well as a host of apparently mundane but vital work below the radar. The famous Falkirk or Millennium Wheel, completed under AWG, was featured in two annual reports: a picture with the Chairman's Statement in 2001 and the on cover in 2002.[19] It seems whatever problems there were with the takeover, generally the quality of work was not a fundamental issue.

The Wheel is, in fact, 'a spectacular rotating boat lift' that enables craft to move between the Union and Forth and Clyde Canals. Replacing a derelict flight of eleven locks, the two canals were not only reconnected, but in the process, the Wheel became a major tourist attraction in its own right. It

Worthy of note: the revolutionary Falkirk Wheel was featured on the reverse of a Bank of Scotland £50 note.

The Falkirk Wheel has become a major tourism destination, attracting visitors from around the world.

thus fulfilled an important business and transport need, yet the project also aimed to regenerate the whole waterway for leisure uses. This connects it to a longer tradition of regenerative works, like Exchange Plaza in Edinburgh, or even the early work in the Highlands designed to bring about economic redevelopment. The Wheel was funded by a range of bodies, including Falkirk Council, Glasgow and Edinburgh City Councils and European Regional Development Fund grants, but the majority of the largest grant – £33.2m, came from the Millennium Commission.[20]

For the contractor, the task was complex. Not only was the design cutting-edge, but the site was of ecological sensitivity and historical interest.[21] Dealing with all this represents points of continuity with the kind of work done by the company before. Fraser considers it as 'an example of an entrepreneurial approach', because after the original plan proved too expensive:

> we proposed to the client a new design… a boat lift… and it is amazing how that design continues to be a focus – I have seen it on tourism brochures recently… [the architectural firm RMJM] the architect talks about producing the design using his child's Lego kit.[22]

The finished work is celebrated on the Bank of Scotland's £50 notes. Undoubtedly, it is a remarkable piece of engineering as 'a row of different sized cogs help turn the vast 1800 tonne Falkirk wheel using only the same power as six kettles'.[23] Hugh England was very proud of this piece of engineering, describing the project as his 'swansong'.[24]

THE MORRISON STORY

Hugh England shows HRH Prince Charles around the Falkirk Wheel site, 2002.

*Olympic Park, 2012*

Rather less glamorous was the remediation of half of the Olympic Park site in London ahead of the 2012 Olympic Games. Delivered on the basis of a strict time-frame, technical specialism and under a framework partnership, this Galliford Try contract had all the hallmarks of Morrison.[25] Morrison had established expertise in land remediation work from the contract at Pride Park, in Derby, where it decontaminated dangerous soil polluted by locomotive, gas and coke works including 'some low level radioactive waste at the base of the landfill'.[26] Such was the complexity of the contamination, options such as 'a clay trap over the site to contain the contamination' was not available.[27] At the Olympic site, the first task was cleaning it to make it usable. The rest of the development hinged upon this, but this was no easy matter, after a century as 'a dumping ground for industrial and domestic waste. Much of the land was polluted with contaminants such as oil, tar, arsenic and lead.' On this site, 1.4 million m³ of soil had to be excavated and cleaned of which 80 per cent were reused; 52 pylons were buried and 200 buildings demolished.[28] Morrison was responsible for half of this.

Works for the Olympics were high pressure, but such was the quality and timeliness of the execution that Ken Gillespie suggests it 'materially changed the perception of Morrison'. Tasks included the canoeing and rowing venues, and 'a lot of the athletes' village'. Altogether, the contracts were worth over £250m. The remediation work was very technically demanding, but also done under time pressure:

> you had factories, bakeries, tips, houses, railway lines, roads, so this whole site had to be cleared and remediated because it had hundreds of years of [detritus] in East London, so it was heavily contaminated, and Morrison became well-known for its ability to deal with contaminated sites… because we had expertise, we could do cradle to grave… [and this all had]… an immovable date'.[29]

The pressure stemmed because other work had to be done after this against the absolute deadline of the start of the Olympic Games.

As was so often the case, after one contract on a major project, Morrison was awarded further ones. Peter Heathershaw noted that '[o]n the back of the Olympic Park we did the water sports centre, which was the canoeing course'. This had been part of the rationale behind the way Morrison had approached the tender in the first place, seeking to price keenly and establish reputation before winning additional contracts:

> I wanted to go in on a tight margin… there has got to be opportunities because of the way the contract is structured and the nature of the sites, [the client] eventually bought into our strategy, and we won the bid. I spent the first nine months actually on the site, so I set all the target costs… it was really rewarding to sit down with the client… and ensure he bought into the way you were structuring your price.[30]

This collaborative approach is a continuation of the public and private sector approaches previously identified under Private Finance Initiatives and partnership models in which Morrison had taken a lead from the start.

## Extreme locations

Under Galliford Try, Morrison has continued to market itself as performing exceptionally in extreme conditions: 'working in climates ranging from −50°C to +50°C', as one recent promotional booklet puts it, showcasing work in South Georgia, Antarctica, and the Falkland Islands.[31] In 1999 a partnering agreement saw Morrison (Falklands) Limited carry out £30m of work for the Falkland Islands Government:

> The projects included remote island jetties, harbour works, water treatment plants, roads and sewers, visitor centre, school extensions, hospital and police station and works on the Military Base.[32]

This task drew on expertise in collaborating, a broad range of construction and civil engineering projects, and logistically challenging locations.

Nearby, in South Georgia, work involved cleaning up the Grytviken Whaling Station site contaminated by the whaling industry, with a toxic mixture of oil, asbestos and sunken ships.[33] The South Georgia Association Newsletter could proclaim that 'Grytviken is now safe', and in particular, Morrison Construction Services (Falklands) Ltd, had done so for £6m, considerably under the original £10m costing.[34] The challenges here included not only remediation, but complex logistics and a highly sensitive environment with 'unique landscape, fauna and flora'.[35] The job was completed successfully,

Taking a cruise, Fraser and Trish Morrison were surprised and delighted to come across a familiar sight in the Falklands.

A snap of the Grytviken whaling station on South Georgia where Morrison did work, taken by Gordon on holiday, January 2013.

and a second contract followed to install hydroelectric power generation facilities which were opened by the Princess Royal in March 2009.[36]

The most challenging location on the planet, at least in terms of logistics must be Antarctica. Morrison has been working here over a number of years. It started when the British Antarctic Survey (BAS) made contact 'via the Morrison website', to tender for a base at Rothera, which was won in April 1999.[37] The company's competence in these most challenging locations was consolidated by all this experience, however, it was the Halley VI contract which was most prominent.

The building, unmistakable in its bright colours has the exceptional feature that it can be moved on the ice, which first became necessary in the 2016/17 season. With temperatures dropping as low as −55°C, the base must

keep the scientists working there safe: technical failures would very likely be lethal.³⁸ Doing work here in perhaps the most uncompromising place on the planet obviously required a particular set of skills, carried real danger, but was a thrilling prospect. Ken Tallant suggested that the number of volunteers always outstripped the postings available. The popularity of location was, in a roundabout way, a reason they bid for the contract. As Michael Martin remembered:

> We had to do site visit in Antarctica, so I sent – or Ken [Gillespie] sent – a young estimator out there to view the site. We bid the job, we won it [and]… it is massive in terms of the profile of the business.³⁹

Morrison won this work because of the reputation established through its work in the Falklands and experience of working in remote locations in Scotland and elsewhere.⁴⁰

One of the key issues in such a location is logistics, which necessitate careful planning. The remoteness meant that shipping containers had to contain all the right equipment and materials but in the right order. Anything forgotten presented a serious problem as 'you could not go around to B&Q'. Peter Heathershaw remembers that this singular contract

> was all about logistics rather than actual price, because you were given windows where you could go in and do actual construction work before you had to come out again… the first container off the ship had to be life support, welfare facilities, emergency facilities… when you look at the [Halley] now and are able to jack the structure up… and pull it along on skis to new locations, there must be a lot of pride in the company in the people who built that… it was where the business culture was.⁴¹

The Halley VI is an instantly recognisable structure. Antarctica Research Station.

Ken Gillespie stressed that it was built 'from a piece of paper. It is a one-off – quite a scary one-off, because once you put people in it and you come away, they have got to survive, so it has to work'. From within Galliford Try, it was Morrison men who built it, 'from the Highlands, because they were used to working in remote locations', including the Falklands.⁴² This was one strand of the company's reputation for quality in play: building in the most difficult, remote environments possible.

### Managing risk: the Queensferry Crossing and other projects

Another articulation of the quality agenda was the completion of major civil engineering works. The Queensferry Crossing which opened in 2017 was the final of the triptych of major Morrison bridges: started by Kylesku and continued by Dornoch Bridge. In building this trio, the company worked in partnerships with other leading firms and architects. Technically they are some of the most sophisticated and innovative civil engineering projects ever undertaken in the UK, monuments to the profession's abilities. The most recent bridge was celebrated in a book written by David Watt, the former Head of Corporate Affairs at Morrison. Michael Martin described the Crossing in his introduction to the book as 'one of the largest and most complex civil engineering projects of any time undertaken anywhere in the world so far in the 21$^{st}$ century', with 'some of the most complex "temporary" works ever attempted in the UK'.⁴³ The figures indicate something of the scale: after 19 million hours of labour, 35,000 tonnes of steel, and 208,000 cubic metres of concrete.⁴⁴

Morrison operated as part of a joint venture, Forth Crossing Bridge Constructions (FCBC), with Dragados, Hochtief, and American Bridge. Michael Martin returned from retirement to take up the pivotal role of project director.⁴⁵ Andrew Aldred calls him '[t]he best engineer I've ever

The beautiful Queensferry Crossing, opened by HM the Queen in September 2017, brings Morrison's involvement with significant bridge building projects right up to date. Sitting alongside the famous Forth Bridge and the Forth Road Bridge, the location is believed to be unique in hosting three major bridges from three different centuries.

come across', and given the quality of the demanding civil engineering projects for which he was responsible in Morrison, it is hardly surprising.[46] The importance of health and safety was underscored by a terrible incident which attracted widespread publicity. An engineer, John Cousin, died when helping a colleague fix a crane. He removed a pin and the fly jib fell on him.[47] It was ruled an accident by the Sheriff court. In the book Michael Martin put it: 'The "race" for safety truly has no finishing line; it's a challenge which must continue indefinitely'.[48]

The Queensferry Crossing was perhaps the first flagship project in which there were noticeable moves towards some gender balance. Whilst the first female member of the Institution of Chartered Civil Engineers was admitted in 1957, this did not lead to an immediate female presence on construction sites.[49] Fraser says that whilst it 'has become more diverse, up until the 1990s, there would have been very few females'.[50] Progress has been slow since then across the sector. Lisa MacInnes suggests 'what would be really great, would be at some point to see [more] female director[s]'.[51] At time of writing, two of seven directors of Galliford Try are female, but none of the executive board.[52] In this respect, the sector lags behind the progress made elsewhere. There is cause for hope. Allan Russell gave a lecture at the University of Edinburgh shortly before being interviewed at which he was struck by the fact that around half his audience were female.[53] Michael Martin, however, notes how few women were found on site:

> When I got into construction, there were very few women. At Arup's there were [some] but in the office. I think Morrison always welcomed

Morrison Utility Services.

women into the workforce. I ran the graduate training programme for a long time, and I was delighted when we did the milk round, if there were any ladies who were interested in joining, I was probably biased towards employing them because it is refreshing.

In more recent years, he has noticed some improvements. In the case of the Queensferry Crossing, there were several female engineers in the team: 'not only my head of safety,… but one of my best section engineers was… and a forklift truck driver… so there has been a lot of changes, for the better'.[54] Even if women are only starting to make an appearance on site, they have been a considerable presence in the office for many years, but not much in the board room. Whilst Liz Urquhart has 'seen a great increase in female engineers, which is great', but still 'we need a few more at board level'.[55] Likewise, Julie Brinkley at Morrison Utility Services observed that 'there were a lot more women working outside when I first started… we do have women digging holes, whereas before there were not that many: women are now doing what they want', which includes fitting metres, management roles and a greater presence in accounting, so that when recruiting, 'it is not about gender, it is about someone that can do that role'.[56] In short, the situation is far from ideal, but compared with 1948 the progress has been considerable, and there are clear grounds for optimism for the future.

The final theme worthy of note returns to that of the central concerns of this history: risk. The scale of the project, at some £1.4 billion meant that risk had to be managed carefully. Even one per cent on this would be a large sum of money. At a project level, two key steps were taken. Firstly, extensive scientific testing ensured the risks of problems in construction were minimised. Secondly, 'the relieving of the contractor from the potentially large inflation risk always inherent in contracts of such long duration' is one way to increase stability. With ever-larger contracts, it becomes increasingly in the interest of both client and contractors to ensure that risks are managed, as was seen with the collapse of Carillion in early 2018, the risks are substantial. Morrison is one of the partners in the joint venture responsible for the Aberdeen Western Peripheral Route (AWPR), as was Carillion: 'we have had to pick up their share of the loss' as Liz Urquhart put it.[57]

Cutting across many of these concerns was the collaborative approach. The Moray Flood Alleviation Scheme completed in 2016 was a major undertaking for the Construction division. The £105 million scheme had five sub-schemes: Lhanbryde, Rothes, Forres, Findhorn and Elgin.[58] Allan Russell was involved in most of them and enthused:

> It was an engineer's dream because you had everything from heavy civil engineering, piling, sheet piles, board piles, bridge building, land remediation. There was all sorts of things involved in these projects, really interesting… and a very good client because they had the foresight to set the thing up early days, they got the contractor involved, and we helped with the design, the buildability of these schemes and worked very closely with them, and they let us get on with it… It was a typical Morrison job, it was everything we had learned through the history, the culture, and how we helped the client.[59]

Stuart Higgins points to the advantages of these contracts. The Moray Flood Alleviation Scheme was a framework project, which means that initially Morrison

> bid for the first flood alleviation scheme, the successful bidder then worked alongside the Moray Council flood alleviation team and there designers on a ECI (early contractor involvement) using the NEC contract to produce a target cost. Also using lessons learnt through each of the flood schemes and a set of KPI (key performance indicators) to ensure value for money. We successfully delivered the flood alleviation to Moray.[60]

## A million holes a year: the rise of Morrison Utility Services

The rise of Morrison Utility Services is an extraordinary story. When Morrison was bought from Charter Consolidated, as noted above, Shand and Biggs Wall were also acquired, at a time when changes in the Utility sector presented a real opportunity. Biggs Wall would evolve into Morrison Utility Services, being called Morrison Biggs Wall in between. Privatisation of the gas (1986), water (1989), and electricity (1990) supply industries from public ownership to private ownership, designed to achieve efficiencies and were flagship policies of the Conservative government of those periods. As was clearly demonstrated through an incident at Royston which happened on 8 March 1991, Biggs Wall and most of their competitors within the sector were little more than labour hire companies with the construction managers and the supervising engineers employed by the utility companies. This was a way of working which was a long way from the collaborative Morrison approach. For example, network drawings were seldom shared with the contractors.

The Royston incident clearly illustrated the flaws in this type of arrangement. When a Biggs Wall operative was asked to connect the medium pressure gas pipe to the low-level network around Royston, he was aware that this was unusual and highlighted the situation to his supervisor and was told to follow instructions. This resulted in every domestic gas appliance failing and caused a number of fires. The *Royston Crow* headline 'Pregnant mum's blaze horror: the great gas crisis', gives some sense of the panic caused.[61]

In a similar transfer of risk seen in civil engineering and construction contracts, so utilities work saw responsibility for management and, therefore, risk transferred to the contractor. Utility contracting became increasingly more sophisticated, challenging and interesting from that point onwards. The innovative and entrepreneurial approach from Morrison saw Biggs Wall well placed to take full advantage with spectacular success. The episode underscores that a central dynamic for both private and public-sector clients is the transfer of all risk, whilst the scale of projects and contracts is constantly expanding.[62]

The nature of the work done by Morrison Utility Services is rather harder to picture than major civil engineering projects. Around 2000, Morrison Utility Services excavated and filled over one million holes in London that year. The logistical and data management needs of a business of this scale is quite awe inspiring.[63] The importance of this work being done safely is, of course, very high. Charles Morrison points a 2017 example of this: work to install a 'gas mains within [Buckingham] Palace, with all the security

## THE MORRISON STORY

Morrison Utility Services have completed many high-profile works, including at Westminster Abbey ahead of a Royal Wedding.

The expanding fleet of vehicles: new Morrison Transit vans purchased in 2005.

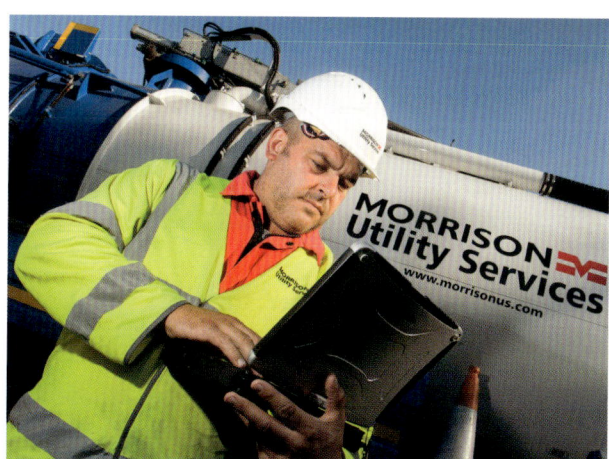

[regulations], plus you do not want to have a gas escape'. Such prominence could have a catalytic effect in securing necessary permissions:

> We had to replace gas mains at Westminster Abbey before the wedding of William and Kate… before the wedding was announced at Westminster Abbey, we were trying to get approvals to get road closures… once the wedding was announced, suddenly the approvals magically arrived! Everything just got cleared.[64]

The issue of scale is managed by technology. A million holes a year might only be possible due to technologies permitting digital invoicing. As Zoe Gentle notes, 'if we did not have the computers we have now, you would have to employ lots of people' to do it manually. The older systems were simply much more labour intensive:

> When we did a purchase ledger, we used to have to input everything manually, so any entries left outstanding… [which] had not been invoiced [at the end of] each month, you would have to… do a tally roll of all the outstanding entries, so they would have an idea what was still to be paid out… that is all done in electronically now.[65]

This process to identify the expenditure for which invoices had not yet been received used to take three or four days, and highlights the hidden elements of all the projects which have been discussed in this book. Right from the first piece of wood being sawn in Alex's workshop in Tain to the cutting edge and mass-scale jobs discussed in this chapter, all required a huge amount of back office work to account and invoice for the work done, to ensure workers and suppliers were paid accurately and on time. For example, the task of processing the purchase ledger and other paper and labour-intensive processes were vital. The best insight into this was from Lawrence Allan. He was one of the first brought in to manage the financial side, part of that first move to run the business on a more formal footing, at a time when wages were paid weekly and in cash, and every cheque required Alex's signature. The distance travelled to state-of-the-art systems capable of handling the scale of operations in 2019, is quite extraordinary.

Other innovations include a lone worker app, and the OptiMUS platform which 'runs on salesforce' and in which Morrison Utility Services has invested a great deal in the last decade.[66] Yet as sites are contacted by email, perhaps there is a downside to this technology. Zoe Gentle suggests that whilst this provides efficiency 'I think you lose the communication: we do not have site visits now... because it has just grown, and everything is done so quickly'.[67] Given the scale, there is simply no choice. With a turnover over of £1 billion, and 8,200 employees, it is hard to imagine that this growth came from the Biggs Wall company, which was 'thrown in' with Morrison when they reversed out of Shand.[68] As David Jeffs put it: 'Gordon did well with that because he saw a market on the utility side – it had not developed yet, and he was one of the first' to see opportunities.[69]

## Quality Built In: a corporate reputation

In late 2018, Morrison still represents two big names in construction and utilities services. The name Morrison Construction can be seen on many major and minor construction and civil engineering projects in Scotland; across the UK, the red M is still often on display when essential utilities services are being fixed. The journey to this position from Alex setting up as a joiner to provide work for some of his ex-military comrades is remarkable. Ultimately, this was a question of people's talent, skill, and loyalty. Ian Smith's grandson was born early, and as another early completion, was promptly placed in Morrison hat and baby grow.[70]

A family business: Ian Smith with his grandson, Martin, in a Morrison hard hat.

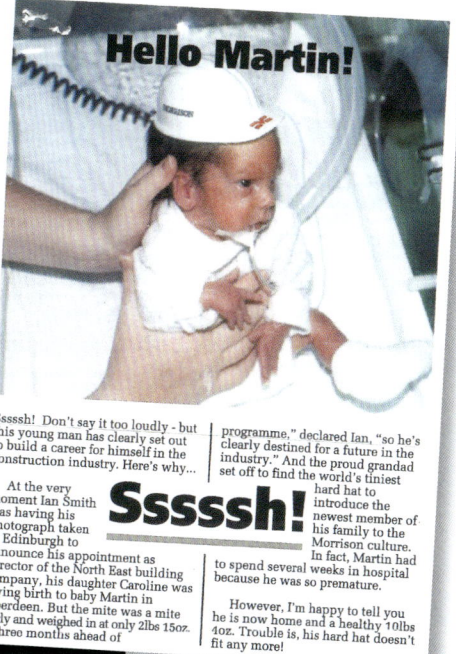

A culture of safety from a young age: Gordon's grandchildren Sophie, James and Kirsty at the Lord Mayor's show in Morrison Utility Services-branded personal protective equipment.

A strand which came through in many interviews was friendships, not of the workplace variety, but of enduring, real ones. After the waning of the Twenty-Five Year Club when it became too large to manage, imitations were established: the Morrison Old Boys by Ian Smith and Donald MacLennan, or the civils board still meets to this day, meeting up once a year in the North of Scotland.

At the heart of these friendships, Stewart MacLeod thought, was the fact that:

> We all shared this creative desire to promote the company's standing, and to come up with creative ideas that would allow the company to go into other areas of contracting that we hitherto had not.[71]

Many enduring relationships were forged with clients as well as colleagues. The collaborative approach meant that business was much less likely to be confrontational, not only making commercial settlement and repeat business easier to seek, but also created friendships which have stood the test of time.

Stuart Higgins suggested that the company was

> very ambitious, at that time they were prepared to take on things which were technically difficult, and in fact that became the motto: take on difficult, technical jobs, and allow us to come up with inventive solutions and the planning and phasing of the works. They were good for us, they were good for the team, who had to rise to the challenge.[72]

This was one way to encourage work of the highest quality. Individual ownership and responsibility were in contrast to working elsewhere. Compared to Morrison, other companies were full of 'Yes men'.[73] Lisa MacInnes found that under AWG, she 'had to get everything approved' in a more bureaucratic way than when Morrison had been independent.[74]

Quality was always a core value. Around it, a whole corporate culture was structured. Stewart MacLeod was emphatic that this culture meant 'everything had to be done to the highest possible standard, and in a nutshell, that is it.'[75] Hugh England summarised 'Morrison Culture' as a set of values which motivated people to give of their best and not just to seek bonuses:

> It was quality, doing it right; it was team work; it was safety; it was innovation, and the best bottom line in the industry. And I put that last… because it came to me last, because I was a great believer that if you do those other things right, the bottom line will come.[76]

When asked if he thought some of the success enjoyed was down to luck, Fraser was emphatic that the company's success was underpinned by hard work:

> I quote Gary Player who said, "You know it is a strange thing, but the harder I practice, the luckier I get", and yes, you have got to have a stroke of luck… but the effort we put into it was absolutely enormous, and it is only by putting that effort into it that you get where you want to be.

Things could have taken a turn in a very different direction:

> at any point in time over those years, from my father convincing Mr Gibson [the bank manager in Tain] that he needed another £250 to

THE MORRISON STORY

pay the wages this week or us convincing the client on Kylesku that he should pay £2 million as an additional payment on a £2.75m contract, whatever it was, the bank manager could have said no, the client on Kylesku could have said sorry, it is not going to happen, and that is the difference between winning and losing.[77]

The corporate culture was fundamentally that of a family business. Even as the scale of the operation became a FTSE-listed company, a strong attachment and regional structures left people with a strong sense of ownership. As the company became ever-more successful, some found this frustrating, as they could not know everybody. Ken Gillespie stressed that on the construction side social activities were arranged in an attempt to maintain the intimacy of the family firm feel:

> I want an organization where everybody thinks they work for a small business. I want to know their names, wives' names, children's names. It spooked me when I walked onto a site when I did not know everyone. I was happiest when there were sixty people and I knew them all. That grows loyalty, commitments; we were interested in our people.[78]

Employees were also brought on board through *Morrison News* and copies of the Annual Reports. The company even recognised 'the right of our employees to be informed and made aware of matters which affect their work'.[79] Alongside this were occasional site visits for those based in offices, and 'we always had regular meetings – he'd get all the sales people from other divisions… so to get everybody together so you know what is going on in other parts of the company, and the thing about Gordon is if he said the meeting would be two hours, it would be two hours; he is so focused'.[80]

## Reward: a family firm

Lawrence Allan, present in the very earliest days found that the company really 'was a family business, and we were part of the family' when he arrived. However, as the company grew, this changed, as 'there were so many people you did not really know'.[81] This echoes what Ken Gillespie felt about sites growing at a much later day. However big the company became, some sense of it being a family business was retained. An enduring sense of being a family firm was created by the leadership shown by both Alex's sons. Adam

Sir Fraser Morrison who very successfully ran the business for 25 years until 2000.

Gosnold found Fraser a 'very engaging character... I found him quite inspirational'. John Morrison saw his prescience around different types of contract as 'visionary'.[82] Ian Smith noted that when Fraser visited his office 'he would listen and learn'.[83] Gordon also was 'entrepreneurial, looking for next big thing', suggests Ian Cusden.[84] Adam Gosnold echoes these views:

> Gordon was very much a thinker... with his quite innovative, creative thinking, just occasionally the seeds would land and would germinate, and we would come up with a strategy, an idea, an approach that would really help develop the business and new ideas.

For Adam,

> Gordon really gave us great leadership in the business, he grew into the role as the lead for the England-based part of the business... one of the things he could do, as I think to great effect... he could talk about my business. And it was not in an arrogant way, it was just in a very personal and taking-ownership-and-accountability kind of way... it was great to have that personal edge that he could bring to the conversations with our client organizations.[85]

What all this shows is that the value of quality and the benefits of entrepreneurship and thinking differently, established by Alexander Morrison, still hold. This is what made Morrison Morrison: tackling any challenge head on and doing any job very well, however big or small or difficult, led to a remarkable business story and brought out the best in those involved. Alex's business started in Tain, but the red "M" logo came to stand for quality wherever it was found – even in Antarctica.

In 2018, Morrison celebrated its seventieth anniversary. Split into Morrison Utility Services and the Scottish construction part of Galliford Try, the casual observer might not imagine that these began in a small Highland town with some saved army pay, a bag of borrowed tools and a desire not to have to answer to a boss. Alex cannot possibly have thought his business would reach such dazzling heights. His ambition, Connie remembers, was much more modest: 'he wanted to provide for Fraser and take care of the family, which would later include Gordon'.[86] As has been shown, it achieved very much more. The accomplishment can be catalogued: using financial data, figures of turnover and profit; the awards and accolades; photographs of the most striking and technically advanced structures. But perhaps all of this fall rather short of the mark, because fundamentally the achievement was human. The machinery and techniques were far less important than those using them. Overwhelmingly, people seem to have been satisfied with their careers, and this satisfaction was noted by many as the thing which was reward enough. These are reflections worth quoting at a little length.

Lawrence Allan is one of the interviewees with the earliest connection to the business:

> The expression that often got used was that they were Morrison Men, there was a range of foremen and the like who had been there for a long time, and they were sort of known as Morrison Men… those in the Twenty-Five Club… had a feeling of pride.[87]

Hugh England:

> For all the risks… we had fun, we enjoyed it… we had a laugh, right from top to bottom, I would say… I come back to people, one of the Shand diehard guys, who lived in a caravan 365 days of the year, and he was always there at weekends, would always fuel the pump that had to be kept going… Totally reliable until he was 65, and was an operative, and he had a first-class retirement "do" from the company… he was an essential member of the team.[88]

Roger Croson:

> I had a happy career. I could not possibly have been in with a better team, better company; that was one of the great things. We still have an annual reunion, my civil engineering comrades and I, the ones who have retired. We meet every year in November, and it is just like we were working together yesterday. That was the great strength of it, there was a real team spirit: there were no bosses and underlings: we were all in it together, a team and that was the great strength of it I felt, and still is; it is always a joy to meet with them.[89]

Donald MacLennan:

> I liked it all. I wish I could turn the clock back. I enjoyed working for Morrison.[90]

Michael Martin:

> We meet up every year for a reunion… that is still my team. Obviously, Morrison was sold, I worked for AWG, I ran Scottish Water Solutions, I ran the biggest infrastructure project in Scotland in a generation [the Queensferry Crossing], but that is still my team.[91]

Ian Smith:

> It has been wonderful being in construction. I look back and say if I had my life to live over again, would it be in construction? Yes, without a shadow of a doubt, because you never do the same thing twice, never in the same place, and never with the same people. So that's what it makes it so enjoyable.[92]

The story of the business, from a tiny outfit to a market-leading FTSE-listed plc with international interests, sold and bought several times, with enduring legacies is remarkable.

Sir Fraser Morrison looks back with no small amount of satisfaction:

> My thirty years, most of them running the business, and seeing it grow and develop from a local company around Easter Ross… the overall experience and the pleasure that it gave us and the life that it has given us has been very special.[93]

Looking across the whole Morrison story, Gordon puts it thus:

> For my father, Fraser and I it was an incredible journey. Yes luck was on our side on many occasions but we worked hard at that. What is very satisfying is that the journey and the good fortune successfully continues under new management and ownership. My father would have been 100 in April 2019, what has been achieved will always be a lasting legacy.

AFTERLIVES 2000–2019

A plate presented to Alex Morrison in 1998, on the 50th anniversary of his company, bearing the signatures of all members of the Twenty-Five Year Club.

# Notes

## Notes for Chapter Two: Alex's war

1. Release Leave Certificate Army Form X 202/A. Family papers.
2. R. Parker, *The Second World War: a short history* (Oxford, 2001), pp.44–45.
3. A. Fairdie, *Queen's Own Highlanders (Seaforth and Camerons)* (Golspie, 1998), p.137; Longden, *Dunkirk: the men they left behind* (London, 2008), pp.150–154.
4. Lieutenant Colonel ----, 'The Seaforth Highlanders: a Message from Battalion Commander', *Ross-shire Journal* (21 June 1940), cutting in Family Papers. Likely from *Press and Journal*.
5. E. A. Cameron, *Impaled Upon a Thistle: Scotland since 1880* (Edinburgh, 2010), p.177.
6. S. P. Mackenzie, *The Colditz Myth: British Commonwealth prisoners of war in Nazi Germany* (Oxford, 2004), p.36.
7. Mackenzie, *Colditz Myth*, pp.36, 43.
8. Mackenzie, *Colditz Myth*, p.45.
9. Mackenzie, *Colditz Myth*, pp.26, 40, 43, 45, 48–49, 64.
10. National Archives. Hereafter NA WO 416/263/1. Alex's prisoner of war record notes that he was captured on 12 June 1940, and his details were recorded at Stalag VIIIB on 15 July 1940; this may not have been the day of his arrival. It seems unlikely that thirty miles were travelled each day, as this is at the upper range of distances travelled, so it can be inferred that at least part of that journey must have been on mechanized transport. Mileage based on Google maps. The name Lamsdorf is used here rather than Łambinowice, to make it clear that it belonged to the Nazi regime and not the Polish state.
11. A specific discussion of the Colditz myth is found in Mackenzie, *Colditz Myth*. As always, powerful media images are very hard to shake off once they are established in the public mind.
12. Imperial War Museum, hereafter IWM Documents.3802/B. C. G. King, 'Left Behind', typescript prepared 4/10/1974.
13. M. A. Mead, *A Long Walk Home: life in my 20th century* (Self-published, n.d. c.2009), p.115.
14. IWM Documents.26373. 17/13/1/2 David's PoW Letters to his parents, Private Papers of D U R Lidstone, letter sent 25/1/1945.
15. Mead, *Long Walk Home*, p.115.
16. IWM Documents.7697, D. M.

16. Elliott, 'Denholm's War' (Typescript, 1984), p.6.
17. IWM 17/13/1/2 sent 6/12/1942; Lidstone, 'An Account of His Time', p.23.
18. Elliott, 'Denholm's war', p.6.
19. Lidstone, 'An Account of His Time', p.26.
20. Lidstone, 'An Account of His Time', p.12.
21. Mackenzie, *The Colditz Myth*, pp.97, 99.
22. IWM Documents.26373, 17/13/1/2 Letter to his mother, 9/8/1942.
23. King, 'Left Behind', p.28.
24. A. J. Kochavi, *Confronting Captivity: Britain and the US and their Prisoners of War in Nazi Germany* (Chapel Hill, 2005), p.54.
25. King, 'Left Behind', p.28.
26. IWM Documents.188845. A. W. Woolley, 'An Account of the War-time Recollections of Major A. W. Woolley, R.A.M.C. (1911–2005)' (typescript dated April 2008), p.19. The authorship of this material is not entirely clear, but large proportions of the text are italicized and clearly Woolley's words. Woolley notes that the old camp was called 344. References are made variously to Stalag VIIIB/344.
27. IWM Film Archive MGH3726 and a duplicate MGH2752.
28. Woolley, 'War-time Recollections', pp.19–20.
29. Kochavi, *Confronting captivity*, pp.30–2, 49.
30. Mead, *Long Walk Home*, p.116.
31. D. Rolf, '"Blind Bureaucracy": the British Government and POWs in German captivity, 1939–45', in B. Moore and K. Fedorowich (eds), *Prisoners of War and their captors in World War II* (Oxford, 1996), p.56.
32. Rolf, 'Blind Bureaucracy', p.57.
33. Mead, *Long Walk Home*, p.125.
34. Mackenzie, *Colditz Myth*, p.130.
35. Mackenzie, *Colditz Myth*, pp.113, 115, 135–150.
36. Mackenzie, *Colditz Myth*, pp.131–2; Longden, *Dunkirk*
37. Lidstone, 'An Account of His Time', p.12.
38. A. J. Kochavi Confronting captivity: Britain and the US and their Prisoners of War in Nazi Germany (Chapel Hill, 2005), p.34.
39. Mackenzie, *Colditz Myth*, p.156.
40. Elliott, 'Denholm's War', p.6; Lidstone, 'An Account of His Time', p.12.
41. Lidstone, 'An Account of His Time', p.14.
42. A highly readable account of this is G. W. Lockhart, *The Scots and their Oats* (Edinburgh, 1998).
43. Lidstone, 'An account of His Time', p.12.
44. Elliott, 'Denholm's War', p.7.
45. Cheffie', 'Stalag Recipes', *Clarion*, 4 (April 1944), p.193; Anonymous, 'Cookery Nook', 4 (May 1943), p.107, reproduced and paginated in G. Whiteside, *The Clarion: WWII memories as a P. o. W.* (San Antonio, 1999). All references to the *Clarion* are to this edition.
46. Lidstone, 'An Account of His Time', p.12; also see, per e.g. Elliott, 'Denholm's War', p.7.
47. Elliott, 'Denholm's War', p.7.
48. King, 'Left Behind', p.27.
49. Mackenzie, *Colditz Myth*, p.161.
50. Mackenzie, *Colditz Myth*, p.155.
51. Elliott, 'Denholm's War', p.7.
52. Mackenzie, *Colditz Myth*, p.160.
53. Elliott, 'Denholm's War', p.7.
54. IWM Documents.3802/A, C. G. King, 'A Wartime Log' (nd but after 24 June 1944), p.96.
55. King, 'Wartime Log', p.106.

## NOTES FOR CHAPTER TWO: ALEX'S WAR

56  Mackenzie, p.162, Elliott, 'Denholm's War', p.8.
57  Mead, *Long Walk Home*, p.137.
58  Mackenzie, *Colditz Myth*, pp.157–8.
59  His son Gordon thinks he had appendicitis, and this was treated; peronitis would explain such a long stay in hospital; however his admission card indicates he had an appendix scar when created on 15 July 1940 on Alex's arrival at the camp. NA WO 416/263/1.
60  Mackenzie, *Colditz Myth*, p.193.
61  Kochavi, *Confronting Captivity*, p.56
62  For example, G. Whiteside cites this as reason in his memoir, *Clarion*, p.9.
63  King, 'Left Behind', p.25.
64  U. Herbert, *Hitler's Foreign Workers: enforced foreign labor in Germany under the Third Reich*, transl. W. Templer (Cambridge, 1997), pp.95–6.
65  Mackenzie, *Colditz Myth*, pp.194–5.
66  On the lack of food, see Kochavi, *Confronting Captivity*, p.34.
67  Longden, *Dunkirk*, p.348.
68  Kochavi, *Confronting Captivity*, p.62.
69  IWM Documents.26373. 17/13/1/4 Private Papers of D U R Lidstone. J. S. Couper to Mrs Lidstone, 4 May 1945, pp.1–2.
70  Longden, *Dunkirk*, p.348.
71  Kochavi, *Confronting Captivity*, p.61.
72  NA WO 416/263/1 Prisoner of War Record for Alexander Morrison; Lidstone, 'An Account of His Time',
73  Lidstone, 'An Account of His Time', p.21.
74  Woolley, 'War-time Recollections', pp.14–15. He also saw mass killings of Jews near Katowice, p.19.
75  The BFC has not featured much in the literature, but a helpful overview with some Australian case studies is provided in R. Goyne, 'British Free Corps (BFC): traitors to the king', *Sabretache*, XLVI, 3 (2005), pp.39–42.
76  G. I. Beck, 'A Prisoner of War's diary from Stalag VIIIB: April to June 1944' online at www.bbc.co.uk/history/ww2peopleswar/stories/13/a8442713.shtml accessed 13 February 2018. Entry for 28 May 1944.
77  Goyne, 'British Free Corps', p.42 suggests this was to avoid publicity.
78  U. Herbert, *Hitler's Foreign Workers: enforced foreign labor in Germany under the Third Reich*, transl. W. Templer (Cambridge, 1997), pp.95–6.
79  Kochavi, *Confronting Captivity*, p.33.
80  NA WO 224/27. Item 575. Gabriel Naville and Dr Hans Wehrle, 'Working Detachment E 46 Mechtel' (6 August 1942), p.24.
81  NA WO 224/27. Item 395. Dr Exchaquet and Dr Rublip, 'Labour Detachment E.46 Preussengrube', (not dated, but reports are numbered and filed chronologically).
82  NA WO 224/27. Item 494. Work Camp E 46 – Mechtal' (6–8 May 1942), p.18.
83  NA WO 224/27. Item 762. Working Detachment Stalag VIIIB' (10 March 1943), p.1.
84  NA WO 224/27. Item 762. Working Detachment Stalag VIIIB' (10 March 1943), p.12.
85  NA WO 224/27. Item 1141. Gabriel Naville, 'E75 Knurow' (14 February 1944), in 'Working Detachments depending upon Stalag VIII B', pp.16–17.
86  J. Rose, *The Intellectual Life of the British Working Classes* (New Haven, 2008), p.464; passim, on failure in 1960s see pp.455–64.
87  The kailyard myth was predominantly a nineteenth-century one,

but the pride taken in Scottish traditions of education continued well through the twentieth century. See A. Nash, 'Re-reading the 'Lad o' Pairts': the myth of the Kailyard Myth', *Scotlands*, 3, 2 (1996), pp.86–102; R. Cook, 'The Home-ly Kailyard Nation: nineteenth-century narratives of the highland and the myth of Merrie Auld Scotland', *ELH*, 66, 4 (1999), pp.1053–1070; L. Paterson, 'The Reinvention of Scottish Liberal Education: secondary schooling, 1900–39', *Scottish Historical Review*, XC, 1, 229 (2011), pp.96–130.

88 'Alexander Morrison 1919–98', *Herald* (17 November 1998), online at www.heraldscotland.com/news/12345353.Alexander_Morriosn, accessed 13 February 2018.
89 J. Rancière, *Proletarian Nights*, revised edition (London, 2012).
90 Mackenzie, *Colditz Myth*, p.163.
91 Mackenzie, *Colditz Myth*, p.163.
92 IWM 17/13/1/2 8 April 1941, 14 April 1941, 30 May 1941, 25 November 1941.
93 IWM 17/13/1/2 8 February 1942.
94 IWM 17/13/1/2 25 October 1942; 1 November 1942.
95 IWM 17/13/1/2 18 July 1943.
96 IWM 17/13/1/2 17 May 1942.
97 *Clarion*, 1 (January 1943), p.33.
98 *Clarion*, 13 (April 1944), p.227.
99 *Clarion*, 1 (January 1943), p.33.
100 *Clarion*, 1 (January 1943), p.36; e.g. 2 (February 19423), p.61.
101 Mackenzie, *Colditz Myth*, p.159.
102 B. Moore and B. Hately, 'Captive Audience: camp entertainment and British Prisoners-of-War in German Captivity, 1939–1945', *Popular Entertainment Studies*, 4, 1 (2014), pp.58–60, 67–68.
103 M. Gillies, *The Barbed-wire University: the real lives of Allied PoWs in the second world war* (London, 2011), p.291.
104 Lidstone, 'An Account of His Time', p.23.
105 Gillies, *Barbed-wire University*, p.293.
106 *Clarion*, 9 (February 1944), p.183.
107 B. Rowe, 'On to Victory! Beethoven's Fifth Symphony', *Social Studies*, XXXV, 7 (1944), p.291. This is linked to the great and humane conductor Bruno Walter's performances of *Fidelio*, Beethoven's only opera which is set inside a prison, in wartime New York, p.292.
108 Gillies, *Barbed-wire University*, p.293.
109 Lidstone, 'An Account of His Time', p.23.
110 Gillies, *Barbed-wire University*, pp.50–51.
111 *Clarion*, 8 (Jan 1944), p.168
112 Gillies, *Barbed-wire University*, pp.293, 50–51.; see discussion in Mackenzie, *Colditz Myth*, pp.211–4.
113 *Clarion*, 12 (May 1944), pp.214–5.
114 V. Emeljanow, 'Popular Entertainments as Survival Strategies in Prisoner-of-War Camps During World War II', in J. Goodall and C. Lee (eds), *Trauma and Public Memory* (London, 2015), p.177.
115 Emeljanow, 'Popular Entertainments', p.180.
116 *Clarion*, 13 (June 1944), pp.228–229.
117 *Clarion*, 15 (August 1944), p.260.
118 Emeljanow, 'Popular Entertainments', p.180.
119 Gillies, *Barbed-wire University*, p.74.
120 Elliott, 'Denholm's War', p.6; Mackenzie, *Colditz Myth*, pp.166, 213.
121 Elliott, 'Denholm's War', p.6
122 See *Clarion*, 1 (1943), p.63; figures

## NOTES FOR CHAPTER TWO: ALEX'S WAR

converted using R. Edvinsson, 'Historical Currency Converter'. http://www.historicalstatistics.org/Currencyconverter.html accessed 30 May 2018 to £1140; inflation calculated using RPI from L. H. Officer and S. H. Williamson, 'Five Ways to Compute the Relative Value of a UK Pound Amount, 1270 to Present (2018), online https://www.measuringworth.com/calculators/ukcompare/relativevalue.php accessed 30 May 2018.

123 *Clarion*, 9 (February 1944), p.174.
124 Lidstone, 'An Account of his time', p.23 noted ball games, as did Beck, 'Prisoner of War's diary', entry for 17 April 1944.
125 Kochavi, *Confronting Captivity*, p.21. Newsletter no 2 (May 1941).
126 Mackenzie, *Colditz Myth*, pp.163–4, p.173.
127 Gillies, *Barbed-wire University*, p.21.
128 D. Rolf, 'Blind Bureaucracy', pp.47, 63.
129 B. Moore and K. Fedorowich, 'Prisoners of War in the Second World War: an overview', in Moore and Fedorowich (eds) *Prisoners of War and their Captors in World War II* (Oxford, 1996).
130 Lieutenant Colonel ----, 'The Seaforth Highlanders: a Message from Battalion Commander', *Ross-shire Journal* (21 June 1940), cutting in Family Papers. Likely from *Press and Journal*.
131 Mead, *Long Walk Home*, pp.139, 141; J. Nichol and T. Rennell, *The Last Escape: the untold story of allied prisoners of war in Germany 1944–45* (Penguin, 20003), p.53; Elliott, 'Denholm's War', p.11.
132 Elliott, 'Denholm's War', p.10.
133 Kochavi, *Confronting Captivity*, pp.218, 220.
134 Nichol and Rennell, *Last Escape*, p.53.
135 Mackenzie, *Colditz Myth*, p.358.
136 Mackenzie, *Colditz Myth*, p.385.
137 Woolley, 'War-time Recollections', p.23.
138 Woolley, 'War-time Recollections', p.22.
139 Mackenzie, *Colditz Myth*, pp.373–8
140 When Nazis came looking for him with search dogs, he filled a can with urine to put them off their scent. Interview with Sir Fraser Morrison, 23 May 2018.
141 On escape mythology see Mackenzie, *Colditz Myth*, p.1; Moore and Fedorowich, 'Prisoners of War in the Second World War: an overview', p.2; on reality, and that 'a great many captives were willing to wait out the war rather than try to make it home, see Mackenzie, *Colditz Myth*, p.319; on the lack of escape from Lamsdorf in particular see Elliott, 'Denholm's War', p.10.
142 NA WO 344/226/1 War Office: Directorate of Military Intelligence: Liberated Prisoner of War Interrogation Questionnaires, Morrison A – Morrison S. Item 84410. No 2822095 Pte Alexander Morrison.
143 Interview with Sir Fraser Morrison, 23 May 2018.
144 http://www.naval-history.net/WW2UScasaaDB-USMCbyNameM.htm accessed 31 May 2018. The name comes from prisoner of war and missing in action.
145 Family papers. Wesley G. Flood came from Philadelphia, joined 13 January 1931 as a private. He had been an electrician with two years of high school education in the National Guard. Army serial number 20324771. AAD Electronic

Army Serial Number Merged File, ca. 1938–1946 (Enlistment Records), record 1923725. He died 11 December 1997. Death Files, 1936–2007 (Last Names E through G). Online at www.aad.archives. gov. Accessed 11 April 2018. He was buried in Coachella Valley Public Cemetery. www.findagrave.com, memorial 137348234.

146  Gordon Morrison, *Men of Tain* (Private press, 2009), p.9. This volume has been extremely useful in preparing the early chapters of this history.

147  Release Leave Certificate Army Form X 202/A. Family papers.

## Notes for Chapter Three: Starting out

1. E. Harwood, *Space, Hope and Brutalism: English architecture 1945–1975* (New Haven: Yale University Press, 2015), p.xix, identifies these three priorities and discusses their consequences for architectural design. Government policy in relation to Scotland was similar to England in these regards.

2. £5.04m calculated using Officer and Williamson, *Measuring Worth*. Inflated by percentage of GDP, accessed 10 August 2018.

3. Parish population in Rev. R. W. A. Begg, 'The Parish of Tain', in A. S. Mather (ed.), *The Third Statistical Account of Scotland: the County of Ross and Cromarty* (Edinburgh: Scottish Academic Press, 1987), p.250.

4. Begg, 'The Parish of Tain', p.240.

5. A royal burgh simply means one which got its charter from the king. It was the most privileged category because this enabled it not simply the right to hold a market, but to trade internationally which was a prerogative reserved exclusively for royal burghs. The original charters have not survived – which is not uncommon. The nine hundredth anniversary of the charter was celebrated in 1966 nonetheless. See W. Ross Napier, *Tain: the oldest royal burgh in Scotland* (Tain, 1994), p.3. Also see R. D. Oram, P. F. Martin, C. A. McKean, T. Neighbour and A Cathcart, *Historic Tain: Archaeology and development* (York and Edinburgh: Council for British Archaeology and Historic Scotland, 2009), p.20.

6. In recent years these have become much less valuable due to a decline in quality. https://www.bbc.co.uk/news/uk-scotland-scotland-business-14861300, accessed 4 December 2018.

7. Letter from Connie Morrison, 1 April 2018.

8. Begg, 'Parish of Tain', p.247.

9. Begg, 'Parish of Tain', p.248, noted 'as at February 18th 1954 [sic]' but this must mean 1945.

10. J. Bryden, 'Scottish Agriculture, 1950–1990', *Scottish Tradition*, XX (1995), pp.44–41.

11. Bryden, 'Scottish Agriculture', pp.48–54.

12. Begg, 'Parish of Tain', p.248.

13. The only modern treatments are found in Oram et al., *Historic Tain*, which is predominately archaeological, and the older R. W. and J.

Munro, *Tain Through the Centuries* (Edinburgh: Birlinn, 2005 [1966]).
14. The complaints are noted in Morrison, *Men of Tain*, p.13.
15. Begg, 'Parish of Tain', p.258.
16. Interview with David Henderson, 1 March 2018.
17. W. R. Napier, *Tain: the oldest royal burgh in Scotland* (1994), p.3.
18. Begg, 'Parish of Tain', p.257
19. https://www2.le.ac.uk/departments/history/heritage/images/post-war-architecture-timeline, accessed 10 June 2018.
20. Gordon Morrison, typescript autobiographical notes.
21. Letter from Connie Morrison, 1 April 2018.
22. Interview with Lawrence Allen, 17 April 2018. Connie's participation confirmed by Sir Fraser Morrison.
23. This is what Gordon Morrison notes in *Men of Tain,* p.9; interview with Lawrence Allen, 17 April 2018.
24. Interview with David Henderson, 1 March 2018.
25. Interview with Sir Fraser Morrison, 23 May 2018.
26. Interview with David Henderson, 1 March 2018.
27. Quoted in Morrison, *Men of Tain*, p.11.
28. The £200 figure comes from Morrison, *Men of Tain*, p.10. By RPI, the purchasing power of 200 in 1948 is £6913 in 2017 money. On borrowing tools: Interview with Gordon Morrison, 30 January.
29. Companies House.
30. Interview with David Henderson, 1 March 2018.
31. Interview with Lawrence Allan 17 April 2018.
32. Morrison, *Men of Tain*, p.22.
33. Morrison, *Men of Tain*, pp.25–26
34. Interview with Gordon Morrison, 30 January 2018.
35. For detailed discussion of this, see N. Hayes, 'Did Manual Workers want Industrial Welfare? Canteens, Latrines and Masculinity on British Building Sites 1918–1970', *Journal of Social History*, 35, 3 (2002), pp.637–658.
36. Interview with Sir Fraser Morrison, 23 May 2018.
37. Morrison, *Men of Tain*, p.15.
38. Morrison, *Men of Tain*, pp.18–21.
39. Morrison, *Men of Tain*, pp.16–17, 74.
40. Morrison, *Men of Tain*, pp.21–22, 31–33.
41. D. Hall, *Cornerstone: a study of Britain's building industry* (London: Lawrence and Wishart, 1949), p.1. Written for the Labour Research Bureau which supports trade unions, this took the perspective of how employment should be arranged in the sector.
42. Hall, *Cornerstone*, p.1.
43. This figure is calculated from, 'Appendix A: Completed Houses – Scotland, 1919–1987', in Richard Rodger (ed.), *Scottish Housing in the Twentieth Century* (Leicester: Leicester University Press, 1989), pp.236–7. The calculation is as follows. Completions 1940–47 were 46,298 against an expected number of 193,936 if the pre-war rate (mean 1933–39 24,242) had been maintained. Given Scotland's small population, Hall's rough figure holds.
44. Begg, 'Parish of Tain', p.250. The figures are not given with any greater breakdown that this, but clearly the construction was focused on the postwar period, with one third of this total under construction in 1952.

45. Begg, 'Parish of Tain', p.251.
46. Harwood, *Space, Hope and Brutalism*, p.50.
47. Interview with Gordon Morrison, 30 January 2018.
48. See for example M. Francis, '"A Crusade to Enfranchise the May": Thatcherism and the "Property-Owning Democracy"', *Twentieth Century British History*, 23, 2 (2012), pp.289–90; P. Malpass, 'The Wobbly Pillar? Housing and the British Postwar Welfare State', *Journal of Social Policy*, 32, 4 (2003), p.589, suggests the Labour party was not good enough on housing, so the conservative view held sway; A. Davies, '"Right to Buy": The Development of a Conservative Housing Policy, 1945–1980', *Contemporary British History*, 27, 4 (2013), pp.421–44.
49. Francis, 'A Crusade to Enfranchise the Many'; D. Torrance, *Noel Skelton and the Property-owning Democracy* (London: Biteback, 2010), notes the term was first used in 1920s.
50. Morrison, *Men of Tain*, p. 56.
51. Interview with Gordon Morrison, 30 January 2018.
52. Letter from Connie Morrison, 1 April 2018.
53. Morrison, *Men of Tain*, p.14.
54. Morrison, *Men of Tain*, p.12; adjusted by earnings index at Officer and Williamson, 'Relative Value', accessed 23 July 2018. Exact figure, £1821.
55. Morrison, *Men of Tain*, p.14.
56. Morrison, *Men of Tain*, pp.45, 55; Highland Council Archive, hereafter HCA CRC/9/3/1/11, County Council Contract Book. Housing 1957–70, pp.105–6.
57. Morrison, *Men of Tain*, p.85.
58. N. Hayes, 'Making Homes by Machine: images, ideas and myths in the diffusion of non-traditional housing in Britain 1942–54', *Twentieth Century British History*, 10, 3 (1999), pp. 283, 287.
59. R. Brown, 'Designing Differently: the self–build home', *Journal of Design History*, 21, 4 (2008), p.361.
60. Harwood, *Space, Hope and Brutalism*, p.51.
61. Thornton Kennedy, MP for Aberdeen and Kincardine, Western. HC Deb 25 February 1949 vol 461, cc.2259–60.
62. HCA CRC3/1/75, Ross and Cromarty County Council, Minutes 1954–55, Property and Works Committee, 9 December 1954, pp.31–2; HCA CRC3/1/78, Ross and Cromarty County Council, Minutes 1957–58, Property and Works Committee, 20 March 1958, p.58; HCA CRC3/1/81, Ross and Cromarty County Council, Minutes 1961–62, Property and Works Committee, 19 October 1961, p.21.
63. Morrison, *Men of Tain*, pp.99–100.
64. https://www.architects-journal.co.uk/news/stroud-council-backs-down-over-swedish-houses/10026751.article; https://www.architectsjournal.co.uk/news/c20-society-urges-stroud-council-not-to-overclad-post-war-swedish-homes/10026687.article, accessed 23 July 2018.
65. The Slingsby was a later variation of the Dorran home designed and manufactured by R. Tarran 1947–51. H. Harrison, S. Mullin, B. Reeves, and A. Stevens, *Non-traditional Houses: identifying non-traditional houses in the UK 1918–75* (Watford: Building Research Establishment, 2004), suggest Dorran was precast and the Slingsby was made with

## NOTES FOR CHAPTER FOUR: GROWING SUCCESS

66. onsite moulded bricks. pp. 310–11, 934. Gordon Morrison, in *Men of Tain*, pp.57–8, suggests they were pre-cast, and Sir Fraser Morrison confirms that this is correct to his knowledge.
66. HCA CRC3/1/74, Ross and Cromarty County Council, Minutes 1953–54, Property and Works Committee, 3 September 1953, p.18; HCA CRC3/1/75, Ross and Cromarty County Council, Minutes 1954–55, Property and Works Committee, 15 June 1954, p.2; HCA CRC3/1/78, Ross and Cromarty County Council, Minutes 1957–58, Property and Works Committee, 20 March 1958, p.56; HCA CRC3/1/80, Ross and Cromarty County Council, Minutes 1959–60, Property and Works Committee, 3 December 1959, p.39.
67. I am grateful to Ian Russell archivist at Glenmorangie for having made enquiries about this.
68. G. Barr and G. Painter, 'Tain', in *Scottish Cinemas and Theatres Project*, online at http://www.scottish-cinemas.org.uk/scotland/tain.html, accessed 23 July 2018.
69. Interview with Lawrence Allan, 17 April 2018.
70. Interview with David Henderson, 1 March 2018.
71. Morrison, *Men of Tain*, pp.66–67.
72. Morrison, *Men of Tain*, pp.34–35, 69.
73. Morrison, *Men of Tain*, pp.62–3.
74. Morrison, *Men of Tain*, p.51.
75. See http://www.tainmuseum.org.uk/imagelibrary/picture/number346.asp, accessed 10 August 2018, for discussion of the Rose Garden and the sundial. Accessed 10 August 2018. The page suggests the sundial is long gone.
76. Morrison, *Men of Tain*, pp. 38–41, 57.
77. Morrison, *Men of Tain*, p.40.
78. Morrison, *Men of Tain*, pp.1, 64–5.
79. Morrison, *Men of Tain*, pp.60–61.
80. Figure inflated using GDP share of £2154 in 1959, using Officer and Williamson, 'Relative Value', accessed 13 August 2018.

### Notes for Chapter Four: Growing success

1. 'Memorandum of Association of Alexander Morrison (Builders) Limited', 28 May 1963, §III (1), pp.1–2. Document was signed and dated by Alex and Connie on 28 May, and received at Companies House three days later on 31 May 1963. Companies House (CH) records for company SC38867. Hereafter referred to as CH SC38867 and date of filing. Annual accounts were not filed until later.
2. Memorandum of Association, § III (19), p.3.
3. Interview with Lawrence Allan, 17 April 2018.
4. Interview with Lawrence Allan, 17 April 2018.
5. Interview with Lawrence Allan, 17 April 2018.
6. Morrison, *Men of Tain*, p.88.
7. Interview with Lawrence Allan, 17 April 2018.
8. Interview with Lawrence Allan, 17 April 2018.
9. C. Sirrs, 'Accidents and Apathy: the construction of the "Robens Philosophy" of occupational safety

and health regulation in Britain, 1961–1974', *Social History of Medicine*, 29, 1 (2015), p.70.
10. Sirrs, 'Accidents and Apathy', p.78.
11. Interview with Lawrence Allan, 17 April 2018.
12. http://www.hse.gov.uk/aboutus/timeline/index.htm The HSE is the 'operating arm' of the Health and Safety Commission.
13. Morrison, *Men of Tain*, pp.59–60.
14. Gordon Morrison, typescript autobiographical notes.
15. C. G. Powell, *An Economic History of the British Building Industry 1815–1979* (London: Methuen, 1982).
16. L. Paterson, 'Liberation or Control?: What are the Scottish education traditions of the twentieth century?', in T. M. Devine and R. J. Finlay, *Scotland in the Twentieth Century* (Edinburgh: EUP, 1996), p.232.
17. S. Cowan, G. McCulloch, and T. Woodin, 'From HORSA huts to ROSLA blocks: the school leaving age and the school building programme in England, 1943–1972', *History of Education* (2012), pp.361–2.
18. HCA CRC5/2/1/5 Educational Building Sub Committee of Ross and Cromarty County Council, 1962–66. Note of Meeting Held at Edinburgh on 9th January, 1964, between representatives of the County Council of Ross and Cromarty and Officials of the Scottish Education Department', p.3.
19. HCA CRC3/1/84, Ross and Cromarty County Council, Minutes 1963/64, Property and Works Committee, 24 October 1963, p.22.
20. HCA CRC3/1/86, Ross and Cromarty County Council, Minutes 1964/65, Property and Works Committee, 8 July 1965, p.6; CRC3/1/90, Minutes 1969/70, Property and Works Committee, 4 September 1969; HCA CRC5/2/4/2/43 Inver School 1969–75, 18 August 1970.
21. HCA: CRC5/2/3/2/120, School Building Programme 1969–70, Revised Cost Limits – Appendix to Circular No 753, p.1. Maximum costs were calculated based on school cost units, plus allowances for pools and games halls. Primary Schools were allowed £222, and Secondary £445.
22. HCA CRC3/1/89, Ross and Cromarty County Council, Minutes 1968/69, Property and Works Committee, 24 October 1963, p.22; 5 September 1968, p.13.
23. HCA CRC3/1/84, Ross and Cromarty County Council, Minutes 1963/64, Property and Works Committee, 24 October 1963, p.25.; 12 March 1964, p.48; 12 September 1963, p.19.
24. HCA CRC3/1/83, Ross and Cromarty County Council, Minutes 1962/63, Property and Works Committee, 16 January 1963, pp.1–2.
25. J. Gifford, *Buildings of Scotland: Highlands and Islands* (London: Penguin, 1992), p.426.
26. HCA CRC3/1/87, Ross and Cromarty County Council, Minutes 1966/67, Report of a Meeting of the Joint Sub-Committee of the Property and Works and Education Committee on School Building held at Invergordon on Friday, 11th November, 1966 at 2:30 pm', pp.1–2.
27. HCA CRC3/1/87, Ross and Cromarty County Council, Minutes 1966/67, Report of a Meeting of

## NOTES FOR CHAPTER FOUR: GROWING SUCCESS

the Joint Sub-Committee of the Property and Works and Education Committee on School Building held at Invergordon on Friday, 11th November, 1966 at 2:30 pm', p.2.

28  HCA CRC3/1/88, Ross and Cromarty County Council, Minutes 1967/68, Property and Works Committee, 9 June 1967, p.3; 2 May 1968, p.63; on Friday, 11th November, 1966 at 2:30 pm', pp.1–2.

29  HCA CRC3/1/91, Ross and Cromarty County Council, Minutes 1970/71, Property and Works Executive, 21 August 1970, p.5. The minutes do not offer any more information about the subject of the claim.

30  Interview with Sir Fraser Morrison, 23 May 2018.

31  HCA CRC/5/2/2/11/2, Ross and Cromarty County Council, Minutes of Tain and Fearn District Education Sub-Committee, 30 Mach 1960, p.1.

32  HCA CRC5/2/4/2/83, Ross and Cromarty County Council, Education Committee, Tain Royal Academy. Invitation to H. A. Rendell, Govan, 5 April 1949.

33  HCA CRC5/2/1/5, Ross and Cromarty County Council, Educational Building Sub Committee, 1962–66, Educational Building Survey 1962: report by the special Sub-committee on Education Buildings, 20 February 1962, p.37.

34  HCA CRC5/2/1/4, Ross and Cromarty County Council, Educational Building Sub Committee, Ross and Cromarty Education Authority Building Programme for 1962–5, 14 June 1962.

35  HCA CRC5/2/4/2/83, Ross and Cromarty County Council, Tain Royal Academy, Property and Works Committee, 8 September 1966, p.16.

36  HCA CRC3/1/88, Ross and Cromarty County Council, Minutes 1967/68, Property and Works Committee, 9 June 1967, p.4.

37  Interview with Sir Fraser Morrison, 23 May 2018.

38  HCA CRC5/2/4/2/83, Ross and Cromarty County Council, Education Committee, Tain Royal Academy, Invitation and Programme, Official Opening.

39  Interview with Gordon Morrison, 30 January 2018.

40  HCA CRC3/1/89, Ross and Cromarty County Council, Minutes 1968/69, Property and Works Committee, 24 October 1963, p.21; 5 December 1968, p.30; 5 September 1968, p.13.

41  HCA CRC3/1/89, Ross and Cromarty County Council, Minutes 1968/69, Property and Works Committee, 24 October 1963, p.20.

42  HCA CRC9/3/1/11, County Council Contract Book, Housing, 1957–70, pp.311–12, 377–8.

43  Interview with David Henderson, 1 March 2018.

44  Interview with David Henderson, 1 March 2018.

45  Interview with David Henderson, 1 March 2018.

46  J. Black, *A History of Britain: 1945 to Brexit* (Bloomington, IN: Indiana University Press, 2017), p.132.

47  LSE Archives SELECTION TRUST/TEMP/M/7, 'Alexander Morrison', Codrington to Directors', 22 March 1974, p.7.

48  W. W. Knox, *Industrial Nation: work, culture and society in Scotland, 1800-present* (Edinburgh: Edinburgh University Press, 1999), p.254.

49 M. Dupree, 'Foreshadowing the Future: health services in remote areas, the National Health Service and the Highlands and Islands of Scotland, 1948–74, in J. T. H. Connor and S. Curtis (eds), *Medicine in the Remote and Rural North, 1800–2000* (Routledge, 2011), p.75. For the more traditional view see W. Finnie, 'Scotland's proto-NHS: the Highland and Islands Medical Service', *Juridical Review*, 1 (1994), pp.78–96.

50 S. Newton, *The Reinvention of Britain 1960–2016: a political and economic history* (London: Routledge, 2018), pp.24–25.

51 HCA D204/5/1/1/2 Moray Firth Development: a growth plan for costal burghs: progress report. June 1967. Jack Holmes Planning Group.

52 F. Wellings, *British Housebuilders: History and Analysis* (Oxford: Wiley-Blackwell, 2006), pp.7–8.

53 Interview with Donald MacLennan, 10 February 2018.

54 HCA CRC3/1/85, Ross and Cromarty County Council, Minutes, Property and Works Committee, 9 July 1964, p.6. Figures are rounded to the nearest pound.

55 Department of Agriculture and Fisheries for Scotland, *Agriculture in Scotland: Report for 1966* (Edinburgh, 1967 [Cmd. 3214], pp.43–44. There were other schemes too, such as the Horticulture Improvement Scheme, which included 'the erection of production buildings', p.46.

56 Ferocious historical debate has raged on this matter. The most readable, but rather dated book is J. Prebble, *The Highland Clearances* (various editions e.g. London, 1982). E. Richards offers good modern accounts, and in particular *Patrick Sellar and the Highland Clearances: homicide, eviction, and the Highland Clearances* (East Edinburgh 1999), on the Sutherland estate's clearances.

57 I. Levitt, 'The Creation of the Highlands and Islands Development Board, 1935–65', *Northern Scotland*, 19 (1999), pp.86–87.

58 Levitt, 'The Creation of the Highlands and Islands Development Board', p.91; E. A. Cameron, 'The Scottish Highlands as a Special Policy Area, 1886 to 1965', *Rural History*, 8, 2 (1997), pp.195, 201.

59 Levitt, 'The Creation of the Highlands and Islands Development Board', p.101.

60 I. Levitt '"Taking a Gamble": the Scottish Office, Whitehall and the Highlands and Islands Development Board, 1965–67', *Northern Scotland*, 20 (2000), p.88

61 C. H. Lee, *Scotland and the United Kingdom: the Economy and the Union in the Twentieth Century* (Manchester: MUP, 1995) p.156, Cameron, 'Scottish Highlands as a Special Policy Area', pp.208–209.

62 Levitt, 'Taking a Gamble', pp.91–92.

63 Morrison, *Men of Tain*, pp.69–71, 89–90, 83–4.

64 R. H. Campbell, 'The Agricultural Revolution of the Twentieth Century', *Scottish Archives*, 1 (1995), p.55.

65 Campbell, 'The Agricultural Revolution of the Twentieth Century', pp.55, 57–58.

66 Board of Agriculture report CMD 3214 (1967).

67 Morrison, *Men of Tain*, pp. 50–51, 54.

68 Morrison, *Men of Tain*, p.72.

69 Interview with Lawrence Allan, 17 April 2018.

NOTES FOR CHAPTER FOUR: GROWING SUCCESS

70  Interview with Lawrence Allan, 17 April 2018.
71  Interview with David Henderson, 1 March 2018.
72  Interview with Gordon Morrison, 20 January 2018.
73  J. S. Smith, 'The Invergordon Aluminium Smelter: growth policy gone wrong? A note', *Scottish Geographical Magazine*, 98, 2 (1982), p.115; Gifford, *Buildings of Scotland: Highlands and Islands* (London: Penguin, 1992), p. 426.
74  G. A. Mackay, *A Study of the Economic Impact of the Invergordon Aluminium Smelter* (HIDB, special report 15, place of publication not given, 1978), p.5.
75  Mackay, *Impact of the Invergordon Aluminium Smelter*, p.86.
76  Smith, 'Invergordon Aluminium Smelter', pp.115–7.
77  Interview with Gordon Morrison, 30 January 2018. For detail and broader context see A. Perchard, *Aluminiumville: global business and the Scottish Highlands* (Crucible, 2012).
78  Ferguson and Chrimes, *Contractors*, p.89.
79  LSE Archives SELECTION TRUST/TEMP/M/7 Assessment of the Market and Competition for Quarried Products in the Cromarty Firth Area, p.1.
80  LSE Archives SELECTION TRUST/TEMP/M/7 Assessment of the Market, pp.1–3.
81  LSE Archives SELECTION TRUST/TEMP/M/7 Assessment of the Market, undated but c. March 1974, p.3.
82  LSE Archives SELECTION TRUST/ADD/26. 'Speech by Mr A. Chester Beatty at the Annual General Meeting of Selection Trust Limited on 18 July 1973'.
83  LSE Archives SELECTION TRUST/TEMP/M/7 Alexander Morrison. H. J. Codrington to Alexander Morrison, 22 February 1974, p.1.
84  SELECTION TRUST/TEMP/M/7. 'Alexander Morrison (Builders) Ltd, Tain', H. J. Codrington to Directors of CAST, 22 March 1974, p.7.
85  Interview with Sir Fraser Morrison, 23 May 2018.
86  SELECTION TRUST/TEMP/M/7. 'Alexander Morrison (Builders) Ltd, Tain', H. J. Codrington to Directors of CAST, 22 March 1974, p.1.
87  SELECTION TRUST/TEMP/M/7, 'Alexander Morrison', Codrington to Directors', 22 March 1974, p.1.
88  SELECTION TRUST/TEMP/M/7, 'Alexander Morrison', Codrington to Directors', 22 March 1974, p.2.
89  SELECTION TRUST/TEMP/M/7, 'Alexander Morrison', Codrington to Directors', 22 March 1974, p.4.
90  SELECTION TRUST/TEMP/M/7, 'Alexander Morrison', Codrington to Directors', 22 March 1974, p.6.
91  Interview with Hugh England, 20 June 2018.
92  Interview with Sir Fraser Morrison, 23 May 2018.
93  SELECTION TRUST/TEMP/M/7. Codrington to AM, 22 February 1974, p.2.
94  SELECTION TRUST/TEMP/M/7. Codrington to AM, 22 February 1974, pp.2–3.
95  Morrison, *Men of Tain*, pp.96–97.
96  Interview with Gordon Morrison, 20 January 2018.
97  Interview with Gordon Morrison, 20 January 2018.
98  Morrison, *Men of Tain*, pp.91–92.
99  Morrison, *Men of Tain*, p.88.

100. It might be noted that it is only profitable due to the extent of negative externalities, and the notion of such profits should be understood in such terms.
101. SELECTION TRUST/TEMP/M/7, 'Alexander Morrison', Codrington to Directors', 22 March 1974, p.5.
102. Interview with Gordon Morrison, 20 January 2018.
103. Morrison, *Men of Tain* pp.92–6.
104. Interview with Gordon Morrison, 20 January 2018.
105. Interview with Hugh England, 20 June 2018.
106. Interview with David Henderson, 1 March 2018.

## Notes for Chapter Five: Building capacities

1. Interview with Stewart MacLeod, 22 February 2018; interview with Sir Fraser Morrison, 23 May 2018.
2. Interview with Stewart MacLeod, 22 February 2018.
3. Interview with Sir Fraser Morrison, 23 May 2018.
4. Interview with Ron McGraw, 26 April 2018.
5. Interview with Allan Russell, 19 April 2018.
6. Interview with Donald MacLennan, 10 February 2018.
7. Interview with Hugh England, 20 June 2018.
8. Interview with Hugh England, 20 June 2018.
9. Interview with Ken Gillespie, 2 February 2018.
10. Interview with Michael Martin, 19 April 2018.
11. 'Morrison Move into North East Scotland', *Morrison News*, 2 (April 1981), p.3.
12. 'Edinburgh Office Opens', *Morrison News*, 8 (August 1983), p.1.
13. 'New Glasgow Office for Morrison Group', *Morrison News*, 5 (August/September 1982), p.2.
14. 'Party Marks Opening of Group Edinburgh Office', *Morrison News*, 9 (December 1983), p.1.
15. Interview with John Morrison, 21 February 2018.
16. Interview with Stewart MacLeod, 22 February 2018.
17. Interview with Stewart MacLeod, 22 February 2018.
18. J. Bamberg, *British Petroleum and Global Oil, 1950–1975: the challenge of nationalism* (Cambridge: Cambridge University Press, 2000), pp.195–6.
19. Cameron, *Impaled upon a Thistle*, p.251.
20. Bamberg, *British Petroleum*, p.212.
21. D. Newlands, 'The Oil Economy', in W. Hamish Fraser and C. H. Lee (eds), *Aberdeen 1800–2000: a new history* (East Linton: Tuckwell, 2000), pp.135–6. Newlands also notes: 'paucity of good statistics relevant to the impact of oil on the Aberdeen area', p.133.
22. C. M. M. McDonald, *Whaur Extremes Meet: Scotland's twentieth century* (Edinburgh: John Donald, 2009), p.76.
23. B. Mackie, *The Klondykers: the oil men onshore* (Edinburgh, Birlinn, 2006), pp.91–7.
24. H. Ryggvik, *The Norwegian Oil Experience: a toolbox for managing resources?* (Oslo: Centre for

## NOTES FOR CHAPTER FIVE: BUILDING CAPACITIES

Technology, Innovation and Culture, 2010). For price see: https://www.nbim.no/en/the-fund/market-value/, accessed 5 January 2019.
25 Interview with Dan MacDonald, 23 February 2018.
26 Interview with Gordon Morrison, 30 January 2018.
27 HRA D204/8/1/1/12. G. A. Mackay, 'A Study of the economic Impact of the Invergordon Aluminium Smleter', (HIDB special report 15, no place given, 1978), p.86.
28 Interview with Lawrence Allan, 17 April 2018.
29 Gordon Morrison, typescript autobiographical notes.
30 Gordon Morrison, typescript autobiographical notes.
31 Interview with Sir Fraser Morrison, 23 May 2018.
32 I. Hargreaves, 'Enterprise Oil begins to draw up its North Sea Shopping List', *FT* (13 December 1983), p.7c.
33 Interview with Gordon Morrison, 30 January 2018.
34 'Takeover of CFE Now Complete', *Morrison News*, 9 (December 1983), p.1.
35 'Cromarty Firth Engineering', *Morrison News*, 12 (November 1984), p.3.
36 Interview with John Morrison, 21 February 2018.
37 Interview with Gordon Morrison, 30 January 2018.
38 Interview with Sir Fraser Morrison, 23 May 2018.
39 Interview with Pamela McKay, 8 May 2018.
40 Cameron, *Impaled upon a Thistle*, p.242.
41 Interview with Donald MacLennan, 10 February 2018.
42 'Building for the Industries of the North', *Morrison News*, 2 (April 1981), p.5.
43 'A new Engineering Division for the Morrison Group', *Morrison News*, 5 (October 1982), p.5.
44 Ferguson and Chrimes, *Contractors*, p.93.
45 C. H. Lee, *Scotland and the United Kingdom: the economy and the Union in the twentieth century* (Manchester: MUP, 1995), p.7.
46 R. Hudson, 'Thatcherism and its geographical legacies: the new map of socio-spatial inequality in the Divided Kingdom', *The Geographical Journal*, 179, 4 (2013), pp.377–81; Cameron, *Impaled upon a Thistle*, p.250.
47 Cameron, *Impaled upon a Thistle*, pp.245–6.
48 A point of departure into this is found in the special number of *British Politics*, 10, 1 (2015): '25 years on…the legacy of Thatcher and Thatcherism'.
49 D. Towey, *Construction Quantity Surveying: a practical guide for the contractor's QS*, 2$^{nd}$ edition (Chichester: John Wiley and Son, 2018), p.295.
50 Note from Roger Croson, 20 December 2018.
51 Interview with Roger Croson, 9 February 2018.
52 Based on timeline from John Morrison, former Company Secretary.
53 Interview with Lawrence Allan, 17 April 2018.
54 Interview with Sir Fraser Morrison, 23 May 2018.
55 Interview with Hugh England, 20 June 2018.
56 'Caledonian Canal Project', *Morrison News*, 1 (December 1980), p.6.
57 'Sill Replacements to Caledonian

Canal Locks', *Morrison News*, 10 (March 1984), p.2. For detail on the works see D. J. Cochrane, 'Caledonian Canal – repairs to locks at Fort Augustus', *Proceedings of the Institution of Civil Engineers*, part one, 80 (1986), pp.1363–83.

58 'Reservoir Complete at Bridge of Don', *Morrison News*, 6 (December 1982), p.5, suggests dimensions of '30 metres square', presumably meaning 27,000m$^3$ Another example of this kind of work was another reservoir at Cults. 'Tapping the Waters of the Dee', *Morrison News*, 7 (April 1983), p.5.
59 'Coastal Protection at Fort George', *Morrison News*, 7 (April 1983), p.4.
60 'Urgent Sea Wall at Banff', *Morrison News*, 8 (August 1983), p.4.
61 Newlands, 'The Oil Economy', pp.129, 136.
62 'Morrison at Aberdeen Airport', *Morrison News*, 9 (December 1983), p.5.
63 'Morrison at Aberdeen Airport', *Morrison News*, 9 (December 1983), p.5.
64 Interview with Roger Croson, 9 February 2018.
65 Interview with Roger Croson, 9 February 2018.
66 'Morrison Construction Stays Ahead with another stretch of the A94 open well before schedule', *Morrison News*, 6 (December 1982), p.5.
67 'Reshaping the Map', *Morrison News*, 4 (April 1981), p.4.
68 'Changing the Face of the North: North East Region: Major Projects including the Elgin Relief Road', 'Reshaping the Map', *Morrison News*, 4 (April 1981), p.4.
69 'Morrison win Perth Bypass contract', *Morrison News*, 10 (March 1984), p.6.
70 'Major Bridge Contract for Morrison Construction', *Morrison News*, 5 (August 1982), p.1.
71 Interview with Michael Martin, 19 April 2018.
72 Interview with Michael Martin, 19 April 2018.
73 Interview with Michael Martin, 19 April 2018.
74 Interview with Michael Martin, 19 April 2018.
75 Interview with Stewart MacLeod, 22 February 2018; a similar point made in interview with Roger Croson 9 February 2018.
76 'Report from Kylesku', *Morrison News*, 6 (November 1982), p.4.
77 Interview with Gordon Morrison, 30 January 2018.
78 Interview with Stewart MacLeod, 22 February 2018; and interview with Roger Croson, 9 February 2018, plus written notes.
79 Interview with Michael Martin, 19 April 2018.
80 Interview with David Jeffs, 2 March 2018.
81 Interview with Hugh England, 20 June 2018.
82 Interview with Sir Fraser Morrison, 23 May 2018.
83 For example, a special number of *Morrison News*, 11 (July 1984).
84 See for example J. R. and M. M. Gold, *Imagining Scotland: Tradition, Representation and Promotion in Scottish Tourism Since 1750* (Routledge, 1995).
85 Interview with Roger Croson, 9 February 2018.
86 HCA CS/5/5/47/d Durness Scrapbook of Opening of Kylesku, unpaginated.
87 Interview with Roger Croson, 9 February 2018.
88 http://portal.historicenvironment.

## NOTES FOR CHAPTER FIVE: BUILDING CAPACITIES

scot/designation/LB52497 accessed 15 February 2019.
89  'Minor Works: a new concept', *Morrison News*, 7 (April 1983), p.4.
90  'Important Developments from Engineering Department', *Morrison News*, 7 (April 1983), p.2.
91  'You Need MORESPACE', *Morrison News*, 2 (April 1981), p.2.
92  Morrison 'A' Frame Chalets: a lucrative investment in the self catering holiday boom', *Morrison News*, 1 (December 1980), pp.3–4.
93  'Morrison Building North East', *Morrison News*, 8 (August 1983), p.3.
94  'Housing Association Works', *Morrison News*, 2 (February 1982), p.20.
95  'Key to Garnett Hill', *Morrison News*, 11 (July 1984), p.3.
96  'Morrison Homes: Autumn feature', *Morrison News*, 5 (August/September 1982), p.5.
97  'News on the Homes Front'; 'Champagne and Christian Aid', *Morrison News*, 8 (August 1983), p.2.
98  'Orkney Housing: efficiency pays dividends', *Morrison News*, 10 (March 1984), p.6.
99  'Morrison Homes in Central Scotland', *Morrison News*, 6 (December 1982), p.3.
100  'Advance of Homes', *Morrison News*, 10 (March 1984), p.6.
101  'Bellahouston Handover', *Morrison News*, 4 (February 1982), p.5.
102  'Building for the Industries of the North', *Morrison News*, 2 (April 1981), p.5.
103  Interview with Donald MacLennan, 10 February 2018.
104  '1983 Superstore now underway', *Morrison News*, 6 (December 1982), p.1.
105  'Superstore Stays in Front', *Morrison News* (April 1983), p.6.
106  'Superstore Handover: Inverness Co-op completed ahead of schedule', *Morrison News*, 9 (December 1983), p.6.
107  J. F. Wilson, A. Webster & R. Vorberg-Rugh; *Building Co-operation: a business history of the Co-operative Group, 1863–2013* (Oxford, 2013), p.294.
108  'New Public Buildings in the Highlands', *Morrison News*, 5 (August/September 1982), p.6.
109  'Linwood Factory for SDA', *Morrison News* (July 1984), p.3.
110  The company also built an extension to 'Perth Grammar School', *Morrison News*, 2 (April 1981), p.6, and the new £2.3m Arbroath High School, as well as a swimming pool on an adjacent site for £840,000, 'Arbroath Progress on Pool and School', *Morrison News*, 10 (March 1984), p.5; 'Arbroath High School takes shape', *Morrison News* 12 (1984), p.1.
111  'New Academy at Culloden: major educational building project for Morrison', *Morrison News*, 2 (April 1981), p.1; 'Culloden Opens for Autumn Term', *Morrison News*, 5 (August/September 1982), p.4.
112  'Art Award at Culloden', *Morrison News*, 10 (March 1984), p.2.
113  Interview with Donald MacLennan, 10 February 2018.
114  'Community School for Barra', *Morrison News*, 5 (August/September 1982), p.4.
115  'Morrison Plant and Transport', *Morrison News*, 3 (September 1981), p.2.
116  Interview with David Jeffs, 2 March 2018.
117  Alasdair MacKay quoted in 'Winning the Raw Materials of Construction', *Morrison News*, 2 (April 1981), p.2.

118 'Imported Cement Gives Morrison Quarries the Edge', *Morrison News*, 7 (April 1983), p.6.
119 'New Quarry Network', *Morrison News*, 8 (August 1983), p.2.
120 'Aggregates Shipped Out', *Morrison News*, 11 (July 1984), p.2.
121 Newlands, 'The Oil Economy', p.129.
122 'Morrison Developments', *Morrison News*, 3 (September 1981), p.6.
123 'Morrison Developments', *Morrison News*, 3 (September 1981), p.6.
124 'Morrison Developments: make going to the office a pleasure!', *Morrison News*, 6 (December 1982), p.2.
125 'More News from Carden Place', *Morrison News*, 8 (August, 1983), p.6.
126 Interview with Dan MacDonald, 23 February 2018.
127 'Developments in Scotland', *Morrison News*, 12 (November 1984), p.5.
128 'Latest Property Development at Byres Road in Glasgow', *Morrison News*, 9 (December 1983), p.2.
129 Interview with Dan MacDonald, 23 February 2018.
130 'Morrison Developments: Current and Recent Projects', *Morrison News*, 10 (March 1984), p.10.
131 LSE Archives SELECTION TRUST/ADD/2 Box 2 File 2: British Petroleum Take-over 1980. To all members of group from Chairman John du Cane, 7 July 1980, p.1.
132 'Charter Consolidated Ltd. New Ultimate Holding Company for Morrison Construction Group', *Morrison News*, 2 (April 1981), p.1.
133 'Group Founder Retires', *Morrison News*, 11 (July 1984), p.1.
134 Interview with Donald MacLennan, 10 February 2018.
135 S. M. Davis, 'Entrepreneurial Succession', *Administrative Science Quarterly*, 13 (1968), p.407, quoted in C. Howorth, M. Rose and E. Hamilton, 'Definitions, Diversity and Development: key debates in family business research', in A. Basu, M. Casson. N. Wadeson, and B. Yeung (eds), *The Oxford Handbook of Entrepreneurship* (Oxford: OUP, 2008), p.226. Bracketed addition Howorth, Rose and Hamilton's.
136 Interview with Donald MacLennan, 10 February 2018.
137 Interview with John Morrison, 21 February 2018.
138 Interview with Roger Croson, 9 February 2018.
139 Interview with Roger Croson, 9 February 2018.
140 Interview with Ken Tallant, 16 May 2018.
141 Interview with Stewart MacLeod, 22 February 2018.
142 Interview with Gordon Morrison, 30 January 2018.
143 'Group Success Brings Change', *Morrison News*, 7 (April 1983), p.2.
144 As examples: 'Manpower for the future', *Morrison News*, 6 (November, 1982), p.6; 'Site Sage '83 – Accidents don't happen – they are caused', *Morrison News*, 7 (April 1983), p.5.

## Notes for Chapter Six: Opportunities beyond the Highlands

1. 'Move to City for Group HQ', *Morrison News*, 15 (May 1986), p.1.
2. 'Morrison Make Capital Move', *Morrison News*, 16 (November 1986), p.1.
3. Royal Scottish Academy Archives, Edinburgh, hereafter RSA. File 150: Morrison Prize. Michael Fraser to Sir Anthony Wheeler, 12 February 1988, p.1.
4. The exhibition catalogue notes 'The exhibition has received generous financial support from the Morrison Construction Group', with the "M" logo. Helen Smailes and Duncan Thomson, *The Queen's Image: a celebration of Mary, Queen of Scots* (Edinburgh: Scottish National Portrait Gallery, 1987), copyright page. Exhibition 9 July to 18 October 1987.
5. Interview with Pam MacKay, 8 May 2018.
6. Morrison Scottish Portrait Award files, Royal Scottish Academy of Art & Architecture archives. Hereafter RSA. Michael Fraser to Sir Anthony Wheeler, 12 February 1988, p.2.
7. 'Scottish Portrait Award impresses the art critics', *Morrison News*, 23 (December 1989), p.8; RSA. Morrison Prize. Press Release, 13 October 1989.
8. RSA. Morrison Prize. James Stuart of Michael Fraser Associates to Sir Anthony Wheeler'.
9. Original is in capitals. RSA. Morrison Prize. From Joyce Cairns to William Meikle. n.d., p.1.
10. '1991 Portrait Award', *Morrison News*, 29 (Winter 1991) p.3.
11. RSA. Morrison Prize. Jean Watson, PA to Fraser Morrison to William Meikle, 7 August 1991; Memorandum, n.d.
12. Interview with Stewart MacLeod, 22 February 2018.
13. RSA. Morrison Prize. William Meikle to Michael Fraser, 10 March 1992.
14. RSA. Morrison Prize. Memorandum from Jeffrey Robinson, 8 September 1993.
15. RSA. Morrison Prize. Memorandum, n.d.; from Jeffrey W. Robinson to Fionn Carlisle, 19 November 1993.
16. RSA. Morrison Prize. RSA Press release, 19 October 1995; List of Prize Winners, 26 September 1997.
17. RSA. Morrison Prize. Margaret A. Wilson to David Watt, 22 September 1999.
18. RSA. Morrison Prize. Memorandum, n.d; Jennifer McRae to Ian McKenzie Smith, 3 October 1999.
19. Interview with Sir Fraser Morrison, 23 May 2018.
20. '…And opening a new office', *Morrison News*, 27 (Spring 1991), p.2.
21. *Morrison Group Review* (Morrison, n.d., c. 1987), p.3.
22. Fraser Morrison, 'Chairman's Statement', *Morrison Group Annual Report 1991* (Morrison, 1991), p.2; the older structure is giving in Fraser Morrison, 'Chairman's Statement', *Morrison Group Annual Report 1990* (Morrison, 1990), p.2.
23. Fraser Morrison, 'The Way Ahead', *Morrison Group Review* (Morrison, n.d., c. 1987), p.1.
24. Interview with Jim Arnold, 3 April 2018.
25. Interview with Hugh England, 20 June 2018.

26 Interview with Ian Cusden, 8 March 2018.
27 Interview with Peter Heathershaw, 17 May 2018.
28 Interview with Ian Cusden, 8 March 2018.
29 Interview with Stewart MacLeod, 22 February 2018.
30 B. Popplewell and A. Wildsmith, *Becoming the Best: How to gain Company-wide commitment to total quality* (Aldershot: Gower, 1988).
31 Y. Kondo, 'Emphases of Japanese Total Quality Management in the 1980s', *Total Quality Management*, 1 (1990), p.23.
32 Gordon Morrison, 'Spreading the New Culture', *Morrison News*, 39 (Spring 1995), p.8.
33 Interview with Ken Gillespie, 2 February 2018.
34 G. K. Kanji, 'Total Quality Management: the second industrial revolution', *Total Quality Management*, 1, 1 (1990), p.4.
35 Anon., 'Morrison's 18-Hole Scorecard', *Measuring Business Excellence*, 2, 2 (1998), p.10.
36 Memorandum from Roger Croson to Liz Urquhart, 30 July 1987, p.5. Copy from Liz Urquhart.
37 Interview with Ken Tallant, 16 May 2018.
38 Interview with Ian MacKay, 18 April 2018.
39 Interview with Stewart MacLeod, 22 February 2018.
40 'Mission Statement', *Annual Report* (Morrison, 1993), p.1.
41 Interview with Charles Morrison, 28 February 2018.
42 Norman MacLennan, 'Building and Property Development Division', *Annual Report* (Morrison, 1991), p.9.
43 Fraser Morrison, 'Chairman's Statement', *Annual Report* (Morrison, 1990), p.3.
44 Fraser Morrison, 'Chairman's Statement', *Annual Report* (Morrison, 1991), p.2.
45 'Quality Wins', *Morrison News*, 36 (Spring 1994), pp.1, 3; Fraser Morrison, 'Chairman's Statement', *Annual Report* (Morrison, 1994), p.4.
46 'Posters make the quality point', *Morrison News*, 19 (May 1988), pp.4–5.
47 Stewart MacLeod, 'Quality Improvement Programmes: new life for a Morrison tradition: quality marks route to further success', *Morrison News*, 19 (May 1988), p.4.
48 Interview with Sir Fraser Morrison, 23 May 2018.
49 Interview with Sir Fraser Morrison, 23 May 2018.
50 Interview with Michael Martin, 19 April 2018.
51 Interview with Adam Gosnold, 8 March 2018.
52 'Morrison Show the Way to Quality at Work', *Morrison News*, 20 (November 1988), p.3.
53 Interview with Adam Gosnold, 8 March 2018.
54 Interview with Andrew Aldred, 4 April 2018.
55 Hamish Robertson quoted in anon., 'Morrison's 18-Hole Scorecard', *Measuring Business Excellence*, 2, 2 (1998), p.10.
56 Interview with Ken Gillespie, 2 February 2018. For detailed discussion of what the metrics were and the basis of the measure see, J. Somerville and H. W. Robertson, 'A Scorecard Approach to Benchmarking for Total Quality Construction', *International Journal of Quality and Reliability*

## NOTES FOR CHAPTER SIX: OPPORTUNITIES BEYOND THE HIGHLANDS

*Management*, 17, 4–5 (2000), pp.453–466.

57 Interview with Stewart MacLeod, 22 February 2018.
58 'Suppliers Soiree', *Morrison Construction*, 30 (Spring 1992), p.8.
59 'Meanwhile in Edinburgh', *Morrison News*, 39 (Spring 1995), p.1.
60 Interview with Dan MacDonald, 23 February 2018.
61 'Prestige Plaza', *Morrison News*, 37 (Summer 1994), p.4.
62 Inflated using Measuring Worth, by GDP share.
63 'Vision of the Future', *Morrison News*, 37 (Summer 1994).
64 Keith Howell, 'Operating Review', *Morrison Annual Report 1999* (Morrison, 1999), p.5.
65 *The Times* (3 December 1997), p.30.
66 A highly readable account is offered in W. R. Polk and W. J. Mares, *Passing Brave* (New York: Alfred A. Knopf, 1973).
67 Interview with Roger Croson, 9 February 2018. It is harder to date this, but Primakov was Prime Minister for only a short period September 1998 to May 1999.
68 Interview with Michael Martin, 19 April 2018.
69 Interview with Sir Fraser Morrison, 23 May 2018.
70 Interview with Andrew Aldred, 4 April 2018.
71 Interview with Dan Macdonald, 23 February 2018.
72 Interview with Dan Macdonald, 23 February 2018.
73 'From Russia with…', *Morrison News*, 35 (Autumn 1993), p.1.
74 'The Kylesku Connection', *Morrison News*, 39 (Spring 1995), p.10.
75 Interview with Dan Macdonald, 23 February 2018.
76 Norman MacLennan, 'Building and Property Division', *Annual Report 1993* (Morrison, 1993), p.5.
77 Norman MacLennan, 'Building and Property Division', *Annual Report 1993* (Morrison, 1993), p.5.
78 'Eastern Promise', *Morrison News*, 31 (Summer 1992), p.1.
79 Interview with Ian Smith, 25 April 2018.
80 Interview with Ken Tallant, 16 May 2018.
81 Interview with Ken Tallant, 16 May 2018.
82 Interview with Roger Croson, 9 February 2018.
83 Interview with Ken Tallant, 16 May 2018.
84 Interview with John Morrison, 21 February 2018.
85 Interview with Ken Tallant, 16 May 2018.
86 'Quickly into Kuwait', *Morrison News*, 28 (Summer 1991), p.1; interview with Allan Russell.
87 'Success in the Sun', *Morrison News*, 29 (Winter 1991), p.1.
88 S. Gall, *A Year in Kuwait* (Edinburgh: Morrison, 1992), p.17.
89 Gall, *A Year in Kuwait*, pp.7, 19–20.
90 Interview with Ken Tallant, 16 May 2018.
91 Gall, *A Year in Kuwait*, p.17.
92 Interview with Allan Russell, 19 April 2018.
93 Interview with Stuart Higgins, 18 April 2018.
94 Gall, *A Year in Kuwait*, p.27.
95 Interview with Ken Tallant, 16 May 2018.
96 Roger Croson, 'Civil Engineering Division', *Annual Report 1991* (Morrison, 1991), p.7.
97 Gall, *A Year in Kuwait*, p.25.
98 Interview with John Morrison, 21 February 2018.

99. Interview with John Morrison, 21 February 2018.
100. Fraser Morrison, 'Chairman's Statement', *Annual Report 1991* (Morrison, 1991), p.2.
101. Roger Croson, 'Civil Engineering Division', *Annual Report 1993* (Morrison, 1993), p.7.
102. Interview with Sir Fraser Morrison, 23 May 2018.
103. 'Building and Property Development', *Annual Report 1994* (Morrison, 1994), p.7.
104. 'Morrison Flies the Flag in Post-War Gulf Project', *Morrison News*, 28 (Summer 1991), p.3.
105. 'Home Sales Improve', *Morrison News*, 13 (April 1985), p.6.
106. E.g. 1991 was poor but not so bad for Scotland. Alistair McDougall, 'Housing Division', *Annual Report 1991* (Morrison, 1991), p.13.)
107. 'Homes Confident', *Morrison News*, 14 (October 1985) p.6.
108. 'Homes sign Rupert', *Morrison News*, 15 (May 1986), p.8.
109. 'Homes sign Rupert', *Morrison News*, 15 (May 1986), p.8.
110. 'Housing', *Annual Report 1994* (Morrison, 1994), p.13.
111. 'Report on Morrison Building', *Annual Report 1990* (Morrison, 1990), p.5.
112. 'Highland complete high standard housing', *Morrison News*, 18 (December 1987), p.3.
113. 'Home Sweet Homes', *Morrison News*, 33 (Spring 1993), p.3
114. Alistair McDougall, 'Housing', *Annual Report* (Morrison, 1993), p.10.
115. 'Developments at Chester City FC, *Morrison News*, 24 (Spring 1990), p.1.
116. S. Mansley, 'Nowhere to Go', *Chester City Supports Club Southern Branch*, 69 (April 1990), p.1.
117. Mansley, 'Nowhere to Go', p.1.
118. Norman MacLennan, 'Building and Property Division', *Annual Report 1993* (Morrison, 1993), p.5. *The Hillsborough Stadium Disaster 15 April 1989: Inquiry by the Rt Hon Lord Justice Taylor: Final report* (London: HMSO, cmd 962, 1990), pp.76–79.
119. Chester sees the future', *Morrison News*, 28 (Summer 1991), p.1.
120. Interview with Sir Fraser Morrison, 23 May 2018.
121. 'Parking a-plenty as Park Progresses', *Morrison News*, 33 (Spring 1993), p.4.
122. 'Italian Request', *Morrison News*, 13 (April 1985), p.3.
123. 'Kylesku on Show', *Morrison News*, 13 (April 1985), p.6.
124. 'Civic Trust Awards', *Morrison News*, 17 (June 1987), p.5.
125. Reay D. G. Clarke, P. Hunter Gordon, and John. J. Smith, *The Crossing of the Three Firths* (Self-published pamphlet, 1969), printed at a cost of £77.7.6 of their own money. HCA D96/1 Crossing of the 3 Firths Radio Programme; HCA D927/1/1 Crossing of the Three Firths; HCA D923/1/4, 'Three Firths Plan "interesting" but Board back round route to North', *Highland News and Northern Chronicle* (30 October 1969), p.1.
126. 'Dornoch Bridge will attract World Interest', *Morrison News*, 19 (May 1988), p.1.
127. 'Joint Venture Bids for Dornoch Bridge', *Morrison News*, 17 (June 1987), p.3; also 'Joint Venture Combines Wealth of Experience', *Morrison News*, 23 (May 1988), p.1.

NOTES FOR CHAPTER SIX: OPPORTUNITIES BEYOND THE HIGHLANDS

128 Fraser Morrison, 'The Last Word', *Morrison News*, 19 (May 1988), p.8.
129 Interview with Ron McGraw, 26 April 2018.
130 'Piling Begins at Dornoch Firth Bridge', *Morrison News*, 23 (December 1989), p.9.
131 Roger Croson, 'Engineering Division', *Morrison Annual Report 1991* (Morrison, 1991), p.11.
132 Interview with Stuart Higgins, 18 April 2018.
133 Interview with Michael Martin, 19 April 2018.
134 'Hands Across the Firth', *Morrison News*, 28 (Summer 1991), p.2; Roger Croson, 'Engineering Division', *Morrison Annual Report 1991* (Morrison, 1991), p.7.
135 Roger Croson, 'Engineering Division', *Morrison Annual Report 1991* (Morrison, 1991), p.7.
136 Interview with Liz Urquhart, 18 April 2018.
137 Reprinted in 'Goodbye, Good bye, it's time to say Good Buy', *Morrison News*, 30 (Spring 1992), p.8.
138 Roger Croson, 'Civil Engineering', *Morrison Annual Report 1993* (Morrison, 1993), p.7.
139 S. Montague, 'Casting for a Long Run', *New Civil Engineer* (21 June 1990), p.21.
140 C. M. MacDonald, *Whaur Extremes Meet: Scotland's Twentieth Century* (Edinburgh: John Donald, 2009), p.77.
141 'Offshore Initiative: Morrison joins forces with Howard Doris', *Morrison News*, 15 (May 1986), p.1.
142 'Cromarty Dock shows Faith in the Future', *Morrison News*, 16 (November 1986), p.7; 'Healthier Prospects for CFE', *Morrison News*, 17 (June 1987), p.2; Fraser Morrison, 'The Way Ahead', *Group Review* (1986/7), p.1.
143 Interview with Ian MacKay, 18 April 2018.
144 'Major Leisure Centre for Strathclyde', *Morrison News*, 13 (April 1985), p.5; 'Paisley Planners Cater for All in Wet Sports Complex', *Morrison News*, 14 (October 1985), p.3.
145 'Perth Bypass Opens Five Months Early', *Morrison News*, 14 (October 1985), p.1.
146 'Cobble Stones win Export Markets', *Morrison News*, 13 (April 1985), p.6.
147 'Small Works Business Grows in the Highlands', *Morrison News*, 16 (November 1986), p.2.
148 'CWS Alliance Strengthens', *Morrison News*, 13 (April 1985), p.5.
149 'Forres Supermarket', *Morrison News*, 14 (October 1985), p.3.
150 'Morrison win Fifth Store Contract from Co-op', *Morrison News*, 15 (May 1986), p.4.
151 'Morrison Skills Help Booming Inverness', *Morrison News*, 22 (August 1989), p.8.
152 Quoted in 'Family Buyout Creates a Strong Base for UK Expansion', *Morrison News*, 21 (March 1989), p.1; a neat summary is contained in Gall, *A Year in Kuwait*, p.18.
153 Anonymous, *Biggs Wall: Centenary 1884–1984: 100 years' service in the construction industry* (Arlesey: Biggs Wall Group, 1984), pp.1–2.
154 Gordon Morrison, typescript autobiographical notes.
155 Gordon Morrison, typescript autobiographical notes.
156 http://www.mgroupservices.com/about-us/our-financial-highlights/ accessed 6 December 2018.

*Notes for Chapter Seven: The Morrison Approach*

1. 'London Share Service', *Financial Times* (14 November 1998), p.20.
2. Interview with Charles Morrison, 28 February 2018.
3. Interview with Allan Russell, 19 April 2018.
4. Interview with Dan MacDonald, 23 February 2018.
5. Interview with Stewart MacLeod, 22 February 2018.
6. Interview with Pam Mackay, 8 May 2018.
7. Interview with David Henderson, 1 March 2018.
8. Interview with Donald MacLennan, 10 February 2018.
9. S. Thompson, J. Brown and J. Kibazo, 'Oil Price Worries Leaders, *Financila Times* (7 October 1995), p.15.
10. 'Successful Stock Exchange Listing for Morrison', *Morrison News*, 40 (Winter 1995), p.1.
11. *The Times* (29 August 1995), p.40; James Buxton, 'Morrison Float Aims to Raise £30m', *Financial Times* (29 August 1995), p.14.
12. 'Smearing Success', *Daily Mail* (2 September 1995), cutting in family papers.
13. Interview with Sir Fraser Morrison, 23 May 2018.
14. Tom Stevenson, 'Morrison Float to Bolster Builders', *Independent* (29 August 1995), cutting in 'Flotation' scrapbook; online at https://www.independent.co.uk/news/business/morrison-float-to-bolster-builders-1598523.html.
15. *The Times* (24 May 2000).
16. Interview with Sir Fraser Morrison, 23 May 2018.
17. Interview with John Morrison, 21 February 2018.
18. 'Internal Announcement: Building and civil engineering divisions: restructuring and senior management changes', Facsimile from Keith Howell (30 January 1998), p.1. and chart 'Building Division: management Boards: 01 July 1998' (ref RAC/gyr/BuildDiv, 2 July 1998). Both provided by Ian Smith.
19. 'The Vision', *Morrison Annual Report 1999* (Morrison, 1999), p.1.
20. See per e.g. D. J. Mayston, 'The Private Finance Initiative in the National Health Service: an unhealthy development in New Public Management', *Financial Accountability & Management*, 15, 3&4 (1999), pp.249–250.
21. G. Plimmer, 'Death Knell Sounded for PFI Contracts', *Financial Times* (30 October 2018), p.8.
22. For example, see Michael Martin, 'PFI-Now that Godot's Here', *Morrison News*, 41 (Spring 1996), p.2.
23. Interview with Michael Martin, 19 April 2018.
24. Interview with Sir Fraser Morrison, 23 May 2018.
25. Interview with Michael Martin, 19 April 2018.
26. Interview with Michael Martin, 19 April 2018.
27. Interview with Sir Fraser Morrison, 23 May 2018.
28. Interview with David Jeffs. 2 March 2018.
29. Interview with Liz Urquhart, 18 April 2018.
30. Interview with Peter Heathershaw, 17 May 2018.
31. 'Road Link's Success', *Morrison News*, 41 (Spring 1996), p.1; interview with Roger Croson.

## NOTES FOR CHAPTER SEVEN: THE MORRISON APPROACH

32. 'Road Link's Success', *Morrison News*, 41 (Spring 1996), p.1.
33. 'PFI-Now that Godot's here', *Morrison News*, 41 (Spring 1996), p.2.
34. Interview with Ian Smith, 25 April 2018.
35. Interview with Gordon Morrison, 30 January 2018.
36. 'PFI Hospital Opens its Doors', *BBC News online* (28 January 2002), online at http://news.bbc.co.uk/1/hi/scotland/1785682.stm
37. Keith Howell, 'Operational Review', *Morrison Annual Report 1999* (Morrison, 1999), p.6; interview with Ken Gillespie, 2 February 2018.
38. For example: A. M. Pollock and D. Price, 'The private finance initiative: the gift that goes on taking', *British Medical Journal*, 341 (15 December 2010), c.7175; https://www.scotsman.com/news/exclusive-we-ll-pay-163-1-2bn-for-pfi-hospital-but-never-own-it-1-1247575, accessed 13 November 2018.
39. 'The New Royal Infirmary of Edinburgh: Full Business Case (Royal Infirmary of Edinburgh NHS Trust, July 1997), §1.4.2, p.4. https://www.nhslothian.scot.nhs.uk/OurOrganisation/KeyDocuments/Royal%20Infirmary%20of%20Edinburgh%20PFI%20Agreements/NRIE_Business_Case_1997.pdf, accessed 13 November 2018.
40. Interview with Ian Cusden, 8 March 2018.
41. Interview with Adam Gosnold, 8 March 2018.
42. Interview with Adam Gosnold, 8 March 2018.
43. Leyla Boulton, 'Scottish Sewerage deal is PFI first', *Financial Times* (17 December 1996), p.14.
44. Bechtel, *Bechtel: Building a century: 1898–1998* (Kansas, 1998).
45. Interview with Hugh England, 20 June 2018.
46. Interview with Hugh England, 20 June 2018.
47. Interview with David Jeffs, 2 March 2018.
48. Interview with Gordon Morrison, 30 January 2018.
49. Gordon notes that this contract was brought to an end soon after John Simpson retired, and his son Peter is now current Chief Executive of Anglian Water. Interview with Gordon Morrison, 30 January 2018.
50. Interview with Gordon Morrison, 30 January 2018.
51. Interview with Ian Cusden, 9 March 2018.
52. Interview with Gordon Morrison, 30 January 2018.
53. Interview with Gordon Morrison, 30 January 2018.
54. Interview with Ian Cusden, 9 March 2018.
55. Interview with Zoe Gentle, 3 April 2018.
56. Interview with Ian Cusden, 9 March 2018.
57. Interview with Hugh England, 30 June 2018.
58. M. Latham, *Constructing the Team: joint review of procurement and contractual arrangements in the United Kingdom construction industry* (HMSO, 1994), p.vii.
59. J. Egan, *Rethinking Construction: the report of the Construction Task Force* (London: Department for Trade and Industry, 1998), pp.1–2; paragraphs 13–14.
60. Fraser Morrison, 'Chairman's Statement', *Morrison Annual Report 1999* (Morrison, 1999), p.3.

61. R. Cole, 'Morrison', *The Times* (26 November 1998), p.32.
62. Keith Howell, 'Operational Review', *Morrison Annual Report* (Morrison, 1999), p.8.
63. Interview with Charles Morrison, 28 February 2018.
64. 'Thames/Morrison Network Partnering Pioneers', *Movement for Innovation*, project 73 (May 2000), p.1.
65. Interview with Jim Arnold, 3 April 2018.
66. Note from Ian Smith; 'Morrison Builds on Reputation as A Market Leader', advertising feature, *Press and Journal* (3 December 1996), p.10.
67. 'Morrison Builds on Reputation as A Market Leader', advertising feature, *Press and Journal* (3 December 1996), p.10.
68. http://portal.historicenvironment.scot/designation/SM90343 http://portal.historicenvironment.scot/designation/LB1872 https://www.historicenvironment.scot/visit-a-place/places/bridge-of-oich/history/, accessed 13 November 2018.
69. J. Hume, 'Scottish Suspension Bridges', *Scottish Archaeological Forum*, 8 (1977), p.98.
70. See for example https://www.lochness.co.uk/castle/, accessed 13 November 2018.
71. Interview with Liz Urquhart, 18 April 2018.
72. Kirkstall Revisited, p.1 and G. C. Cunningham, 'Brains are replacing Brewing', *Morrison News* 40 (Winter 1995), pp.4–5.
73. Interview with Ken Gillespie, 2 February 2018.
74. Interview with Peter Heathershaw, 17 May 2018.
75. Specific withheld.
76. Specific withheld.
77. Interview with Jim Arnold, 3 April 2018.
78. Interview with Charles Morrison, 28 February 2018.
79. Specific withheld.
80. Interview with David Jeffs, 2 March 2018.
81. Interview with David Jeffs, 2 March 2018.
82. Interview with Julie Brinkley, 3 April 2018.
83. Interview with Adam Gosnold, 9 March 2018.
84. Interview with Ian MacKay, 18 April 2018.
85. http://www.morrisonconstruction.co.uk/sustainability/health-and-safety/, 10 November 2018.
86. Interview with Liz Urquhart, 18 April 2018.
87. Interview with Allan Russell, 19 April 2018.
88. Interview with Stewart MacLeod, 22 February 2018.
89. http://www.mgroupservices.com/about-us/our-financial-highlights/ accessed 6 December 2018.

## Notes for Chapter Eight: Afterlives 2000–2019

1. M. Jones, 'Anglian pays £262m for Morrison', *Financial Times* (25 August 2000), p.19.
2. 'AWG International', *Anglian Water Annual Report 1995* (Anglian Water, 1995), p.3; 'International Business',

## NOTES FOR CHAPTER EIGHT: AFTERLIVES 2000–2019

*Anglian Water Annual Report 1996* (Anglian Water, 1996), p.3.

3  Robin Gourlay, 'Chairman's Statement', *Anglian Water Plc Annual Reports and Accounts 2000* (Anglian Water, 2000), p.3.

4  Robin Gourlay, 'Chairman's Statement', *awg plc Annual Reports and Accounts 2001* (Anglian Water, 2001), pp.8–9.

5  Elliott Mannis, *awg plc Annual Report and Accounts* (AWG, 2002), p.20; N. Tait, 'Morrison Settles £130m Damages Claim with AWG', *Financial Times* (7 February 2006), p.22.

6  Robin Gourlay, 'Chairman's Statement', *awg plc Annual Reports and Accounts 2001* (Anglian Water, 2001), p.9.

7  Chris Mellor, 'Chief Executive's Review', *awg plc Annual Report and Accounts* (AWG, 2001), p.14.

8  Robin Gourlay, 'Chairman's Statement', *awg plc Annual Report and Accounts* (AWG, 2002), p.8.

9  'Morrison', *awg plc Annual Report and Accounts* (AWG, 2005), pp.13, 18.

10  'Operating and Financial Review', *awg plc Annual Report and Accounts 2002* (AWG, 2002), p.10.

11  Interview with Adam Gosnold, 8 March 2018.

12  http://www.awgproperty.co.uk/who-we-are.cfm accessed 6 December 2018.

13  http://www.awgproperty.co.uk/what-we-do.cfm, accessed 6 December 2018.

14  A timeline is found here http://www.mgroupservices.com/about-us/our-history/, accessed 6 December 2018.

15  Quoted in L. Frampton, 'PAI Partners acquires M Group Services', online at https://missioncriticalpower.uk/pai-partners-acquires-m-group-services/ (22 May 2018), accessed 16 November 2018.

16  Interview with Charles Morrison, 28 February 2018.

17  Interview with Ken Gillespie, 2 February 2018.

18  https://www.rospa.com/awards/categories/sir-george-earle-trophy/ accessed 6 December 2018.

19  Robin Gourlay, 'Chairman's Statement', *awg plc Annual Report and Accounts 2001* (AWG, 2001), p.9; *awg plc Annual Report and Accounts 2002* (AWG, 2002), p.9.

20  R. A. Paxton, J, M. Stirling, and G. Fleming, 'Regeneration of the Forth & Clyde and Union Canals, Scotland', *Proceedings of ICE*, Civil Engineering, 138 (May 2000), pp.61, 67, 69.

21  R. A. Paxton, J, M. Stirling, and G. Fleming, 'Regeneration of the Forth & Clyde and Union Canals, Scotland', *Proceedings of ICE*, Civil Engineering, 138 (May 2000), p.70.

22  Interview with Sir Fraser Morrison, 23 May 2018.

23  D. Hayward, *The Falkirk Wheel* (Glasgow: British Waterways Scotland, 2003), p.2.

24  Interview with Hugh England, 20 June 2018.

25  'Business Review', *Galliford Try Annual Report and Financial Statements 2012* (Galliford Try, 2012), p.13.

26  D. Bunce and P. Braithwaite, 'Reclamation of Contaminated Land with Specific Reference to Pride Park, Derby', in I. Jefferson, E. J. Murray, E. Faragher, and P. R. Fleming (eds), *Problematic Soils* (London: ICE Publishing, 2001),

p.122; P. A. Braithwaite and S. P. Wade, 'Pride Park, Derby (UK)', in R. W. Sarsby (ed.), *Contaminated and Derelict Land: the proceedings of GREEN2: the second international symposium on Geotechnics Related to the Environment held in Kraków* (London: Thomas Telford, 1998), p.421.

27 'Winner Civil Engineering Sponsored by Thomas Telford: Pride Park Reclamation, Derby', *New Civil Engineer* (21 October 1999), online at https://www.newcivilengineer.com/winner-civil-engineering-sponsored-by-thomas-telford-pride-park-reclamation-derby/838281.article, accessed 8 December 2018.

28 Olympic Delivery Authority, *Building the Olympic Park 2005–2011* (London: Olympic Delivery Authority, 2011), pp 12,.34. It should be noted this relates to the site as a whole, not just the half for which Morrison were responsible.

29 Interview with Ken Gillespie, 2 February 2018.

30 Interview Peter Heathershaw, 17 May 2018.

31 'Strength in Diversity' (Galliford Try, n.d.), p.2.

32 'Strength in Diversity' (Galliford Try, n.d.), p.3.

33 'Strength in Diversity' (Galliford Try, n.d.), p.3.

34 G. Liddle, 'Grytviken is now safe', *South Georgia Association Newsletter*, 8 (April 2005), pp.1–2.

35 'Initial Environmental Evaluation for Proposed Reintroduction of Hydroelectric Power at Gryviken, South Georgia' (Morrison, Falklands, April 2006), p.1.

36 http://www.gov.gs/NewsArchive/newsletters/%28h%29South_Georgia_Newsletter%2C_December_2007.html and http://www.gov.gs/NewsArchive/newsletters/%28h%29South_Georgia_Newsletter%2C_March_2009.html, accessed 3 January 2019.

37 David Watt, 'Morrison Life in the Freezer', *Morrison People*, 19 (June 2000), pp. 6–8.

38 https://www.bas.ac.uk/polar-operations/sites-and-facilities/facility/halley/, 20 November 2018.

39 Interview with Michael Martin, 19 April 2018.

40 Interview with Ken Tallant, 16 May 2018.

41 Interview with Peter Heathershaw, 17 May 2018.

42 Interview with Ken Gillespie, 2 February 2018.

43 Michael Martin, 'The Challenge', in David Watt, *The Queensferry Crossing: vision to reality* (Ramsey, Lily Publications, 2017), p.14.

44 Watt, *Queensferry Crossing*, p.18.

45 Interview with Ken Gillespie, 2 February 2018.

46 Interview with Andrew Aldred, 4 April 2018.

47 Determination by Sheriff W. A. Gilchrrist, 2018 FAI 1 B139/17, 5. https://www.scotcourts.gov.uk/docs/default-source/cos-general-docs/pdf-docs-for-opinions/2018fai01.pdf?sfvrsn=0 and https://www.bbc.co.uk/news/uk-scotland-edinburgh-east-fife-42662814, accessed 5 December 2018.

48 Martin, 'The Challenge' pp.16–17.

49 G. Ferguson and M. Chrimes, *The Civil Engineers: the story of the Institution of Civil Engineers and the People Who Made It* (London: ICE, 2011), p.66.

## NOTES FOR CHAPTER EIGHT: AFTERLIVES 2000–2019

50. Interview with Sir Fraser Morrison, 23 May 2018.
51. Interview with Lisa MacInnes, 3 April 2018.
52. https://www.gallifordtry.co.uk/about-us/our-group/our-board, accessed 5 December 2018.
53. Interview with Allan Russell, 19 April 2018.
54. Interview with Michael Martin, 19 April 2018.
55. Interview with Liz Urquhart, 18 April 2018.
56. Interview with Julie Brinkley, 3 April 2018.
57. Interview with Liz Urquhart 18 April 2018
58. http://www.morrisonconstruction.co.uk/projects/moray-flood-alleviation-scheme/, accessed 20 November 2018.
59. Interview with Allan Russell, 19 April 2018.
60. Interview with Stuart Higgins, 18 April 2018.
61. *Royston Crow*, 15 March, 1991, p.1.
62. Interview with Gordon Morrison, 30 January 2018.
63. Interview with Gordon Morrison 30 January 2018.
64. Interview with Charles Morrison, 28 February 2018.
65. Interview with Zoe Gentle, 3 April 2018.
66. Interview with Lisa MacInnes, 3 April 2018.
67. Interview with Zoe Gentle, 3 April 2018.
68. http://www.mgroupservices.com/about-us/our-financial-highlights/, accessed 6 December 2018.
69. Interview with David Jeffs, 2 March 2018.
70. Interview with Ian Smith, 25 April 2018.
71. Interview with Stewart MacLeod, 22 April 2018.
72. Interview with Stuart Higgins, 18 April 2018.
73. Interview with Ian Smith, 25 April 2018.
74. Interview with Lisa MacInnes, 3 April 2018.
75. Interview with Stewart MacLeod, 22 April 2018.
76. Interview with Hugh Morrison, 20 June 2018.
77. Interview with Sir Fraser Morrison, 23 May 2018.
78. Interview with Ken Gillespie, 2 February 2018.
79. Directors' Report, *Morrison Annual Report 1990* (Morrison, 1990), p.14.
80. Interview with Sally Bond, 7 March 2018.
81. Interview with Lawrence Allan, 17 April 2018.
82. Interview with John Morrison, 21 February 2018.
83. Interview with Ian Smith, 25 April 2018.
84. Interview with Ian Cusden, 9 March 2018.
85. Interview with Adam Gosnold, 8 March 2018.
86. Letter from Connie Morrison, 1 April 2018.
87. Interview with Lawrence Allan, 17 April 2018
88. Interview with Hugh England, 20 June 2018.
89. Interview with Roger Croson, 9 February 2018
90. Interview with Donald MacLennan, 10 February 2018.
91. Interview with Michael Martin, 19 April 2018.
92. Interview with Ian Smith, 25 April 2018.
93. Interview with Sir Fraser Morrison, 23 May 2018.

# General Index

accounting
   purchase ledger  238
   technology and computerisation  238
A-Frame chalets  128
aggregates
   Hamburg  132
   Holland  132
   international sales  132
   quarries network  132
   retail sales  132
Alexander Shand, *see* Shand
Alexander Sutherland of Golspie, *see* Sutherland
AQS limited  113

Balfour Beattie  199
bank managers, as a figure of respect and local importance  39–41, 243
Bechtel  203
Biggs Wall  146–7, 184–7, 216, 239, 245
BP, purchase of Selection Trust  135
bridges, *see* Kylesku Bridge, Dornoch Crossing, Queensferry Crossing, Ochiltree
British Antarctic Survey  227–9
buyback of business  139

CALA, Edinburgh  161–4
   second phase  164
   celebration on banknote  164
Carillion  234
CAST  97–9, 134–5
Central Scotland, expansion into  106

Charter Consolidated  123, 135, 139, 142, 184–5, 187, 235
Chester City FC  174–5
civil engineering
   entry to  67–8
   expansion  116–18
climate and weather  106–8, 131
   Eastgate Shopping Centre, Inverness  106–7
   leave at Christmas  106–7
   technology as response to challenges  107
coastal protections
   Banff sea wall  119
   Fort George  118–19
collaboration
   against competitive tendering  203–4
   nomenclature in private sector work  203–4
Consolidated African Selection Trust, *see* CAST
Co-op, *see* CWS
corporate social responsibility  142
CRINE, *see* oil industry
Cromarty Firth Engineering  113–14, 134, 181
CWS  130–1, 181–4
   Castlebay, Barra  184
   expansion of Inverness store  184
   Forres  184
   Tain  184
   Thurso  184

design and build  137
　Inverness CWS superstore  130
divisional structure  142

ecological challenges  209
Edinburgh head office  140
Edinburgh office  108–9
engineering
　move to mechanical and electrical
　　engineering  115
European Free Trade Area  111
extreme locations
　Antarctica  226
　Falkland Islands  226
　Grytviken, South Georgia  226–7
　logistical challenges of these  228–9

fabrication yards  113–16
　Ardersier  114–5
　Nigg  114–15
family business  213–46
　Alex remains in charge  99
　Alex retires  135
　Fraser enters business  99–101
　Fraser steps up  135–6
　Gordon enters business  99–101
　Gordon steps up  135–6
　intergenerational leadership  136
　persistence during sale  243–5
First Reserve  217
flotation  139
football, see Chester City FC

Galliford Try  244
gender
　female employees, division of
　　labour  41–3
　maleness of working
　　environment  41–3
　support of wives and partners  140–1
　more women in more recent
　　projects  232–3
Glasgow office  109

Hayden  199
health and safety
　business case for  210–11
　CBAB  212
　embedding safety culture  210–12
　HSE  77, 211–2
　initial regime  76–7
　MUS as market leader  212–13, 218–20
　need for cultural change  77–8
　No Accident Behaviour  211–12
　Nurse's house, Tain  89
　reputation  210–11
　Strategic Safety Conversations  211–12
　TQM  211
HIDB (Highlands and Islands
　Development Board)  89–92, 103,
　115–16, 120–1, 128
　Farm Improvement Scheme  90, 92–3
Highland economy and
　demography  88–93, see also HIDB
Highland Fabricators  113–14
Highland hospitality  140
Highland Regional Council  122, 127
Highlanders, Seaforth, see Seaforth
　Highlanders
housing
　and company's development  173–4
　Balintore  86
　Bloomfield Road, Aberdeen  128
　context of Tory ideology  172
　council provision of  45–8
　Dingwall  173
　Dunfermline  129
　Dunkeld  129
　East Berlin  166–7
　Edderton, Tain  86
　Edinburgh  129
　Falkirk  129
　Fearn  92
　Alness  98
　for Tain Town Council  98
　Garnett Hill, Strathclyde  129
　Glasgow  129
　housing association work  128–9
　Invergordon  97–8
　Kirk Care Housing Association  128–9
　Kirkwall  129
　Kyle of Lochalsh  92

Langstane Housing Association  128
Lema Homes  173
Local Authority housing  173
marketing to specific socio-economic groups  172–3
Milton  86
Nairn  173
nature of private demand vs. public provision  172–3
Old Edinburgh Road, Inverness  129
Pitlochry  129
Polmont Bank, near Falkirk  129
Portree, Skye  128–9
postwar  45–8
pre-fabricated and non-traditional types  53
private housing  48–53, 98
publicity and marketing  129
Rupert Bear  173–4
Scandinavian type, and remedial work to  53–6
Scottish Homes, subsidy  173
Seaforth Road, Aberdeen  128
sheltered housing  129
Strathpeffer  173
Howard Doris Cromarty Firth  181
Hugh Mackay, takeover of  45

industrial and mixed developments
 Leicester  134
 London  134
 Oxford  134
industrial welfare  43
inflation
 Baxter and Osborne  116
 price fluctuation contracts  116
international work
 Accra, Ghana  167
 Azerbaijan  165–7
 East Berlin, housing work  166–7
 Eastern Europe  166
 International Centre for Business Co-operation  165
 Kuwait City, Kuwait  168–72
 Kuwait  139, 165
 Marriott hotel, Georgia  167
 Moscow  165
 Quality Built In in desert  172
 risk management  167–8
 Russia  139, 165
 Saudi Embassy, Moscow  166
 St Petersburg, Russia  165
 tax demands and international work  167
 US Army Corps of Engineers  169
 USSR, see Russia
Invergordon aluminium smelter  93–6
Invergordon Sand and Gravel  99
IPO  139

Kylesku whisky  166

leadership  110
Lehane Mackenzie and Shand  116–18, see also Shand
 good corporate fit  118
leisure complex, Paisley  181
Lema Homes  173

M Group Services, see Morrison Utility Services
McDermott  113–14
Minor Works Division  127
modernity  1, 59, 64, 76, 119, 130
Moray Flood Alleviation Scheme
 Lhanbryde  234
 Elgin  234
 Findhorn  234
 Forres  234
 Rothes  234
Moray Flood Alleviation Scheme  234
MORESPACE cabins  128
Morrison
 collaborative approaches  187
 corporate development  187
 corporate entertaining  187
 corporate structure  142
 diversification  56
 employee investments at flotation  194
 expanded structure  105
 family regains control  184–5
 governance and public status  195

growth in 1950s  67–8
hiring accountant for the first
    time  72–6
incorporation as limited
    company  71–2
Inverness HQ  108–9
loyalty  185
management restructure
    195–6
Morrison approach  3, 189, 196–203,
    203–7, 216, 235
Morrison culture  240–3
*Morrison News*  105, 243
Morrison Old Boys  137
Morrison Portrait Prize  141–2
name changes  185
Noble Grossart advisors for IPO  194
postwar story and Alex's company  69
regional offices  108–9
shift in corporate focus to central
    belt  150
speedy success in early years  45
stockmarket  189, 191–6
utilities, growth of  187
working at, conditions  41–3
Morrison Utility Services
    data and logistics  235–7
    health and safety reputation  212–13,
        218–20
    million holes in one year  235–8
    scale  235
    turnover  213
MUS, *see* Morrison Utility Services

National Economic Development
    Organisation  116
National Portrait Gallery  140–1
networks  110
New Public Management  116, 189, 197,
    *see also* PFI
numismatic celebrations
    CALA  164
    Falkirk Wheel  220–1
office developments
    Bath Street, Glasgow  134
    Byres Road, Glasgow  133

Carden Place, Aberdeen  133
Queen's Gardens  133
Rubislaw Terrace, Aberdeen  133
oil industry  103, 108, 111–15, 132–3,
    178–81
    Aberdeen, and oil industry  111
    and Highland economy  93–6
    Collaborative working  178–81
    CRINE  181
    Cromarty Firth Engineering  181
    ethos clashing  114
    government policy on oil industry  112
    Nigg  113–4
    Piper Alpha  112
    SNP and oil industry  111–2
    Sullom Voe Oil Terminal,
        Shetland  113

OptiMUS  238

PAI Partners  217
partnerships
    accounting needs  204–5
    and stockmarket success  205–6
    Anglian Water  204
    Egan Report, and Total Quality
        Morrison  205
    housing associations  128–9
    Latham Report  205
    New Engineering Contract  205
    nomenclature  206
    open-book accounting  205
    practical example of savings  204
    Sainsbury supermarkets  207
    sheltered housing  129
    Thames Water Agility Alliance  206
    Thames Water  204, 206
people
    employment of veterans  45
    grandchildren  239, 240
    teamwork  246
PFI  140, 189, 194, 196–203
    A69, 199
    accounts in JVs and partnerships  203
    CityCare, Norwich  201–3
    collaborative approaches  200

facilities management 201–3
hospitals 196
infrastructure needs 196
Michael Martin director of
need for longer term view 199–200
Newcastle to Carlisle 199
North of Scotland Water
  Authority 203
partnerships in PFI 203
PF2, 196
profitability 198–9
Roadlink 199
Royal Infirmary of
  Edinburgh 199–201
schools 196
transfer of risk to contractor 198–9, 201
value for money 199–200
water 203
Pipe-coating factory 115
postwar
  economy 33–4
  housing 45–56
  political economy 37
pre-cast concrete methods 107
prisoner of war camp, see Lamsdorf
prisoners of war
  end of the War 28–30
  handcuffing after the Dieppe
    raid 13–14
  surrender of 7
  see also Lamsdorf, Seaforth
    Highlanders
privatisation of utilities 235
property development
  Morrison Developments Limited 132
  not capital intensive 133
publicity and marketing
  and private housing 129
  marking move to Edinburgh head
    quarters with sponsorship 140–1

Quality 151–61
  cartoons 156–9
  communicating idea of 154
  Five-Star Sites 155

health and safety as part of 155
Jackie Stewart see biographical index
KPIs and golf course analogy
  160–1
Popplewell and Wildsmith, origins of
  Total Quality Morrison 152
Quality Built In in translation 166
Quality College 155
scorecards 160–1
slogans, etc 152–4
wheelbarrows 160–1
and international acclaim 206
quarries
  acquisition of 92
  Bristol 181
  Holland 181
  Moraystone cobbles 181
  Sullom Voe 101
  supply RAF Leuchars 101
  see also aggregates
Queen's image exhibition 140–1

recreation
  all-weather centre, Fort William 130
  Invergordon Sports Centre 130
remediation work, see Pride Park, Derby;
  Olympic Park
remoteness 131
remuneration 101
risk 150–1
  and large projects 233–5
  and new markets 150
  and overseas contracts, forex rates 151,
    164–5
  and PFI 150–1
RMJM 221
roads
  A69 199
  A894 119–20
  A9 121
  A94 121–2
  Auldearn Bypass 154
  Dundee-Forfar 110–11
  Elgin Relief Road 122
  Newcastle to Carlisle 199
  Parkford 121–2

Perth Western Bypass  122, 181
Perth-Aberdeen  121
Roadlink  199
RoSPA awards  218–20
Ross and Cromarty District Council
    Edderton housing  53
    Evanton housing  53
    Mansfield Estate, Tain  53
Royston Incident – risk transfer  235
Rupert Bear  173–4

Sainsbury's, Garthdee Road, Aberdeen  207
sale to Galliford Try  217
sale to private equity  217
Salesforce  238
satisfaction  244–6
schools
    Barra Community School  131
    buildings to withstand children  131
    Conon Bridge School  79
    Coulhill Primary School, Alness  98
    Culloden Academy  131
    Gledfield, Ardgay  79
    Inver School  79
    South Lodge Primary School, Invergordon  98
    Tain Primary School  79
    Tain Royal Academy  78–86
Scottish Arts Council commission  131
Scottish Development Department  122
Scottish economy, separate character from rest of UK  116
Scottish Tourist Board  128–9
Seaforth Highlanders  5–8
    capture at St Valery  6–8
    Scottish culture at Lamsdorf  24–5
Selection Trust  134–5
Selection Trust, purchased by BP  135
sewage treatment  119–20
    Carbans  120
    Crieff  120
    Dalbeattie  120
    Elgin  120
    Norwich  120
    Ochiltree  120
    Pitlochry  120
Shand North Thames  142
Shand  101, 102, 106, 118, 122–5, 135–6, 143–5, 164–5, 184–5
Small Works Division  181
sources and selection  1–3, *see also Morrison News*
Stalag VIIIB, *see* Lamsdorf
Standard Life  165
Sterling rates  132
Strathclyde Development Agency  131
supermarkets, Alness  98
Supermarkets, *see* Co-op, CWS, Sainsbury
Sutherland (Alexander Sutherland of Golspie)  102, 116, 134
    acquisition  116
Swimming pool, Dingwall  98

takeover
    AWG Property  217
    AWG  215–16
    institutional shock  216–18
    integration  216–7
    Morrison name  217–18
    Red M Logo  217
Tayside Regional Council  122
technology and computerisation  238
Total Quality Morrison, *see* Quality
Transition economy  165
transport and plant
    flights to get to remote locations  131
    Glass model of Trojan  64
    growth of division  132
    Hillman Minx  64
    internal tendering  132
    Landrover  61
    lorry 'DJS 4'  41
    mobile concrete batching  132
    Motors
    Trojan  64
Twenty-Five Years Club  101–2, 136–7, 240
    and Matlock  102

Utilities, *see* Morrison Utility Services

War, *see also* World War II
weather, *see* climate
whisky
    Glenmorangie  58, 130
    Invergordon  59–60, 77, 89, 97

Wight Construction
    purchase of  127
    Wight Ring Pile system  127–8
Wight Engineering  134
World War II
    Dunkirk  5–6
    end of the Battle of France  5–6

# Projects and Places Index

A69  199
A894  119–20
A9  121
A94  121–2
Aberchalder  208
Aberdeen Airport  119
Aberdeen Western Peripheral Route  234
Aberdeen  111, 128, 133, 207
Accra, Ghana  167
All-weather centre, Fort William  130
Alness police station  92
Alness  98
Antarctica  226
Ardersier  114–5
Auldearn Bypass  154
Azerbaijan  165–7

Baillieston, Glasgow  134
Balintore  86
Banff  119
Barra Community School  131
Barra  184
Bath Street, Glasgow  134
Bellahouston Hotel, Glasgow  129
Berlin  166–7
Bloomfield Road, Aberdeen  128
Bridge of Don reservoir  118
Bridge of Oich, Aberchalder  208
Bristol  181
Buckingham Palace  235–8
Byres Road, Glasgow  133

Caledonian Canal  118
Caledonian Club, London  142

Carbans  120
Carden Place, Aberdeen  133
Castlebay, Barra  184
Central Scotland, expansion into  106
Chester  174–5
CityCare, Norwich  201–3
Clydesdale Bank, Edinburgh,
    *see* CALA
Conon Bridge School  79
Coulhill Primary School, Alness  98
Crieff  120
Culloden Academy  131
Culrain School  56

Dalbeattie  120
Derby  224
Dingwall  98, 173
Dornoch Crossing awards  178
    Christiani and Nielsen  177
    commemorative whisky  180
    lord lieutenants  178
    push and launch  177–8
    royal opening  178
    technological demands of  177
    temporary works  177
Dundee-Forfar  110–11
Dunfermline  129
Dunkeld  129
Dunkirk  5–6

East Berlin, housing work  166–7
Eastern Europe  166
Eastgate Shopping Centre,
    Inverness  106–7
Edderton, Tain  53, 86

Edinburgh head office  140
Edinburgh office  108–9
Edinburgh  129, 199–201
Elgin Relief Road  122
Elgin  120, 234
Evanton  53

Falkirk Wheel  220–1
   entrepreneurial approach taken  221
   Lego modelling of  221
Falkirk  129
Falkland Islands  226
Fearn  92
Findhorn  234
Forres  184, 234
Fort George  118–19
Fort William  130
France  5–6, *see also* Dunkirk, St Valery

Garnett Hill, Strathclyde  129
Garthdee Road, Aberdeen  207
Germany, *see* Berlin
Glasgow office  109
Glasgow  129, 133–4
Gledfield, Ardgay  79
Glenmorangie  58, 130
Grytviken, South Georgia  226–7

Hamburg, aggregate sales to  132
Holland  181
Holland, aggregate sales to  132

Inver School  56, 79
Invergordon  57–60, 77, 89, 93–9
Invergordon Distillery warehouses contract, pivotal for business  59–60
Invergordon Sports Centre  130
Inverness  106–9, 129–30, 184
Inverness CWS superstore  130

Kilmuir Easter School  56
Kinlochbervie Pier  67–8
Kirkstall Lock  208–9
Kirkwall  129
Kuwait  139, 165, 168–172
Kuwait City, Kuwait  168–172

Kyle of Lochalsh  92
Kylesku Bridge  122–7, 243
   Civic Trust award  176
   demonstrative of risks of prestigious projects  124
   estimating  125
   importance to company  126–7
   listed  122
   nearly bankrupted company  125
   Ove Arup  123
   reputation  176
   royal opening  126–7
   Saltire Society award  176
   special number of *Morrison News* for Kyleksu  125

Lamsdorf  24–5
   books  22–3
   Carnivals and other festivities  24–5
   conditions in  12–13
   economic life of: cigarette-based economy  25–6; collective welfare  25–6
   food  14–17
   intellectual life of prisoners reflective of working-class culture  21–2
   letters home  25–7
   mining, prisoner labour  18–21
   Music including bagpipes  23–4
   order in camp  14
   Red Cross parcels in  13, 14–17, 17–18, 22
   the camp  9–12
   The Clarion  23
   Theatre  24–5
Leeds Metropolitan University  208–9
Leicester  134
Leuchars  101
Lhanbryde  234
Linwood factory  131
London  134, 224–5, 235–8

Mansfield Estate, Tain  53
Marriott hotel, Georgia  167
Matlock  102

## PROJECTS AND PLACES INDEX

Milton  86
Moscow  165

Nairn  173
Naples, Florida  206
New Tarbat, Kilmuir Easter  24
Newcastle to Carlisle  199
Nigg, Easter Ross  108, 113–5, 132
Norwich  120, 201–3

Ochiltree  120
Old Edinburgh Road, Inverness  129
Olympic Park, London  224–5
Oxford  134

Parkford  121–2
Perth Western Bypass  122, 181
Perth-Aberdeen  121
Pitlochry  120, 129
Poland, occupied, *see* Lamsdorf
Polmont Bank, near Falkirk  129
Portree, Skye  128–9
Pride Park, Derby  224

Queen's Gardens  133
Queensferry Crossing  229–34

RAF Leuchars  101
Rockingham Speedway  209–10
Rothes  234
Royal Infirmary of Edinburgh  199–201
Rubislaw Terrace, Aberdeen  133

Russia  139, 165

Saudi Embassy, Moscow  166
Scotsburn Road  52–3
Seaforth Road, Aberdeen  128
Shetland, *see* Sullom Voe
Skye  128–9
St Petersburg, Russia  165
St Valery en caux  6–8
Strathclyde  129
Strathpeffer  173
Sullom Voe Oil Terminal, Shetland  101, 113
Swimming pool, Dingwall  98

Tain  53, 72–3, 86, 89, 98, 184
Tain
    early history  34–7
    portrait of life in the town in 1951, 34–7
    weather and climate  43
Tain Cinema  59
Tain Primary School  79
Tain Royal Academy  78–86
Tain, Lawrence Allan's first impression of  72–3
Taylor's Garage, Invergordon  57–8
Thurso  184

Urquhart Castle  208
USSR, *see* Russia

Westminster Abbey, London  235–8

# People Index

Aldred, Andrew  160, 165, 229
Alexander, Bill  206–7
Allan, Lawrence  38, 41, 59, 72–3, 76–7, 93, 113
Arnold, Jim  150, 206, 210, 217–8

Bathurst, Philip  111
Bond, Sally  243
Brinkley, Julie  211–2
Broom, James  240
Broom, Kirsty  240
Broom, Sophie  240
Butler, Vincent  142

Cairns, Joyce  141
Cathcart, Jim  131
Christie, Angus  115
Codrington, H. J.  97–9
Croson, Roger  116–8, 124, 126, 136, 153, 165, 167, 245
Currentzski, Olag  124
Cusden, Ian  151, 201, 205, 244

Davidson, Roy  202
Devereux, Alan  129
Dredge, James  208
Duff, Sandy  86, 135, 191

England, Hugh  98, 102, 107, 118, 123, 125, 150, 203, 205, 221, 224, 241, 245

Fraser, Alexander 'Sandy'  141, 188
Fraser, Andrew  26–7
Fraser, Don  27
Fraser, Michael  105, 140–2, 178

Gall, Sandy  169
Gentle, Zoe  205, 238
Gillespie, Ken  107, 152, 160, 218, 225, 228–9, 243
Gosnold, Adam  201, 217, 244
Gourlay, Robin  215
Grant, Jackie  45

Hamilton, Alistair  194
Heathershaw, Peter  151, 199, 209, 225, 228
Henderson family  86–8
Henderson, David  36, 38, 86–8, 93, 103, 190
Henderson, Eric  87
Higgins, Stuart  177, 234, 241
Howell, Keith  194, 206
Hunter, Bill  93

Jeffs, David  124, 132, 198, 211

Keith, Ian  118

Landau, D. M.  130
Lang, Ian  141
Louden, Billy  43, 45, 57, 61

MacDonald, Dan  107, 112, 133–4, 164–5, 184, 190
MacInnes, Lisa  165, 241
MacKay, Alasdair  100–2, 114, 132
MacKay, Ian  153, 181, 212
MacKay, Pam  114, 140–1, 190
MacLennan, Donald  89, 107, 114, 118, 130–1, 133–4, 136, 240, 245

MacLennan, Norman  153, 166, 175, 194
MacLennan, Robert  121
MacLeod, Stewart  105–6, 110, 123–4,
    141, 152–4, 178, 190, 212, 240–1
Mannis, Elliott  216
Martin, Michael  108, 122–4, 164, 177–8,
    196–9, 228–32, 246
McGraw, Ron  106
McRae, Jennifer  142
Morrison, Alex
    being own boss after being subject to
        Nazi regime  31
    competitiveness  88
    death  189–90
    dreaming from prisoner of war
        camp  23
    fond memories of  189–91
    home life at Scotsburn Road  86–8
    importance of family life to AM  37–8
    kindness to employees  61
    kindness to friends  86–6
    Mr Shilling a Foot  60
    rapid success of business  52–3, 68–9,
        86
    retires  135
    setting up business promptly after
        returning home  33, 38–9
    wartime experience  2–3, 5–26, 28–30
    way home from War and discharge
        from army  28–31
    welcoming Lawrence Allan  72–3
    work and family life  38
Morrison, Charles  153, 190, 206, 210,
    217–8, 224, 235
Morrison, Connie  35, 37–9, 41, 43, 49,
    51–2, 55, 63, 65, 71, 73, 86–8, 93, 135,
    244
Morrison, Fraser  37–8, 49, 86–7, 98,
    99–101, 106, 116, 130, 135–7, 139,
    140–2, 151, 152, 165, 167, 169, 176,
    177, 184, 195, 197, 210, 205, 215, 216,
    221, 226, 241, 244, 246
Morrison, George  45
Morrison, Gordon  1–2, 37–8, 39, 46, 49,
    57, 59–60, 65, 68, 77, 86–7, 95, 99–102,
110, 112–3, 116, 136, 139, 184–5, 187,
    190, 200–1, 203–4, 213, 215–16, 218,
    227, 239–40, 243–4, 246
Morrison, John  110, 114, 167, 195, 244
Morrison, Johnny  45
Morrison, Mary  86
Morrison, Trish  141–2, 226

Paterson, Billy  45
Peacock, Alan  142
Polk, Bill  164–5
Popplewell, Barry  152
Primakov, Yevgeny  164
Princess Royal  227

Queen Elizabeth II  viii, 122, 124–6, 232
Queen Mother  65, 178–9

Robertson, Hamish  155
Robertson, Nelson  195
Ross, Frank  86
Ross, John Fisher  45
Russell, Allan  106–7, 190, 232, 234

Sanderson of Bowden, Lord  194
Semple, Alec  38, 57, 93, 101, 135
Simpson, John  204
Sinclair, David M.  142
Smith, Ian  167, 199, 207, 239–40, 244,
    246
Smith, Martin  239
Stewart, Jackie  154–5, 209–10
Strong, Roy  141

Tallant, Ken  153, 167–9, 228
Telford, Thomas  118
Thatcher, Margaret, declining Scottish
    support  115–6
Thomson, Frank  59–60

Urquhart, Alexander  45
Urquhart, Liz  178, 199, 208, 212,
    233–4

Wildsmith, Alan  152